OXFORD MID-CENTURY STUDIES

The Oxford Mid-Century Studies series publishes monographs in several disciplinary and creative areas in order to create a thick description of culture in the thirty-year period around the Second World War. With a focus on the 1930s through the 1960s, the series concentrates on fiction, poetry, film, photography, theatre, as well as art, architecture, design, and other media. The mid-century is an age of shifting groups and movements, from existentialism through abstract expressionism to confessional, serial, electronic, and pop art styles. The series charts such intellectual movements, even as it aids and abets the very best scholarly thinking about the power of art in a world under new techno-political compulsions, whether nuclear-apocalyptic, Cold War-propagandized, transnational, neo-imperial, super-powered, or postcolonial.

Series editors
Allan Hepburn, McGill University
Adam Piette, University of Sheffield
Lyndsey Stonebridge, University of East Anglia

Public Opinion Polling in Mid-Century British Literature

The Psychographic Turn

MEGAN FARAGHER

OXFORD
UNIVERSITY PRESS

OXFORD

UNIVERSITY PRESS

Great Clarendon Street, Oxford, OX2 6DP,
United Kingdom

Oxford University Press is a department of the University of Oxford.
It furthers the University's objective of excellence in research, scholarship,
and education by publishing worldwide. Oxford is a registered trade mark of
Oxford University Press in the UK and in certain other countries

First Edition published in 2021

Impression: 1

Published in the United States of America by Oxford University Press
198 Madison Avenue, New York, NY 10016, United States of America

British Library Cataloguing in Publication Data
Data available

Library of Congress Control Number: 2021936028

ISBN 978-0-19-289897-5

DOI: 10.1093/oso/9780192898975.001.0001

Printed and bound in Great Britain by
Clays Ltd, Elcograf S.p.A.

Acknowledgements

This book originates from research I began while earning my PhD at State University of New York at Buffalo. I am immensely grateful to all the advisors and colleagues I met there who have continued to encourage me and support my work. Particular thanks are due to Damien Keane, who has always embodied a model for astute, thoughtful scholarly work and intellectual integrity; his reflections on this work have been characteristically insightful. I am honored to have the continued friendship of Kenneth James, whose support has been invaluable, and whose expertise has provided profound inspiration as this book has developed. I am also indebted to my colleagues at Wright State University—Lake Campus, who have provided support in this process, including Christine Junker and David Wilson.

I am fortunate to have encountered a wonderful network of inspirational academics whose feedback at yearly conferences has been essential to this book's development. After attending my first Space Between Society conference in 2015, I was warmed to find such a collaborative, generous, passionate, and authentic group of scholars, every one of whom I wish I had time to thank here; this book would not exist without colleagues I found there. Luke Seaber generously introduced me to the work of Celia Fremlin, which was a revelation; her work became foundational to this project. Janine Utell acted as a skilled editor of the Space Between journal, in which some of my argument in this book was previewed with superb editorial care; I have benefitted from her generosity and mentorship. I want to thank other colleagues and collaborators from the Space Between, whose insights have guided my work: Michael McCluskey, Melissa Dinsman, and Caroline Krzakowski, a skillful collaborator. I particularly want to thank Debra Rae Cohen, whose energy and vitality in the field continues to be a palpable force, and whose enthusiasm for my work continues to motivate me. I am also grateful for my participation in the Modernist Studies Association, without which I would not have been acquainted with Shawna Ross, whose friendship throughout the production of this book has been vital. I also wish to thank those who have reviewed parts of this work throughout the early drafting process, including Rebecah Pulsifer, Krystal Cleary, and Jess

Waggoner; the book has grown due to their suggestions and insights. Further thanks to Elizabeth Evans and Stella Deen, who helped me through the last hurdles.

The series editors of the Oxford Mid-Century Studies series have been generous in their guidance throughout this project. Allan Hepburn, Adam Piette, and Lyndsey Stonebridge were generous with their time and insights. Allan has provided additional essential guidance along the way with astounding care and efficiency, for which I am extremely grateful. The generous feedback of Oxford University Press's anonymous readers was enormously useful in helping this book take its final shape. Additional thanks are due to Jacqueline Norton, Aimee Wright, and Rebecca Lewis for help in the process of bringing this book to print.

Friends and family—and friends who have become family—have always encouraged me and given me levity throughout this process. Thanks to all of my league mates at Gem City Roller Derby, who have been the source of my sanity, and a grounding force in my life. To Roland, my grandfather, I give my undying gratitude for always telling me to "keep my mind neutral." Thanks to my mother, Maggie, for helping me continue to grow into myself. Posthumous thanks go to my father Tom, a generous man who would have been proud of this book. With extreme patience and love, my partner Eamon (and cat Celia) have made this book possible.

Funding for research from this book has been provided thanks to the Lake Campus Professional Development Grant and the Mark Diamond Dissertation Fellowship. I am grateful to the staff at the British Library and the University of Sussex Special Collections for their professionalism and guidance. The generosity of estates and executors has enabled much of the research of this book to be published for the first time. Material from the Mass-Observation Archive has been reproduced with the permission of Curtis Brown Group Ltd, London on behalf of The Trustees of the Mass-Observation Archive © The Trustees of the Mass-Observation Archive. I am thankful that I have been able to republish materials from Woolf's journals for *Three Guineas* and *Between the Acts*, housed in the Monks House Papers, courtesy of The Society of Authors as the Literary Representative of the Estate of Virginia Woolf. BBC copyright content has been reproduced courtesy of the British Broadcasting Corporation. All rights reserved. "The Unknown Citizen" copyright 1940 and © renewed 1968 by W.H. Auden; from *Collected Poems by W.H. Auden*, edited by Edward Mendelson. Used by permission of Random House, an imprint and division of Penguin Random House LLC. All rights reserved. Figures I and II from The Psychology of Radio by Hadley Cantril, Gordon Allport. Copyright 1935 by Harper & Row, Publishers, Inc., renewed © 1963 by Hadley Cantril. Used by permission of HarperCollins Publishers.

Table of Contents

List of Illustrations

Introduction

From the Era of the Crowd to the Psychographic Turn

Knowing the "Unknown Citizen"

Few works capture public opinion polling's rapid institutionalization in the mid-century as candidly as W.H. Auden's 1939 poem "The Unknown Citizen." Blithely, though not inaccurately, scholars have appreciated this poem as a "neat uncomplicated satire on the corporate state."[1] But while Auden's poem cynically memorializes a citizen via statistics and averages, it also highlights new technological and methodological innovations that enabled the rise of public opinion polling as an elementary force in modern democracy. The poem, which readers are told is an epitaph affixed to a "marble statue," memorializes, I would argue, *not* the citizen it supposedly commemorates (who is only known in the poem by the identification number "JS/07 M 378"), but the techniques by which individual interiority had become increasingly reified, quantified, and conceptualized as part of a mass. Throughout "The Unknown Citizen" Auden makes repeated reference to bureaucratic networks that aid the government in materializing the depths of the psyche. Through these institutional references he outlines the state's two goals in public opinion research: the norming of behavior through amassing collective psychological data and the management of populations through ubiquitous mastery of psychographics—the quantitative study of mass psychology. A few lines frame the life of JS/07 M 378 as it transects various bureaucratic networks and crystalizes a picture of the citizen based on the psychological data he produces:

> ...he wasn't a scab or odd in his views,
> For his Union reports that he paid his dues,
> (Our report on his Union shows it was sound)

---

[1] Edward Mendelson, *Early Auden, Later Auden: A Critical Biography* (Princeton, NJ: Princeton University Press, [1981] 2017), p. 369.

Public Opinion Polling in Mid-Century British Literature: The Psychographic Turn. Megan Faragher, Oxford University Press. © Megan Faragher 2021. DOI: 10.1093/oso/9780192898975.003.0001

And our Social Psychology workers found
That he was popular with his mates and liked a drink.
The Press are convinced that he bought a paper every day
And that his reactions to advertisements were normal in
every way.[2]

Auden captures the entire cyclical process whereby psychological interiority is quantified and interpreted, stressing the institutional framework that makes such data legible within a wider sociological context. Observable behaviors—paying for dues, drinks, or newspapers—are only valuable insomuch as they reveal something otherwise obscured—beliefs, feelings, or thoughts. But conjuring authentic psychological interiority from the citizen-subject depended on an infrastructure of coordinated public opinion research that had only come into full bloom by the time Auden was writing this poem.

Auden's ventriloquized state observes that, when it comes to JS/07 M 378, "Our researchers into Public Opinion are content / That he held the proper opinions for the time of year; / When there was peace, he was for peace: when there was war, he went."[3] By 1939, such researchers, survey cards in hand, would have been enveloping the country like locusts to assess public opinion of a nation at the brink of war. But not a decade earlier, these pollsters had been nearly non-existent; public opinion research was in its pupal stage, not yet ready to unleash itself upon society and forever change our conceptualization of collective psychology. In the first decades of the twentieth century, monographs by Walter Lippmann, Hadley Cantril, William McDougall, and Floyd Allport, among others, formalized the academic field of social psychology, quietly constructing the methodological frameworks for future polling efforts.[4] But by the mid-1930s, public awareness of quantitative social psychological techniques was nearly universal. This was in part due to George Gallup, whose advanced sampling techniques famously predicted Roosevelt's electoral victory in 1936, upending the dominant

---

[2] W.H. Auden, "The Unknown Citizen," copyright 1940 and © renewed 1968 by W.H. Auden; from *Collected Poems* by W.H. Auden, edited by Edward Mendelson, pp. 252–3. Used by permission of Random House, an imprint and division of Penguin Random House LLC. All rights reserved.

[3] Auden, "The Unknown Citizen," p. 253.

[4] See Walter Lippman, *Public Opinion* (New York: Harcourt, 1922); Hadley Cantril, "The Social Psychology of Everyday Life," *The Psychological Bulletin* 31, no. 5 (1934), pp. 297–300; Floyd Allport, *Social Psychology* (Boston, MA: Houghton Mifflin, 1924).

straw-polling technique *Literary Digest* had formalized only decades prior.[5] Polling flourished in the mid-1930s on a variety of other fronts as well. In 1937, the journal *Public Opinion Quarterly* debuted, with editors declaring that "[n]ow, for the first time in history, we are confronted nearly everywhere by *mass* opinion as the final determinant of political, and economic action."[6] That same year, Charles Madge and Tom Harrisson's Mass-Observation published *May the Twelfth*, a study of public sentiment during the abdication crisis; they hoped the observational praxis they defined would allow the citizen-observer to "[heighten] his power of seeing what is around him and [give] him new interest in and understanding of it."[7] And while Madge and Harrisson published their observations on the Coronation, Henry Durant was founding the British Institute of Public Opinion, instituting the Gallup methods in England.[8] This rapid evolution of institutionalized polling, which reached its apex in the 1930s, was the necessary prerequisite for Auden's poem, which memorializes the crescendo of what I am calling the "psychographic turn."

Public Opinion Polling in Mid-Century British Literature: The Psychographic Turn follows the winding path of psychography—the writing of the group mind—from the early twentieth century through World War II, demonstrating that the new methods of inquiry into individual and, more importantly, *collective* psychology galvanized an understudied subfield of mid-century aesthetics. Turning away from the individual interiority of Clarissa Dalloway or Molly Bloom, writers like H.G. Wells, Olaf Stapledon, Evelyn Waugh, Naomi Mitchison, Celia Fremlin, Cecil Day-Lewis, and Elizabeth Bowen looked instead to the political ramifications of collective psychological inquiry to inspire their literary practice. The desire to read the minds of myriad others, to find out what they thought and desired, eventually inspired a whole range of academic and psychological practices, including the emergence of the most powerful "thought-reading" infrastructure society has ever produced: scientific public opinion polling. But these technologies and infrastructures brought with them a slew of anxieties, many of which emerged in literary discourse. This book is fueled by a

---

[5] Henry Durant, "Proceedings: Yorkshire Section, Gallup Surveys," *The Journal of the Textile Institute* 32, no. 12 (December 1941), p. 108.

[6] Poole, Dewitt Clinton, et al., "Foreword," *Public Opinion Quarterly* 1, no. 1 (January 1937), pp. 3–5.

[7] Mass-Observation, *May the Twelfth*, edited by Humphrey Jennings and Charles Madge (London: Faber and Faber, [1937] 2009), p. iv.

[8] Mark Roodhouse, "'Fish and Chip Intelligence,' Henry Durant and the British Institute of Public Opinion, 1936–63," *Twentieth Century British History* 24, no. 2 (2012), p. 225.

series of questions and concerns which remain understudied in the field of twentieth-century culture. What were the implications of understanding what one's fellow citizen was thinking? How was the writerly vision of interiority transformed by technologies that quantified mass opinion? Could these sociological methods open up new avenues for understanding collectivity and democracy? Or, conversely, might new psychographic infrastructures only further ensconce heretofore powerful organizations?

As the infrastructure of public opinion research in Britain became increasingly centered in governmental institutions, particularly during World War II, a new series of problems emerged, inspired by these questions. If, as Foucault argues, "statistics is the knowledge of the state," facilitating the means of governmental power, it was possible that the state's collection of public opinion data might facilitate fascistic control.[9] But if overseen by benevolent experts, it was equally possible that public opinion technologies might make transparent, for the first time, the range and diversity of the public's thoughts and beliefs, ushering in a revitalized age of democracy. As discourse over the role of public opinion research transformed radio, newspapers, government, and academia, literature of the time responded to these debates, expressing emergent anxieties about the quickly evolving psychographic age. And while these discussions heighten in the mid-century, they have become even more prevalent in deliberations over privacy of thought in the internet age, fueled by the resurgence of the algorithmic market research that experts now call "psychographics."

The Psychographic Turn: A Brief Pre-History

When Dracula forces Mina's mouth onto his open vein ("a child forcing a kitten's nose into a saucer of milk"), the consumption of blood offers a new opportunity to the vampire-hunter Van Helsing and his compatriots who seek to destroy the villain.[10] Building from popular Victorian theories of hypnosis and telepathy, Stoker treats Dracula's blood as a medium of suppressed knowledge; consumed orally, the blood catalyzes a psychic infection, leading to changes in Mina's mental state. Just as Freud toyed with

---

[9] Michel Foucault, *Security, Territory, and Population. Lectures at the Collège de France, 1977–1978* (New York: Picador, 2009), p. 274.
[10] Bram Stoker, *Dracula*, edited by Nina Auerbach and David Skal (New York: Norton, 1997), p. 247.

hypnosis as a means of exposing hidden recesses of the patient's mind, Van Helsing discovers that hypnosis exposes a telepathic link to Dracula, facilitated through Mina's involuntary blood feast. After the discovery of this mental link, Mina undergoes hypnosis every morning and evening, with Van Helsing exploiting her trance-like state to better locate the Count, identifying, as Van Helsing states in his broken English, "what the Count see and hear."[11] The crew is able to locate the Count, ascertain his next moves based on this psychic intelligence, and finally defeat Dracula, thwarting his efforts to vampirize England and "create a new and ever-widening circle of semi-demons" from London's "teeming millions."[12]

Irish novelist Bram Stoker was exposed to theories of hypnosis when, in 1893, he attended a meeting of the Society for Psychical Research, where members discussed Freud's theory of hypnosis as a way of exposing repressed trauma.[13] In "On the Psychical Mechanism of Hysterical Phenomenon" (1893), Freud, inspired by Jean-Martin Charcot, promoted the use of hypnotism in patients subjected to psychic trauma. Repressed trauma, according to Freud, acted "like a foreign body [...] even long after its penetration"; hypnosis could reproduce, "with hallucinatory vividness," the masked traumatic events.[14] It should come as no surprise then that this theory of hypnosis and trauma emerged in the pages of Stoker's *Dracula* only a few years later.[15] But hypnosis, a term coined in the Victorian period, was not just a method of accessing one's own mental trauma; it might also provide a means of materializing the minds of others, just as Mina channeled the sights and sounds of Dracula's environs. A decade before *Dracula*'s publication, *The Century Dictionary* first defined "psychography," a concept that pooled with others in describing the pseudo-scientific practices that promised to make interiority legible.[16] This term, I would argue, more aptly

[11] Stoker, *Dracula*, p. 281.   [12] Stoker, *Dracula*, p. 51.
[13] Barbara Belford, *Bram Stoker: A Biography of the Author of Dracula* (New York: Knopf, 1996), p. 212–13.
[14] Sigmund Freud, "On the Psychical Mechanism of Hysterical Phenomenon," in *Studies on Hysteria*, translated by James Strachey (New York: Basic Books, 2000 [1893]), p. 9.
[15] Anne Stiles has recognized the tie between Stoker and established neurological sciences of the Victorian period. Alyssa Straight notes that Mina's body becomes, literally, "the battlefield upon which the fate of England is decided." Talia Schaffer recognizes that Mina gains "special erotic jolt from distributing packets of knowledge" through her hypnotic state (418). Ann Stiles, "Cerebral Automatism, the Brain, and Soul in Bram Stoker's *Dracula*," *Journal of the History of the Neurosciences* 15, no. 2 (2006); Alyssa Straight, "Giving Birth to a New Nation: Female Mediation and the Spread of Textual Knowledge in *Dracula*," *Victorian Literature and Culture* 45, no. 2 (2017), p. 391; Talia Schaffer, "'A Wilde Desire Took Me': The Homoerotic History of Dracula," *ELH* 61, no. 2 (1993), pp. 381–425.
[16] "Psychography," *The Century Dictionary* (New York: The Century Co, 1889).

describes both the nature of Mina's mind-meld with Dracula, as well as Dracula's impact on London's potential vampiric hoards. Psychography was described as the practice of "spirit-writing at the hand of a medium" but, additionally, it was defined as "the description of the phenomenon of the mind"—better known as mind-reading.[17] As psychography emerged as a term to capture the extant parapsychological trends of the late Victorian and early modernist periods, it blended the ability to channel the dead with the concept of making legible the mental interiority of the subject. For some, automatic writing, famously exercised by W.B. and Georgie Yeats in the production of their theosophical treatise *A Vision*, allowed the minds of the dead—or the undead, as in *Dracula*—to be revealed.[18] But such psychographic efforts also had political ramifications, as allegorized in *Dracula*; the vampire's mental attunement with his victims facilitates his control, threatening to create a population that not only shares Dracula's instincts, but expedites his will to power. To read the mind—to transmit its interiority to another and make legible its inner workings—is also to control the mind, to lead it to new beliefs, to reprogram it to the design of the reader. *Dracula* was ahead of its time in establishing a connection between individual mind-reading and collective mind-control, as the rise of modernity brought with it many tools to interpret, assess, write, and change the collectivized mind. Dracula's psychographic mastery of his subjects would be a haunting precursor to the psychographic age to come, when all interiority could potentially be made legible and controllable.

In an effort to demystify the private realm of the mind, Adolphus Wagner patented the "psychograph" in 1853: "an apparatus for indicating a living person's thoughts by the agency of nervous electricity."[19] Bearing striking similarities to the traditional planchette, the device harvested "nervous electricity" from the user's hands, enabling them to spell out their hidden thoughts to the public. Such pseudo-scientific theories on thought transmission had become increasingly popular; even *Dracula* suggests that such ideas had become part of mainstream scientific thought by the end of the nineteenth century, as when Van Helsing expresses astonishment that

---

[17] "Psychography."
[18] See Margaret Mills Harper, *Wisdom of Two: The Spiritual and Literary Collaboration of George and W.B. Yeats* (Oxford: Oxford University Press, 2006) and Brenda Maddox, *Yeats's Ghosts: The Secret Life of W.B. Yeats* (New York: Harper Collins, 1999).
[19] Adolphus Theodore Wagner, "Apparatus for Indicating a Person's Thoughts by the Agency of Nervous Electricity," in Provisional Specification, Office of the Commissioners of Patents, no. 173 (London: Eyre and Spottiswood, January 23, 1854).

Dr. Steward could "accept [Charcot's] hypnotism and reject the thought reading."[20] This citation of thought-reading in *Dracula* registers the secularization of such practices, which had expanded beyond the occultist desire to recover the will of the dead (or undead); slowly, the burgeoning desire to transform the inscrutable human mind into a material, legible resource was transforming the landscape of social science.

To this day, the symbolic association between polling and occultism permeates our discourse: to learn the thoughts of the masses is to read tea leaves, act as a diviner, or tap into an amorphous zeitgeist. Pierre Bourdieu suggested that the rise of public opinion polling acted, more or less, as a reprisal of "the ancestral art of the fortune-tellers, palmists and other clairvoyants."[21] To Bourdieu's point, as psychography became increasingly secularized, academics who also studied parapsychology shifted their attention from spiritualism to the various mysteries of the living human mind. While in the late nineteenth and early twentieth century "psychography" primarily described the process of channeling the thoughts of the dead, within a few decades the term described more than just ghost-facilitated scribbling, appropriating a veneer of academic authority in the process. Most fascinating among such newly scientific concerns was the mystifying psychological composition of individuals within a crowd. Twentieth-century scholars like William McDougall, Gustave Le Bon, and Wilfred Trotter eventually transformed the interest in parapsychological mind-reading into legitimate studies of the psychological dynamics between individuals and groups. If Wagner's 1853 mind-reading planchette promised to manifest the opaque workings of the individual psyche, by the mid-century sociologists and social psychologists had begun to articulate how individuals formed their thoughts and, furthermore, how these views or opinions might be understood vis-à-vis the collective. The desire to manifest individual belief went a step further when, by the mid-century, Gallup formalized a method for studying individual opinions, collecting the data, and distributing it to the masses. The public was, for the first time, confronted with its own beliefs, rendered statistically.

"Psychography"—mind-writing—underwent radical transformation from its occultist roots in the Victorian period; a capacious and sprawling

---

[20] Stoker, *Dracula*, p. 171.
[21] Pierre Bourdieu, "Opinion Polls: A 'Science' Without a Scientist," in *In Other Words: Essays Towards a Reflexive Sociology*, translated by Matthew Anderson (Stanford, CA: Stanford University Press, 1990), p. 170.

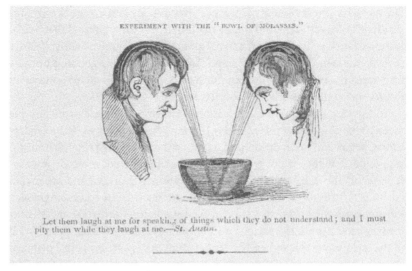

Figure 0.1 Title page of Robert H. Collyer's *Psychography* (Philadelphia: Zieber, 1843).

term, psychography spread its tentacles into multiple fields and took on multiple valences, transforming the literary sphere in the process. Robert Collyer, who experimented with mind-transference utilizing a bowl of molasses ("any other dark fluid will answer the same purpose," he assures us), remarks his pleasure in 1843 when he found "the subject of Psychography [...] occupying the attention of the ablest minds" in Europe (see Figure 0.1).[22] But the generous concept of "mind-writing" soon migrated into literary discourse. Gamaliel Bradford reprised "psychography" during World War I to christen the new method of biography proffered by Lytton Strachey's *Eminent Victorians*. In Bradford's *A Naturalist of Souls: Studies of Psychography* (1917), the psychographic biographer avoids the approach of the portrait or historical biography, instead capturing the "condensed, essential, artistic presentation of character" by "grasp[ing] as many particular moments as he can to give his reader not one but the enduring sum total of them all."[23] Looking into the dark water of the

---

[22] Robert Collyer, *Psychography, or the Embodiment of Thought* (Philadelphia, PA: Zieber & Co, 1843), p. 39.

[23] Gamaliel Bradford, *A Naturalist of Souls* (New York: Dood, Mead, and Company, 1917), p. 5.

subject's life, the biographical equivalent to Collyer's molasses bowl, the literary psychographer distills the essence of the dead from the sum total of their life stories. The subject's deepest, most opaque essence is therefore materialized in written form, with the writer mining epiphanic moments of the subject's life that elucidate an otherwise impervious interiority. Reinterpreting psychography as a literary motif, Bradford argues it "represent[s] definite phases of literary or historical production, phases not only worthy of a distinct name, but of careful study and consideration."[24] Of course, one can see these psychographic visions of biography throughout Bloomsbury modernism; Virginia Woolf's ethereal vision in "New Biography" (1927), which describes the form as emitting "for ever and ever grains of energy" and "atoms of light," suggests a Bradfordian psychographic perspective.[25] And while modernist Bloomsbury did not use the term "psychography" to describe literary technique, the psychographic turn, all the same, bubbled just beneath the surface—a repressed subtext of literary modernism that would become an undeniable force by the mid-century.

While it had expanded into the literary sphere, psychography at the end of World War I remained anchored to the singular mind made manifest: writing the mind of the dead subject, or the living, but bounded by the privileged status of the individual spirit. Expanding this further, Surrealists, influenced by Victorian spiritualism, looked to, as Lefebvre writes "illuminate the nature of the transition from [...] subjective space to the material realm [...] and thence to social life."[26] The Surrealists, articulating the tie between interiority and the social realm, argued that the "psychic automatism" of automatic writing expresses "the actual functioning of thought [...] in the absence of any control exercised by reason, exempt from any aesthetic or moral concern."[27] Countering the Surrealist's efforts to isolate and explore interiority divorced from the social realm, others hoped to uncover a version of psychological experience completely immersed in collective identity. Influential interwar theorist Gerald Heard looked back to so-called

---

[24] Bradford, *A Naturalist of Souls*, p. 4.

[25] Virginia Woolf, "New Biography," in *The Essays of Virginia Woolf. Volume 4: 1925 to 1928*, edited by Andrew McNeille (London: The Hogarth Press, 1984), p. 473.

[26] Henri Lefebvre, *The Production of Space*, translated by Donald Nicholson-Smith (Malden, MA: Blackwell, 2016), p. 18.

[27] See André Breton, "Surrealism (1924)," in *Modernism: An Anthology of Source Documents*, edited by Vassiliki Kolocotroni, Jane Goldman, and Olga Taxidou (Chicago, IL: University of Chicago Press, 1998), p. 309; Katharine Conley also explores the "repressed ghost of spiritualism within Surrealism." Katharine Conley, "Surrealism's Ghostly Automatic Body," *Contemporary French and Francophone Studies* 15, no. 3 (June 2011), p. 298.

primitive culture, which "excludes the self as we understand it" as a model of how to achieve global collective consciousness, further arguing that psychological evolution would inevitably privilege a new form of collective interiority buttressed by tools like telepathy.[28] While such fledgling theories were met with varying levels of enthusiasm, the interpolation, interpretation, replication, and explication of the individual mind as a material, social concern would inevitably, and rapidly, infect the scientific study of increasingly larger groups of minds in the mid-century. This is best noted by Gordon Allport, a pioneer in the use of personality charts and group character traits in theorizing collective psychology. Introducing his innovative "psychographic" chart, Allport recalls the multivalent history of psychography before he expands it, yet again, to assess the notion of collective "averages." He reminds readers that the term "psychography" is sometimes "synonymous with literary biography, sometimes with any random listing of disparate psychological facts," before he describes his own adaptation of the term. Allport then adopts "psychography" to describe his "printed graph" where one can plot "the actual magnitude of common traits attained by any individual," then study them in light of the "average American population."[29] A systematized version of the planchette, a personality chart Gordon Allport labeled "Illustrative Psychograph" represents a wave of psychographic studies of the 1930s, no longer moored to the individual as its subject of study but invested in the use of individual data to assess the dialectical relationship between individual and collective psychology.[30] No longer interested in divining the precise thoughts of the individual, Bradford's methods of reproducing the individual as a "condensed, essential," and even "artistic" presentation of character find a scientific allegory in a slew of new psychographic tools used to collate, average, and assess individuals in comparison to the collective.

In his 1895 book *The Crowd*, Gustave Le Bon predicted an inexorable onslaught: "The age we are about to enter will in truth be the ERA OF CROWDS."[31] And as mid-century psychographic efforts like those of Allport promised a standardized way of materializing, quantifying, and writing collective psychology, the dominant era of the crowd consumed

---

[28] Gerald Heard, *The Ascent of Humanity* (New York: Harcourt, Brace and Company, 1929), p. 28.
[29] Gordon Willard Allport, *Personality: A Psychological Interpretation* (London: Constable, 1938), p. 402.
[30] Allport, *Personality*, p. 403.
[31] Gustave Le Bon, *The Crowd* (New York: Macmillan, 1897), p. xv.

these new efforts like a tidal wave. Scientific interpretations of psychological interiority quickly superseded the validity of individual experience itself. As Sarah Igo writes, "by presenting collections of facts as more authoritative than individuals' perceptions [...] surveyors helped to manufacture the idea and perhaps even the experience of 'the mass.'"[32] Of course, modernism is well-known as the age of the crowd. We need only think of the crowds of workers streaming into the factory in the opening sequence of *Modern Times*, or the group staring up at the Kreemo Toffee advertisement in *Mrs. Dalloway*, to recognize the consequence of crowd dynamics to modernity. And yet, little attention has been given to the way that this psychographic turn—the study of a mass-mindset through the manifestation of psychological interiority as a form of data—impacted literature and culture.

When Auden cynically recorded the institutionalization of public opinion in "The Unknown Citizen," he had been privy to another branch of the psychographic turn—one that expressed optimism about the democratic and egalitarian possibilities underlying collective consciousness. His early unpublished poem of 1932, "In the Year of My Youth...," imagines the psychographic thinker Gerald Heard guiding him, like Virgil, through modern life, trying to theorize "'The barrier' [...] which divides / That which must will from that which can perceive, / Desire from data.'"[33] Auden described and discussed the poem with other luminaries featured heavily in this book, including novelists Naomi Mitchison and Harold Nicolson. The emergence of this understudied network of such pychographically oriented writers in the mid-century speaks to the impact that these public opinion technologies had on the writerly imagination. Olaf Stapledon imagined telepathically linked interstellar utopias; Naomi Mitchison repurposed Scottish lore to theorize a diviner of pure public opinion; H.G. Wells theorized a world-state dominated by academic social psychologists. Public opinion research, at its best, might coordinate the establishment of democratic utopias, based on authentic decision-making. Optimistic visions of social psychology were fueled by public opinion experts, who imagined that polling could usher in a stronger, more vibrant, democracy. In *The Pulse of Democracy* (1940), Gallup argued that polling might shepherd in both "an advance in human relationships and a forward step in self-government."[34] So though some

---

[32] Sarah Igo, *The Averaged American: Surveys, Citizens, and the Making of a Mass Public* (Cambridge, MA: Harvard University Press, 2007), p. 21.
[33] Mendelson, *Early Auden, Later Auden*, p. 142; Lucy S. McDiarmid, "W.H. Auden's 'In the Year of My Youth...,'" *The Review of English Studies* 29, no. 11 (August 1978), pp. 267–312.
[34] George Gallup, *The Pulse of Democracy* (New York: Simon & Schuster, 1940), p. vi.

remained skeptical as to its negative consequences, others viewed polling as a technologically and informatically inflected medium aiding in the fostering of a more robust and responsive democracy. But as political turmoil of the 1930s led inexorably towards another world war, the tension over public opinion polling heightened. While some viewed polling as the next stage in democracy, others viewed polling and its methods as an invasion of privacy. A pollster asking an interviewee a question was also asking for the establishment of a certain form of intimacy and vulnerability. In the war years, anxiety over the sanctity of private thought rose alongside the increased institutionalization of public opinion polling. As the Ministry of Information, the British Broadcasting Corporation (BBC), and newspapers publicized the results of public opinion polls, and armies of pollsters trawled for respondents, people became nervous about the cost of this new form of democratic practice. This book will reframe mid-century aesthetic concerns in light of this emergent psychographic discourse, highlighting both canonical and non-canonical writers who brought attention to debates over the evolving field of social psychology.

The Psychographic State of Twentieth-century Literary Studies

Theorizing the opaque realm of the psyche has long been seen as the very quintessence of the modernist project. Raymond Williams suggests that modernist "access to the 'unconscious'" is but a rendition of earlier methods of artistic divination that include the "literal possession by gods or spirits," the "personifications of inspiring muses," and the "Romantic vision of creative access to the all-purpose personification of nature."[35] For the most part, discussions of modernist interiority have been read in light of this philosophy of the unconscious. Modernist approaches tend towards representation of the unconsciousness as an anti-rationalist aesthetic praxis, resistant to systematization and the reifying influence of the mass. In response to early theorizations of the group mind by French psychologist Gustave Le Bon, Jules Romains's theory of unanimism expressed anxiety about the "ever-larger imprint of the public on the private, of the collective on the individual."[36] Understood in light of this anxiety, the modernist

---

[35] Raymond Williams, *The Politics of Modernism* (New York: Verso, [1989] 2007), p. 72.

[36] Jules Romains, "Poetry and Unanimous Feelings," translated by Louis Cabri, *The Capilano Review* 3, no. 13 (2011), p. 46.

privileging of interiority can be read as a retreat from this "imprinting" function of the masses. Early group psychology in the twentieth century reinforced this fear of collectivity's hypnotic influence, with Le Bon's suggestion that group identity was but a form of hypnotic contagion, and Wilfred Trotter's argument that group identification originated from animalistic and instinctual impulses. But for Romains in 1905, science was limited in its ability to truly understand group psychology: "Not one satisfactory result has been obtained. Observation has remained summary, superficial, and has resulted in but a few ready comparisons." Romains concludes: "The procedures of scientific analysis end there."[37] But, as I argue, the science of group psychology did not end there. As sociologists continued to build on the frameworks of early statisticians, the stakes of the unconscious identity of groups became radically distinct from the monadic autonomy of the individual consciousness so often cited as the mainspring of literary modernism.

Before the popularization of public opinion polling in 1930s Britain, the privileging of consciousness adopted, as Williams attests, a sublime status, capable of transcending the alienating monadic experience of modernity. Virginia Woolf, in "Modern Fiction," captures this essence, presenting life as a "luminous halo, a semi-transparent envelope surrounding us from the beginning of consciousness to the end."[38] In contrast to the ethereal essence of modern fiction, Woolf denigrates the Edwardians for what she calls their "materialism": "They have looked very powerfully, searchingly, and sympathetically out of the window; at factories, at Utopias, even at the decoration and upholstery of the carriage; but never at her, never at life, never at human nature."[39] While Woolf's accusation of Edwardian aesthetic stagnation in the 1910s and 1920s—in the wake of the high modernist experimentation of James Joyce, T.S. Eliot, Ezra Pound, and herself—aptly identifies a chasm between two branches of twentieth-century writing, the mid-century brought with it a reprisal of the materialist approach. But while early Woolf saw materialism masking the spirit in favor of the body, mid-century psychographic aesthetics staged the luminous world of interiority as a material concern whose further study might allow for the restoration of social and cultural stability. Just as William James and Sigmund Freud's conceptions of the unconscious manifested themselves in the writings of high modernism,

---

[37] Romains, "Poetry and Unanimous Feelings," p. 46.

[38] Virginia Woolf, "Modern Fiction," in *The Essays of Virginia Woolf: Volume 4: 1925 to 1928*, edited by Andrew McNeille (London: The Hogarth Press, 1984), p. 160.

[39] Virginia Woolf, "Character in Fiction," in *The Essays of Virginia Woolf: Volume 3*, edited by Andrew McNeille (London: Hogarth Press, 1966), p. 430.

this new materialization of psychology, rendered collectively, provided new avenues for aestheticizing interiority as a social and political concern. Once tapped, mined, and processed, thoughts and desires cease to be a safe haven away from the hegemonic landscape of ideology. Rather, when a pollster or rater records your beliefs on a candidate or your feelings about a radio broadcast, your beliefs become points on the map itself. The self becomes commodified at a psychic level, and, for data-miners, "the numbers are the product."[40] As varied as the responses to public opinion research have been since the introduction of modern polling techniques, they all share an underlying concern over the role of polling in the public sphere and its potential to change the relationship of individuals to a national, or even global, collective. Unlike a citizen-on-the-street interview, the dissemination of polling data to the public presented the views of the individual as objective, quantifiable, and representable. When *News Chronicle* first published the results of Gallup polling for the enlightenment of its reading public it touted that, for the first time, readers could uncover "What Britain Thinks."[41] In the mid-century, poll-mindedness materialized the "luminous halo" of psychological experience onto the printed page and into the public square. Public opinion research, as Foucault argues, inevitably reframed and bolstered the importance of national identity, forcing the individual to become a "subject-object of a knowledge," seeing their consciousnesses— for the first time—as quantifiable objects of study.[42]

The return of psychography in our cultural discourse over the last decade coincides with trends in literary studies retracing the origins of information cultures in the twentieth century, with the rise of the digital humanities further contributing to an increased interest in the intersection between information and culture. As one example, James Purdon's *Modernist Informatics* traces the impact of new informational institutions on culture, discovering ties between institutionalized information networks and the works of Joseph Conrad, Ford Madox Ford, and Graham Greene, among others. Purdon's book reminds us that institutional practices often considered non-literary can help us better understand aesthetics and give us new insights into our contemporary informatic society. Other scholars have attended to such supposedly non-literary infrastructures in their studies of modernism;

---

[40] Gale Metzger quoted in Mark Balnaves and Tom O'Regan, *Rating the Audience: The Business of Media* (London: Bloomsbury, 2012), p. 17.
[41] "What Britain Thinks," *The News Chronicle*, October 17, 1938, p. 10.
[42] Foucault, *Security, Territory, and Population*, p. 275.

Lori Cole's *Surveying the Avant-Garde* reclaimed the aesthetic importance of the questionnaire for literary modernism. In it, she argues that the questionnaire "provided a formula that contributors and readers recognized, at once engaging in, mocking, and usurping social scientific discourse to bolster aesthetic platforms."[43] And, not to be omitted, the rise of scholarly interest in Mass-Observation (M-O) has led to increased awareness of the relationship between aesthetics and the organization's efforts at a poll-minded autoethnography. The concurrent resurgence in studies on the mid-century has also led to a renewed curiosity about polling, a field that only came to be in its modern form through the emergence of George Gallup's method in the 1930s. Opening with a discussion of Gallup's rise, Ian Afflerbach uses surveys in the *Partisan Review* to explore the political ramifications of surveys in the wake of high modernism.[44]

But while psychographic praxis has, with a few notable exceptions, evaded scholarly attention, the institutionalization of polling and public opinion research from the early twentieth century into the years of World War II, working hand-in-glove with the concomitant rise of social psychology and sociology, codifies a new epistemic approach to individual and group psychology—one that remains dominant to this day. It also helps us better understand the myriad divergences between high modernist and mid-century writing. Just as imperial contraction and social turmoil contributed to the aesthetic style Tyrus Miller and Jed Etsy call "late modernism," I argue that the turn towards a psychographic logic in the 1930s is an equally important contributing factor to the aesthetic shifts in the mid-century.[45] The institutionalization of social psychology and the evolution of polling methodologies in this period had their own influence over the scope and scale of the late modernist scene. While aesthetic focus shifted from the individual scale of Virginia Woolf's *Mrs. Dalloway* to the expansionist world-state of the late H.G. Wells, psychological collectivity concurrently

[43] Lori Cole, *Surveying the Avant-Garde: Questions on Modernism, Art, and the Americas in Transatlantic Magazines* (Philadelphia, PA: Pennsylvania University Press, 2018), p. 28.

[44] Ian Afflerbach, "Surveying Late Modernism: *Partisan Review* and the Cultural Politics of the Questionnaire," *Modernism/Modernity Print Plus* 4, no 1 (March 18, 2019).

[45] Tyrus Miller's theorization of "late modernism" frames it as a reaction to modernist fiction, understanding the "pressure of historical circumstances" which threatens the "aesthetics of formal mastery." Jed Esty contrasts high modernist responses to imperial contraction to late modernist ones, which he says, "absorbed the potential energy of a contracting British state and converted it into the language not of aesthetic decline but of cultural renewal." Tyrus Miller, *Late Modernism: Politics, Fiction and the Arts Between the World Wars* (Berkeley, CA: University of California Press, 1999), pp. 18–19; Jed Esty, *A Shrinking Island: Modernism and National Culture in England* (Princeton, NJ: Princeton University Press, 2004), p. 8.

emerged as an aesthetic concern. If world events seemed larger in the interwar, so too did psychology, whose scale and scope had likewise expanded. Individual consciousness swelled outwards and, as it did, people began to contemplate the intricacies of group psychological dynamics. This "psychographic turn," as I am calling it here, captures the evolution and transformation of social psychology as it was expressed in the mid-century.

The Scope of Public Opinion Polling in *Mid-Century British Literature*: *The Psychographic Turn*

This book is structured by two principles. The first is chronological and captures the genealogy of the psychographic turn, beginning from the origins of academic sociology at the turn of the century but centralizing on the mid-century use of public opinion research by institutions like the BBC, Mass-Observation, and the Ministry of Information. The rise of academic sociology, detailed in Chapter 1, was the first front of the psychographic turn. While H.G. Wells's primary reputation is as a science fiction juggernaut, few scholars address his abiding interest in the early field of sociology. This chapter traces Wells's investment in sociology, beginning with his early aspirations of being the first professor of sociology in England and his controversial refutations of academic sociology at the British Sociological Society. In sparring with early sociologists like Wilfred Trotter and Gustave Le Bon, Wells presents an unexplored pathway of early sociological study. In his turn to future historiography in his fiction, particularly in his 1933 novel *The Shape of Things to Come*, Wells proffers a late-life argument about how sociology might restructure and reorganize society after its collapse. But when this novel is transformed into a film in 1936, the inherent contradictions between Wells's utopian vision in his late novel and the corresponding film emerge. These contradictions set the stage for the remainder of the chapters, which take this ambivalence as their primary focus, as authors unpack and theorize the potentiality of social psychology to reorganize and restructure the body politic.

Alongside following the history of psychography, this book also traces the transmigration of psychographic approaches across multiple public-facing British institutions. Though academic sociology was the foundation of public opinion polling research, newspapers became the first medium by which the public understood this new academic innovation. The second chapter of this project looks at the convergence—and competition—of polling and newspapers in the 1930s, with particular focus on the publicity surrounding the Peace Ballot, a survey registering the opinions of an astounding eleven million English participants. Journalism had long been seen as an agent for the management of public opinion, but the emergence of early polling as a primarily journalistic concern during this decade led to increased scrutiny over the role of newspapers in this new scientific field. Conducted by non-experts with a very particular bias, the League of Nations's Peace Ballot muddied the waters as to the goal of public opinion research, and the media's advocacy of the Ballot further exacerbated these concerns over polling's credibility. While authors like Olaf Stapledon and A.A. Milne found inspiration in the aims of the League that overshadowed methodological concerns, the chapter looks to Evelyn Waugh's short story "An Englishman's Home" to demonstrate skepticism over the Peace Ballot, to which the short story ambivalently alludes in its allegory about uniting communities against war. The chapter then transitions to address Evelyn Waugh's *Scoop*, which takes to task both the newspaper industry's manipulation of public opinion and the burgeoning field of public opinion analysis through its allusions to Mass-Observation's Tom Harrisson. These texts emphasized the critical role of journalism in early polling, as well as its potential contribution to a dangerous overdetermination of public opinion in the 1930s.

Poll-mindedness was not only a concern for the broader public; more formal institutions likewise developed an interest in psychographics. The BBC's Listener Research Department began to use methods informed by the Gallup survey to collect data on listener habits and practices. Building on the discussion of print media in Chapter 2, Chapter 3 focuses on radio and anxieties about listener reception that led to the establishment of the BBC's Listener Research Department; the chapter looks to both the internal development of public opinion research at the BBC as well as the perspective of outsiders as to how the radio could facilitate in the expansion of collective consciousness. Opening with a discussion of BBC drama producer Val Gielgud's co-written detective dramas about the BBC, *Inspector Silence Takes the Air* and *Thirteen to the Gallows*, the chapter articulates the BBC's internal hesitation about radio's ability to reach its audience in wartime, even as it instituted its revolutionary Listener Research Department. Despite hesitation from some conservative BBC administrators, producers like Gielgud expressed enthusiasm that statistical methods like those instituted in newspaper polling and market research could aid the BBC in assuaging concerns about audience. Correspondingly, authors outside the BBC, already conditioned by the psychographic turn, revised their visions of the future with an emphasis on collective consciousness, incorporating the wireless as a key medium to facilitate the construction of consensus-based utopias. The second half of the chapter shifts focus from the internal workings of the BBC to the 1930s fictions of Olaf Stapledon and Virginia Woolf, two writers inspired by the promise of collectivism and whose depictions of the wireless as a potentially revolutionary medium epitomized both the legibility of collective consciousness and the consequent imagination of new egalitarian societies made possible by the harnessing of group psychology for the social good.

We can also locate the emergence of psychography in the work of Mass-Observation (M-O), a group whose early experiments with more qualitative methodologies provided the field of social psychology with a path that remained widely under-explored amidst the fetishization for quantitative analysis within institutionalized polling. The fourth chapter of this book proffers a path unfollowed in the history of sociological research by declaring the importance of qualitative methods of sociological analysis in literature of the interwar period, inspired primarily by M-O's efforts in the field. M-O's self-described position as the "black sheep" of social psychology enabled it to explore a variety of methods for collecting data outside of the "scientific" standards set by research firms like the Gallup-inspired British Institute of Public Opinion. For M-O, statistical methods were bolstered by, and made relevant through, the amassing of volunteer diaries and the collection of anecdotes and overheard conversation gathered by M-O's amateur "observers." Highlighting the novels of two women who performed research at the behest of M-O, Naomi Mitchison and Celia Fremlin, this chapter emphasizes that the new field of quantitative public opinion research was an a priori exclusionary one. The practice and study of polling not only excluded women, considered non-experts, but pollsters themselves often excluded women as interviewees, citing their inability to form independent opinions about politics outside of male authority. Both Mitchison's *We Have Been Warned* and Fremlin's *The Hours Before Dawn* present cautionary tales of the dangerous repercussions of not listening to women's stories, and thus stand as allegories for the necessity of qualitative methods of polling as a means of making women's voices heard, speaking back against the overarching trend towards exclusive quantitative methods of public opinion research.

The concluding chapter of this project looks specifically to the controversial institutional adoption of public opinion polling within the Ministry of

Information (MoI) during World War II. The inclusion of public opinion and morale surveys as a significant weapon of war symbolized the concretization of the field as a valid and respectable social science, thus making a fitting concluding chapter for this book. However, the integration of sociological study into the MoI was not without its failures. The chapter takes on two historical examples of this failure, bolstered by archival evidence from the Home Intelligence Department, including the "Silent Column" campaign of 1940 and the mishandling of propaganda to Ireland. While the "Silent Column" campaign inadvertently prohibited citizens from sharing information, even from pollsters, Home Intelligence and the MoI were looking for novelists and poets who might help them better understand civilian morale; among those were writers Cecil Day-Lewis and Elizabeth Bowen, both of whom provided service to the Ministry during the war. I contend that the fiction of both these writers, particularly Bowen's depictions of psychological interiority and Day-Lewis's institutionally oriented pseudonymous detective fiction, demonstrates an emergent skepticism about public opinion research. When wielded by the government, polling became increasingly viewed as a method to control populations it supposedly sought to represent, while at the same time becoming a cornerstone of administrative culture in the twentieth century.

Where political exigency first set the path for the emergence of the psychographic turn in Britain, the postwar global economy led to its rapid escalation. The world it created is highly recognizable to us today. Market research, focus groups, political polling, and customer surveys are all part of the milieu of modern capitalism, and with them psychography has returned as a term with as much importance now as any other political or social movement of the last several decades. The world of big data now makes us fully aware of our susceptibility to group mentality and our exposure to corporate and political manipulation. The increasingly nuanced work of twenty-first-century market demographics makes us at risk, both individually and collectively, for consumption of propaganda. In modern discourse, polls are no longer considered reflective of a political reality. As we live in a world that, as Walter Lippmann wrote in 1922, has become "altogether too big, too complex, and too fleeting for direct acquaintance," polling has increasingly acted as an agent in the construction of the pseudo-environments in which we live our lives.[46] Recent elections have been

---

[46] Lippmann, *Public Opinion*, p. 16.

fraught with controversy over the role polling plays in democracy; it is undeniable that polling has become a political influence sui generis. And while representations of polling as a malignant force that overdetermines our political life have become increasingly dominant, it is vital to recall that this visceral reaction to polling was not always thus. At its inception, the psychographic turn was met with equal parts hope and dread. The tension between these two positions has accelerated the psychographic age and led to an obsession with polling beyond what George Gallup could have ever foreseen. Such fetishization, I argue, begins in this formative mid-century period, as people began to understand the ramifications of hearing, for the first time, what their fellow citizens were thinking.

1

A Science So-Called

H.G. Wells's Reprisal of Academic Sociology

Introduction: H.G. Wells and the Le Bonian Crowd

As the comet rockets towards earth in H.G. Wells's *In the Days of the Comet* (1906), protagonist Willie Leadford shoots his revolver into the impervious night, blasting at the vague forms of his former lover Nettie Stuart and her wealthy paramour Edward Varrell. As the comet collides with the earth's crust, penetrating its layers, Leadford's interior is also transformed by an invasive force. As Leadford falls unconscious, the comet's vapors infiltrate his mind, subjecting him to "a bath of strength and healing for nerve and brain."[1] The comet's serene fumes traverse the planet; the world's population finds itself, like Leadford, psychologically transformed by this interstellar intrusion. As Ruth Levitas notes, the comet "open[s] humanity to the light of reason and extinguish[es] sexual jealousy and exclusive monogamy," thus fictionalizing the theories of sexual evolution prevalent in Wells's non-fiction, particularly *Socialism and the Family* (1906) and *A Modern Utopia* (1905).[2] But before interstellar peace gas benevolently breaches Leadford's interiority, Wells theorizes a literal collective body contaminated by social strife, in desperate need of detoxification. Wells describes group dynamics before the comet's strike in terms of biological disorder:

> The ordinary healthy flow of people going to work, people going about their business, was chilled and checked. Numbers of men stood about the streets in knots and groups, as corpuscles gather and catch in the blood-vessels in the opening stages of inflammation. The woman looked haggard

---

[1] H.G. Wells, *In the Days of the Comet* (Lincoln, NE: University of Nebraska Press, [1906] 2001), p. 147.
[2] Ruth Levitas, "Back to the Future: Wells, Sociology, Utopia and Method," *Sociological Review* 58, no. 4 (2010), pp. 531–2.

Public Opinion Polling in Mid-Century British Literature: The Psychographic Turn. Megan Faragher,
Oxford University Press. © Megan Faragher 2021. DOI: 10.1093/oso/9780192898975.003.0002

and worried. The Ironworkers had refused the proposed reduction of their wages, and the lockout had begun.[3]

People flow as blood does, through the organism of the body politic and the streets of the city, with economic instability acting as an inflammatory agent, causing individuals in the group to malignantly clot. The comet's calming clouds, therefore, not only recalibrate the individual mind, but also ameliorate civic arterial congestion.

It is not only in describing social dysfunction that Wells evokes bodily symbolism. In diagnosing various causes of social disruption, he invokes similar biological metaphors of contagion and disease. Citing journalism as a cause of violent rhetoric, he designates the fictional *New Paper* as "one of a flood of disease germs."[4] Leadford views himself as a part of this biological corpus. He describes himself as "one corpuscle in the big amorphous body of the English community, one of forty-one million such corpuscles," reflecting that "all over the country that day, millions read as I read, and came round into line with me, under the same magnetic spell."[5] Prefiguring Wells's potent critiques of nationalism between the wars, Leadford recognizes his singularity within the larger, "amorphous" body of England.[6] As "one of forty-one million...corpuscles," Willie's subjectivity is nearly decimated by the extensive scale of the national body. But the newspaper—a media infecting readers as contagions infect hosts—initiates the individual as part of an ailing collective, prefiguring McLuhan's account of the impact of new media.[7] Additionally, in successfully linking metaphors of biological contagion to group psychology, Wells parrots the work of early social psychologists. Early academic sociologists had similarly borrowed metaphors of illness from the established biological sciences to invent the new field of study that would be called, interchangeably, group psychology, social psychology, or sociology. It was the development of this new academic discourse that would catalyze polling culture and transform theories of collective consciousness.

---

[3] Wells, *In the Days of the Comet*, p. 52.   [4] Wells, p. 71.   [5] Wells, p. 71.

[6] John S. Partington dates Wells's more virulent anti-nationalism to the armistice, after which "he sought the supersession of nationalist sentiment in favour of a more tolerant cosmopolitanism which advanced world citizenship and collective responsibility." John S. Partington, *Building Cosmopolis: The Political Thought of H.G. Wells* (Aldershot: Ashgate, 2003), p. 82.

[7] McLuhan writes of "electric" media as a hot media that forces us to go "through the three stages of alarm, resistance, and exhaustion that occur in every disease or stress of life, whether individual or collective." Marshall McLuhan, *Understanding Media* (Cambridge, MA: MIT Press, 1994), p. 164.

At the dawn of social psychology, the field's earliest scholars would liken the mental transformation of groups to a form of biological illness as well. In 1895, a decade before Wells published *In the Days of the Comet*, Gustave Le Bon published *Psychologie des Foules*, translated a year later in English as *The Crowd: A Study of the Popular Mind*. This book constructed an early framework for social psychology as a field of scientific and academic discourse, which it accomplished partly by likening the phenomena of group behavior to the dynamics in established scientific fields like biology and chemistry. To assert a fruitful analogy between established science and its more fledgling form in group psychology, metaphors of illness and disease loom large throughout *The Crowd*. Le Bon defines the "psychological crowd" as "a provisional being formed of heterogeneous elements, which for a moment are combined, exactly as the cells which constitute a living body form by their reunion a new being which displays characteristics very different from those possessed by each of the cells singly."[8] The individual in the crowd, in Le Bon's view, subsumes his desires to that of the larger group, his personality deracinated and melded with traits of others. In this process, the crowd adopts some characteristics of individual members while developing qualities entirely unique to itself, creating a new "cellular" collectivity. And when attempting to identify why crowds evolved new characteristics as individual will resigned itself to the mental unity of the crowd, he cited as one reason the impact of a complex concept he calls "contagion." "Contagion," he articulated, "is a phenomenon of which it is easy to establish the presence, but that is not easy to explain. It must be classed among those phenomena of a hypnotic order [...] In a crowd every sentiment and act is contagious, and contagious to such a degree that an individual readily sacrifices his personal interest to the collective interest."[9] Reframing crowd behavior through the epidemiological logic of contagion, Le Bon stages the psychological phenomenon of group identification at the intersection of nineteenth-century rhetorics of biology and spiritualism, merging a prevalent fascination with biological science—the contagious body—with one from Victorian psychological occultism—mesmeric influence.[10] We see the same convergence in the aforementioned sections of *In the Days of the Comet*, when Wells describes the newspaper's influence as a "disease germ" that produces

---

[8] Le Bon, *The Crowd*, p. 6.   [9] Le Bon, *The Crowd*, p. 10.
[10] Alison Winter traces how Victorians explored the "physiology of volition to explore how individuals could be part of a 'mass' experience without losing their sanity or identity." Alison Winter, *Mesmerized: Powers of Mind in Victorian Britain* (Chicago, IL: University of Chicago Press, 2000), p. 331.

a "magnetic spell" on Willie, thus "defining *fin-de-siècle* crisis in terms of a disease of society."[11] The mechanisms of control applied to biological contagions are analogous to those between the mesmerist and the mesmerized, as they reconstruct a population's psychological interiority as a possible subject for the exercise of biopolitical control.[12] In so doing, *The Crowd* represents the first significant intervention transforming group psychology into a formal scientific pursuit, prefiguring later usages of polling by state institutions like the wartime Ministry of Information.

The contagion theory of crowds became, in its own way, contagious. Le Bon's work inspired an epidemic of work on group psychology, all of which cited *The Crowd* as a foundational text in the burgeoning field, and all of which had to engage with his foundational theories about contagion and mesmerism, even if they did not fully cosign his deductions. British-born Harvard psychologist William McDougall, the "father of the professionalization of modern parapsychology," cites *The Crowd* as one of the "most notable" books in the burgeoning field.[13] A few years later Sigmund Freud would also directly respond to Le Bon and McDougall in *Group Psychology and the Analysis of the Ego* (1921). Freud begins his inquiry by looking to Le Bon's theory of contagion: "why [...] do we invariably give way to this contagion when we are in a group?"[14] And though *In the Days of the Comet* is just one example of the Le Bonian contagion thesis emerging in Wells's mid-career work, the contagion metaphor was recurrent throughout his oeuvre. We see the theme emerge in novels like *Tono-Bungay*, with scholars like Maria Teresa Chialant suggesting that, like Dickens, Wells ties "the idea of

---

[11]   William Bellamy, "The Novels of Wells, Bennett and Galsworthy," in *The Critical Response to H.G. Wells*, edited by William J. Scheick (Westport, CT: Greenwood Press, 1995), p. 72.

[12]   In his *Security, Territory, Population* lectures, Foucault seeks "a 'governmentality' that would be to the state what techniques of segregation were to psychology." What he arrives at is the invention and creation of "population": "a set of processes such as the ratio of births to deaths, the rate of reproduction [...] a whole series of related economic and political problems." Michel Foucault, *Security, Territory, Population: Lectures at the Collège de France: 1977–1978*, edited by Michael Senellart (New York: Palgrave Macmillan, 2007), p. 120; Michel Foucault, *"Society Must Be Defended": Lectures at the Collège de France: 1975–1976*, edited by Mauro Bertani and Alessandro Fontana, Translated by David Macey (New York: Picador, 1997), p. 243.

[13]   Egil Asprem, "A Nice Arrangement of Heterodoxies: William McDougall and the Professionalization of Psychical Research," *Journal of the History of the Behavioral Sciences* 46, no. 2 (2010), p. 135; William McDougall, *The Group Mind* (Cambridge: Cambridge University Press, 1927), p. 20.

[14]   Sigmund Freud, *Group Psychology and the Analysis of the Ego*, edited and translated by James Strachey (New York: Norton, [1921] 1959), p. 35.

change" to "disease and decay."[15] But years later, when Wells wrote the screenplay version of his 1933 novel *The Shape of Things to Come*, he revived—and revised—many of the contagion tropes from *In the Days of the Comet*, foregrounding the role of institutional structures in the formation of public opinion. In *The Shape of Things to Come*, a peace gas cures society of its warmongering, just as it had in *In the Days of the Comet*; however, in the filmic rendition, Wells would replace his interstellar comet with a plane flying at the behest of an international governing body, dropping peace-bombs from the sky. Despite the increasing militarism of the contagion trope, Wells's film continues to promote the links between group psychology and illness. While authoritarian leaders have turned the film's Everytown into a militaristic state, an epidemic of "sleeping sickness" allegorizes the fascist scourge, infecting citizens who wander the streets like zombies, subject to execution from the townspeople bent on protecting themselves from this mental contagion. In both the film and novel, sleeping sickness symbolizes humanity in a state of political decline. And, in a typically Wellsian fashion, the most troubling consequence of human devolution was depicted in the form of unintelligent wanderers plagued by a sickness of mind and body, constitutionally incapable of creating the technocratic utopia of intellectual experts about whom Wells fantasizes throughout his writing career.[16]

It is worth emphasizing that the unmoored status of the wandering ill in *Things to Come* marks a firm distinction from the dynamics of group psychology suggested by *In the Days of the Comet*, where mental persuasion of the crowd originates from the malignant and unilateral influence of the press. And yet, these two examples, pulled from varied points of Wells's life, demonstrate his dedication to understanding social psychology and the shifting beliefs about the dynamics and goals of such a field. As Patrick Parrinder argues, the period of Wells's writing following the rapid-fire publication of his scientific romances, which he specifically dates to 1906, initiates his efforts "to establish his credentials as a serious sociological essayist" and inaugurates a sociological turn in his writing and thought.[17] Wells's

[15] Maria Teresa Chialant, "Dickensian Motifs in Wells's Novels: The Disease Metaphor in *Tono-Bungay*," in *H.G. Wells under Revision: Proceedings of the International*, edited by Patrick Parrinder and Christopher Rolfe (London: Associated University Press, 1990), pp. 98–9.
[16] Keith Williams argues that *Things to Come*'s Cabal, who arrives in the aftermath of the Everytown apocalypse, is "[t]he mouthpiece for Wells's technocratic solution." Keith Williams, *H.G. Wells, Modernity and the Movies* (Liverpool: Liverpool University Press, 2007), p. 114.
[17] Patrick Parrinder, *Shadows of the Future: H.G. Wells, Science Fiction and Prophesy* (Liverpool: Liverpool University Press, 1995), p. 27.

restaging of group psychology in the mid-century film *Things to Come* followed a nearly life-long interest in the subject that tracks as far back as the early twentieth century and his contentious relationship with the British Sociological Society. While Wells maintains an investment and fascination in the concept of psychological contagion, a deeper examination of his works reveals a slightly more complicated relationship with the figureheads of early academic social psychology. This chapter traces Wells's shifting vision of psycho-social dynamics in his work, finding the author sitting, unexpectedly, at the intersection of sociology and mid-century visions of collectivity, as both established themselves as institutional fields in the first half of the twentieth century. In part, this chapter argues that at the core of Wells's aesthetics, accentuated in his latter writings, sociology becomes an increasingly dominant institutional presence, providing an intellectual justification for his technocratic utopianism. Even as a young man, Wells was interested in the emergence of an intellectual elite. But in his later works, Wells's reprisal of academic sociology provides a new praxis for such an elite class and a new vision of how social groups might be reconstructed.

For his contemporaries, Wells's sociological aesthetics positioned him squarely outside the terrain of the other moderns; Woolf famously dismisses Wells, writing that by "taking upon his shoulders the work that ought to have been discharged by Government officials" he forgets "the crudity and coarseness of his human beings."[18] Along these lines, Wells's sociological aesthetics have continually impacted his reception within canonical modernism, as R.D. Haynes notes when he draws a distinction between modernist fiction, in which "characters were studied in depth as individuals [...] in comparative isolation from their backgrounds and society" and Wells's fiction, which "stress[ed] [...] the role of the individual in *society*, not in isolation."[19] Partly, this is due to the division of Wells's oeuvre. His early scientific romances, including *The Time Machine* (1895) and *The Island of Doctor Moreau* (1896), have been readily appropriated by scholars of genre fiction, while his social realism of *Love and Mr Lewisham* (1899) and *Kipps* (1905) have been read as late-Victorian exemplars of social realism. But, as William Bellamy notes, the titular comet in Wells's 1906 novel likewise brings with it a "transition" in his fiction "from a preoccupation with isolated individuals [...] to a speculative concern for the equality of individual

---

[18] Woolf, "Modern Fiction," p. 159.
[19] R.D. Haynes, *H.G. Wells, Discoverer of the Future* (London: Macmillan, 1979), p. 194, italics in original.

life within society as a whole."[20] The aesthetic struggle to adapt his scientific romances to problems of social class parallels the institutionalization of social psychology which, as demonstrated by the early works of Le Bon, prioritizes the use of biological discourse as a way of exploring social experience. In other words, the evolution of Wells's oeuvre is an aesthetic effort to cohere the scientific and the social in his writing practice. In this effort Wells produced what I am calling a psychographic aesthetics: a style that attempted materialist mastery over the complex interior life of the collective social body; it is this style that I will be attending to most diligently in what follows. In addition to shedding light on a broader trend towards psychographic aesthetics in the mid-century, Wells's dedication to psychography also helps us better interrogate his displacement from the modernist canon. If Wells's literary output is not often considered sufficiently modernist—too materialist, as Woolf argued—it is because of Wells's position as a vanguard of sociological aesthetics, as he looks to find coherence between the messiness of interiority and the orderliness of academic theorem. From this position, Wells naturally constructed a vision of group identity that differed from his modernist contemporaries. This aesthetic vision is perhaps best captured by the semi-autobiographical Wellsian figure Dick Remington who, in *The New Machiavelli* (1911), queries his own identity: "[s]omewhere between politics and literature my grip needs to be found, but where?"[21] The tension between public and private, between politics and art, repeatedly stage themselves at the center of Wells's aesthetic project. Building on Sarah Cole's reclamation of Wells, I contend that Wells represents an underdeveloped strain of twentieth-century writing, born of his investment in a more scientifically and statistically informed relationship to group psychology, which matures in his mid-century writings.[22] But I would argue that it is not only Wells being recovered in this process. Further examination of Wells's place in the literary canon forces a reconsideration of academic studies of group psychology before the politicized environment of the 1930s, when the stakes of sociological discussions became more elevated and the debates more intense.

[20] Bellamy, "The Novels of Wells, Bennett and Galsworthy," p. 72.
[21] H.G. Wells, *The New Machiavelli*, edited by Norman Mackenzie (London: Everyman, [1911] 1994), p. 146.
[22] Sarah Cole, *Inventing Tomorrow: H.G. Wells and the Twentieth Century* (New York: Columbia University Press, 2020).

Early Sociology: A Failed Utopian Science

Throughout his career, Wells expressed interest in group dynamics, evinced by his engagement with the academic field of group psychology, or sociology, in its earliest stages. But to understand the relationship between Wells and sociology it is best to begin with a dust-up he caused in British sociological circles in 1905, a year before the publication of *In the Days of the Comet*.[23] Wells had been a member of the Sociological Society for several years, but in a lecture combatively titled "The So-Called Science of Sociology" he mapped an innovative vision of the new science's aims and political impacts. In an effort to expand sociology's scope to incorporate a more utopian praxis, Wells aggressively challenged a foundational premise of sociology, which had been bolstered by the works of Gustave Le Bon and British social psychologist Wilfred Trotter. Early pioneers of social psychology insisted upon the evacuation of individual subjectivity in its subservience to a new collective identity. Wells contrarily insisted that ignoring the prevalence of individual will weakened sociology as a field. In his autobiography, Wells remembers the controversy: "I insisted that in sociology there were no units for treatment, but only one single unit which was human society, and that in consequence the normal scientific method of classification and generalization breaks down."[24] In short, Wells considered the entire focus on crowd theories rather misguided; instead of beginning with a proscribed unit of society, sociology needed to begin from the level of the individual and reframe collectivity from below. *In the Days of the Comet* suggests the dangerous ramifications Wells saw in the institutionalized sociological position, with Willie's self-defeating reflection on himself as one of "forty-one million such corpuscles" standing in for Wells's critique of academic sociology. Responding to the propensity for social psychology to fetishize the crowd as an undifferentiated mass, Wells's essay begins with the bombshell that "[m]y trend of thought leads me to deny that sociology is a science," further arguing that "[s]ociology must be neither art simply, nor science in the narrow meaning of the word at all, but knowledge rendered imaginatively and with an *element of personality*, that is to say, in the highest sense of the word, literature."[25] Wells imagined sociology taking a more

---

[23] Michael Sherborne states that Wells staged this question first in *The Fortnightly Review* in 1905, then in May 1906 in an article for *Independent Review*. Michael Sherborne, *H.G. Wells: Another Kind of Life* (London: Peter Owen, 2012), p. 174.

[24] H.G. Wells, *An Experiment in Autobiography* (London: Victor Gollancz, 1934), p. 657.

[25] Wells, *An Experiment in Autobiography*, p. 658, emphasis added.

capacious view of its subject matter and integrating the notion of individual agency in the models of collectivity, which had marked the field to date. He wanted sociology to adopt an aesthetic and utopian tenor. Wells likewise rejected the typical efforts of sociology to, as Krishan Kumar described it, "observe, compare, classify, establish regularities and formulate testable laws."[26] Michael Sherborne goes further in describing Wells's critique of a sociology that is a smidgen too scientific to embrace its utopianism: "In the hard sciences it may be possible to aggregate data into sound generalizations, but in the study of people laws are harder to achieve [...] there will never come a day when the sociologist will wield the seemingly value-free authority enjoyed by, for example, a 'sanitary engineer.'"[27] Wells wanted a sociology that was part art and part science, a balance he would continue to work towards well into his mid-century writings.

His remarks about sociology were coolly received. But that did not stop Wells from briefly pursuing a career in the field he hoped to create. Wells's opposition to institutional sociological approaches would not only help define sociology; it would also significantly alter his thinking and aesthetics thereafter.[28] In the end, "The So-Called Science of Sociology" had as much of an impact on Wells as it had on the burgeoning field of academic sociology, as has been noted by Ruth Levitas, Duncan Bell, and others.[29] Wells remembered the aftermath of his lecture in detail, writing that, "Mr. Wilfred Trotter thought [the essay] was an 'Attack on Science.'"[30] Despite his harsh reception, Halsey's A History of Sociology in Britain notes that Wells still sought a position as Chair of Sociology at the University of London, a claim corroborated by Wells's letters; in a letter to Beatrice Bell, Wells was apoplectic to find that there was not a "chair of sociology for me," since he felt he had written his best work gratis for the Sociological Society.[31] The position was eventually given to Leonard Hobhouse, who bested Wells to be, alongside Edward Westermarck, the first professor of sociology in England.

[26] Krishan Kumar, "Wells and 'the So-Called Science of Sociology,'" in H.G. Wells under Revision: Proceedings of the International, edited by Patrick Parrinder and Christopher Rolfe (London and Toronto: Associated University Press, 1990), p. 193.

[27] Sherborne, H.G. Wells: Another Kind of Life, pp. 174–5.

[28] Levitas, "Back to the Future," pp. 530–47.

[29] Duncan Bell, "Pragmatic Utopianism and Race: H.G. Wells as Social Scientist," Modern Intellectual History 16, no. 3 (2017), pp. 1–33.

[30] Wells, An Experiment in Autobiography, p. 658.

[31] A.H. Hasley, A History of Sociology in Britain: Science, Literature, and Society (Oxford: Oxford University Press, 2004), p. 22.; H.G. Wells, The Correspondence of H.G. Wells: Volume 2, edited by David C. Smith (London: Pickering and Chatto, 1998), p. 25.

The snub would further pigeonhole Wells as a novelist first and foremost, a field in which he had already made significant contributions by 1906.

Le Bon's theory of the "mental unity of crowds" was furthered in the circle of British psychologists, particularly by Wilfred Trotter—the same man who lambasted Wells's sociology lecture. Trotter, who emphasized the animalistic nature of crowds, continued to challenge Wells's utopian sociology even into the 1920s.[32] The introduction to Trotter's *Instincts of the Herd in Peace and War* (1921) acts as a rebuttal of Wells, who he calls out by name. Trotter contends that "the two fields [of psychology]—the social and the individual—are regarded here as absolutely continuous."[33] Trotter then heaped scorn on those who dared to think otherwise, remembering Wells's 1906 lecture, declaring his offense that Wells "maintained that as a science sociology not only does not but cannot exist."[34] Foundational to Trotter's thinking on the subject is the concept embodied in his title: herd instinct. Trotter saw no distinction between individuals and groups because, in part, the psychology of the individual was always already embodied in the social animal. To that extent, human psychology was animalistic at its base, incapable of being divorced from instinctual drives. For Wells, the problem with this vision of psychology was that it, by definition "[ignored] individualities," ceding ground to theories that prioritized animalism and the intractability of group cohesion. For a man whose aborted career in sociology made way for a prolific career as a novelist, the abandoned field of sociology, and the aims such a field might hold, would be replaced by a utopian literary aesthetics. If deracinated from the conflict between individuals and groups, Wells envisioned sociology as a form of utopian thinking, not a study of humanity's base instincts; it was a project, not a discipline. Wells eventually argued that sociology reject itself as a science and embrace its unconscious desire to "accept Utopias as material," informed by his Platonic vision of an ascendant working-class elite.[35] Sociology's institutionalization focused on symptoms and not the disease of the social structure; it was a claim he would allude to in *In the Days of the Comet* when he lambasted reformist policies for attacking "not the disease, but the consequences of the disease."[36]

---

[32]   Le Bon, *The Crowd*, p. 2.
[33]   Wilfred Trotter, *The Instincts of the Herd in Peace and War* (London: T. Fisher Unwin Ltd, 1916), p. 12.
[34]   Trotter, *The Instincts of the Herd*, p. 12.
[35]   H.G. Wells, *An Englishman Looks at the World* (London: Cassell and Company, 1914), p. 204. Michael Sherborne notes the influence of Plato's *Republic* on his vision of the working-class elite. Sherborne, *Another Kind of Life*, p. 50.
[36]   Wells, *In the Days of the Comet*, p. 34.

Wells's revisionist medico-social rhetoric implies that, rather than looking to simply manage institutional failures, more wide-ranging social reforms should take root in sociology, stating that "the creation of Utopias—and their exhaustive criticism—is the proper and distinctive method of sociology."[37]

It is not difficult to see how Wells's maturing theories of group psychology were reflected in his evolving literary style. Having emerged, as cynical as he was about the conservative aims of academic sociology, Wells began a process of transition in his work, beginning an uncomfortable marriage between the scientific romances of his first books and his subsequent social novels. As early as 1911, Wells saw himself "in a position to put both sociology and fantasy behind him and write nothing but novels for some years."[38] Arguably, he succeeded at the latter by failing to do the former. Whereas the earliest renditions of Wells's social novels focused on the perils of working-class identity—Lewisham an aspiring schoolmaster who fails to climb the social ladder, and Kipps only able to make it out of poverty by the chance success of a play—later manifestations of the "social" Wells, including *Tono-Bungay* (1909) and *The New Machiavelli* (1911), take up the struggles of the social elite and their abilities to manipulate and massage public opinion. This shift in attention, from working-class struggle to the power-wrangling elite, begins Wells's new investment in social realism, but also a new investment in a top-down system of social reorganization. As the protagonist of *The New Machiavelli*, Dick Remington, states, "We must have an aristocracy—not of privilege, but of understanding and purpose—or mankind will fail."[39] We can find the germs of Wells's social elitism here, but this is only one stage in a life-long project that took sociology and public opinion formation as its basis, with the goal of, as Remington puts it, "resuscitat[ing] a Public Opinion and prepar[ing] the ground for a revised and renovated ruling culture."[40] By the publication of *World Brain* in 1938, Wells would wholeheartedly call for a "reconditioned and more powerful public opinion" which would "replace our multitude of unco-ordinated ganglia, our powerless miscellany of universities, research institutions," and "literatures."[41] It was only then, when a new World War thundered on the horizon, that Wells could imagine a populous of "competent receiver[s]" capable of really understanding world affairs.[42]

[37] Wells, *An Englishman Looks at the World*, p. 203.
[38] Michael Sherborne, *H.G. Wells: Another Kind of Life*, p. 196.
[39] Wells, *The New Machiavelli*, p. 241.   [40] Wells, *The New Machiavelli*, p. 281.
[41] H.G. Wells, *World Brain* (New York: Doubleday, 1938), p. xv.
[42] Wells, *World Brain*, p. xv.

Wells's new vision of the masses comes into finest relief in his 1933 novel *The Shape of Things to Come*, only to be further extrapolated in *Things to Come* (1936), the film adaptation of the published novel. In both, Wells provides several analogies for the representation of group psychology. These symbolic connections to mass psychology strike the reader as distinct from those of earlier works like *Anticipations*. Ironically, by 1933, as Wells imagines a new version of institutional sociology successfully wrested from its anti-utopian roots, the emergence of wide-scale polling suggested a recognition of something Wells had long suggested: that theorizing groups as homogenous masses failed to take into account the variation of opinion within populations. The necessity of polling evinced this more complex view of the relationship between individuals and the masses, recognizing that it was only through advancing scientific study that such a relationship might be materialized, managed, or controlled. So, why did Wells reverse his vision of group psychology, embracing institutions as a way of realizing his utopian sociology? And why, conversely, did the sociologists and psychologists flip their own positions on mass psychology in the late 1920s and 1930s to more readily accept the heterogeneity of groups?

Statistical Collectivity in *The Shape of Things to Come*

After his death, Wells would become an unwitting spokesperson for statistically minded social scientists everywhere. This posthumous status, as a defender of national poll-mindedness, derived from a misquoted bit of his writing, which first came to the public in 1951 when Samuel Wilks attributed the following pithy quote to Wells: "Statistical thinking will one day be as necessary for efficient citizenship as the ability to read and write."[43] Wells never did write this, though it became "[o]ne of the most frequently cited quotations championing statistics" according to James Tankard, who uncovered the misquotation.[44] But the quote's spirit, if not its concision, can be traced to Wells's 1903 book *Mankind in the Making*. In it, Wells contends that,

---

[43] Samuel Wilks, "Undergraduate Statistical Education," *Journal of the American Statistical Association* 46 no. 253 (March 1951), p. 5.

[44] James Tankard, "The H.G. Wells Quote on Statistics: A Question of Accuracy," *Historica Mathematica* 6 (1979), p. 30.

endless social and political problems are only accessible and only thinkable to those who have had a sound training in mathematical analysis, and the time may not be very remote when it will be understood that for complete initiation as an efficient citizen of one of the new great complex world-wide States that are now developing, it is as necessary to be able to compute, to think in averages and maxima and minima, as it is now to be able to read and write.[45]

The basic thrust of the actual quote mirrors the misattributed one, but the additional caveats of Wells's version provide awareness as to his reasoning, giving us a sense of why Wells was thinking of a statistical citizenry decades before the Gallup poll. It also provides insights into the core of Wells's theory of sociological utopia that becomes more prevalent in his later work. In both versions of the quote, *efficient* citizenship is highlighted, but it is only in the *Mankind in the Making* version that we get a sense of the circumstances of this citizenship, why it has become so complex, and why it needs to be made more efficient to start with. For Wells, the instantiation of the quantitatively minded citizen develops in tandem with the "great complex world-wide States," as he links the complicated restructuring of worldwide institutions to the reorientation of the citizen's mind towards her statistical value.[46]

As Wells developed these ideas from *Mankind in the Making* throughout his oeuvre and integrated the lessons he learned from his interactions with academic sociology, Wells's vision of a sociological technocracy slowly crystallized. Wells's interwar social realism works at the edges of this vision, documenting the social and economic ascent of charismatic intellectuals like George Ponderevo in *Tono-Bungay* or Dick Remington in *The New Machiavelli*. But in the 1930s, the rise of demagoguery and the significant threat it posed for the formation of public opinion altered Wells's "religious" vision of how a "social science, if properly taught could demolish the walls separating the various atoms of humanity" in the form of the world-state.[47] Wells is an early adopter of the world-state vision he maintains throughout the 1930s. In Wells's early vision of this globalized culture, a progressive

[45] H.G. Wells, *Mankind in the Making* (London: Chapman & Hall, 1904), p. 204.
[46] Wells, *Mankind in the Making*, p. 204.
[47] W. Warren Wagar, "Science at the World State: Education as Utopia in the Prophetic Vision of H.G. Wells," in *H.G. Wells under Revision: Proceedings of the International*, edited by Patrick Parrinder and Christopher Rolfe (London and Toronto: Associated University Press, 1990), p. 44.

citizenry would always be necessarily informed by the tools of sociological analysis that had only just begun to emerge when he was writing of them.[48] But as Wells witnessed the shifting of sociology as a field away from the kinds of utopian visions he proffered, we find in his later fiction a reinvention of sociology's role, as the discipline itself begins to replace and usurp the role of world leaders. Looking to replace the role of the singular charismatic leader that he developed in his social realist novels of the early twentieth century, Wells turns to academic sociology as the vanguard of a new social structure throughout the 1930s. The rise of authoritarians makes it increasingly impossible to wax whimsically about the appealing autocrat on a soapbox, as he would do in texts like *Anticipations*.[49] And so, turning away from individual revolutionaries like Ponderevo and Remington, Wells looks to concentrate authority in an institutional center, fueled by statistics and data. In this case, that center would be a newly reimagined academic field of sociology.

Published nearly three decades after *In the Days of the Comet*, *The Shape of Things to Come* appears, at first blush, to follow much-trodden ground in its reprisal of contagion as a metaphor for collective consciousness. But careful dissection of this renewed trope throughout the novel reveals something new in Wells's return to this sociological analogy. While Wells revisits the metaphors of infection, which had been prevalent in sociological circles since the dawn of the twentieth century, to describe the infectious nature of public opinion and crowd behavior, it is clear that Wells's appropriation of these metaphors maintains a complicated, even contradictory, relationship to their first instantiations. While Le Bon saw group mentality as manifesting contagious features in itself, Wells actually argues that the underdevelopment and amateurism of academic sociology is the true disease from which society finds itself ill. It would be a point he reinforces in the preface of his 1938 *World Brain*—that his work on "constructive sociology, the science of social organization" constitutes the premier source of his scientific

[48] Krishan Kumar notes that, beginning with *Anticipations*, there would be a "new middle class of scientists, technicians, and managers as most fitted to direct the scientific civilization of the modern world" into which "practically everyone would be absorbed." Kumar, "Wells and 'the So-Called Science of Sociology,' " p. 211.

[49] Wells predicts that, "It is improbable that ever again will any flushed undignified man with a vast voice, a muscular face in incessant operation, collar crumpled, hair disordered, and arms in wild activity, talking, talking, talking [...] rise to be the most powerful thing in any democratic state in the world. Continually the individual vocal demagogue dwindles, and the element of bands and buttons, the organization of the press and procession, the share of the machine, grows." H.G. Wells, *Anticipations of the Mechanical and Scientific Progress upon Human Life and Thought* (London: Chapman & Hall, 1902), p. 159.

contributions in his last years.[50] *The Shape of Things to Come* similarly centers around Wells's innovations in sociology and social psychology, as he describes the nadir of human civilization around the year 1955, when a global conflict is trailed by a devastating "macular fever" that "halved the population of the world."[51] Wells, transforming the Le Bonian contagion metaphor, depicts an illness that would eventually catalyze the conversion of the global order to a cosmopolitan world-state system, which Wells calls the "Modern State" in the novel. In altering Le Bon's metaphor, Wells revises the original theses of early social psychology by amending the nature of group susceptibility to contagion. Le Bon considered this to be an inherent feature of the crowd, contending that "the figurative imagination of crowds is very powerful, very active, and very susceptible of being keenly impressed."[52] But Wells puts pressure on this preternatural susceptibility, and his unpacking of contagion in *The Shape of Things to Come* underscores his disagreement. He frames the wandering disease as a more mysterious form of contagion, stating that "[it] swept the whole world and vanished as enigmatically as it came. It is still a riddle for pathologists."[53] After highlighting the limitations of traditional scientific inquiry, Wells cites a fictional scientist, Mackensen, who proffers another theory of the disease. Mackensen suggests that "the real disease [...] may have been *not* the maculated fever at all, but the *state of vulnerability to the infection* [...] The actual pestilence was not the disease but the harvest of a weakness already prepared."[54] This description of the disease is less epidemiological and increasingly sociological. In other words, the problem of contagion was not born of the crowd, but from the failure to study and understand the crowd through an effective institutional sociology. Wells contradicts Le Bon, Trotter, and their guild, diagnosing group susceptibility as a function of institutional and structural failures. Group psychology is, for Wells, not like a pathogen at all. Rather, such dysfunction is a psychological state prepared by sociological and cultural conditioning. Lacking a culture of what Wells calls "sociological awareness," the citizens become disorganized, ill, and prone to wandering.

Aside from describing the contagion of the "sleeping sickness" infecting the wandering masses as an institutional, and not organic, phenomenon, Wells also adopts biological metaphors in respect to social organization in

[50] Wells, *World Brain*, p. v.
[51] Wells, *The Shape of Things to Come* (New York: Penguin, [1933] 2005), p. 228.
[52] Le Bon, *The Crowd*, p. 53.   [53] Wells, *The Shape of Things to Come*, p. 226.
[54] Wells, *The Shape of Things to Come*, p. 226, emphasis added.

the distant future—specifically the year 2106, the last date recorded in the novel's imagined future. The novel traces human history from the interwar period to this long-distant date, outlining how society reorganized itself in the wake of two global wars and a pandemic, eventually reconstituting itself as a sociological pseudo-utopia.[55] When he describes how society came to invent new, revolutionary social institutions, Wells cheekily recalls Le Bon yet again, suggesting that "[a] pathological analogy may be useful."[56] He cites that before the study of organisms, people suffered "dreadfully from all sorts of irregularities of growth in their bodies."[57] Victims were "made to look grotesque," "crippled and at last killed."[58] But *instead* of using this metaphor to describe organic crowd dynamics, as Le Bon had once done, Wells is actually describing sociological institutions *themselves* as the ones suffering from this metaphorical disease, only liberated from the illness by the creation of new sciences of social organization that had not existed, even in the age of Le Bon:

> In the early twentieth century there was still no adequate estimate of economic forces and their social reactions. There were only a few score professors and amateurs of these fundamentally important studies scattered throughout the earth. They were scattered in every sense; even their communications were unsystematic. They had no powers of inquiry, no adequate statistics, little prestige; few people heeded what they thought or said.[59]

Instead of looking to crowds as carriers of a social epidemic, the diagnosis of sociology itself as the cause of social illness revises the original Le Bonian thesis significantly. By cleverly redeploying the contagion metaphor, Wells promises to cure society of its feeble academic sociology and build, in its place, a robust sociological technocracy.

In *The Shape of Things to Come*, Wells makes clear that technologies of public opinion assessment lagged behind the more robust industrial and military technologies of the twentieth century. Beginning with the early

---

[55] Michael Sherborne states that "[w]hile part of Wells's mind does seem to have been excited by his dictatorial fantasy […] he remains clear about its monstrosity," also noting that "the book fails to come to terms with its political themes or with Wells's personal ambivalence" Sherborne, *Wells: Another Kind of Life*, p. 304.
[56] Wells, *The Shape of Things to Come*, p. 42.
[57] Wells, *The Shape of Things to Come*, p. 42.
[58] Wells, *The Shape of Things to Come*, p. 42.
[59] Wells, *The Shape of Things to Come*, p. 43.

technological revolutions of modernity, the novel moves forward into the future, imagining global conflicts and revolutions that would aid in the production of his utopian vision. Wells, the acknowledged writer of the novel, speculates on the future through the records and dream-diary of the farsighted Philip Raven, who died and presumably left Wells his papers, from which Wells prognosticates the eponymous things to come. The form of the novel—the "dream book"—harkens to Wells's utopian sociology, which Duncan Bell likens to "a vast compendium of utopian texts, a palimpsest of visions of a better society." As Wells, via Raven, contrasts the historical past to the utopian future, he theorizes a sociology bound up in, as Bell describes it, "a dialectical dance of the imagination."[60] Comprising one half of this dialectical dance, Wells's recording of the present moment highlights extant technological innovations which, in Raven's hindsight, only reveal their failures in facilitating social cohesion. While he notes that "mechanical invention" was responsible for "increasing the power and range of every operating material force," little had been done to match this level of invention in respect to the apparatuses that explained human drives and the formulation of group psychology.[61] "Biological and especially social invention," he claims, lagged "behind the practical advances of the exacter, simpler sciences."[62] Wells emphasizes that the material changes brought about by railways and cars necessitated "new social institutions" that must develop more slowly and with more difficulty than their predecessors.[63] Here, with these new social institutions, came the future, acting as the other half of the dialectical dance of which Bell writes.

As Wells records Raven's future history before the establishment of his beloved Modern State, he repeatedly identifies the failure of sociology to master the political sciences that had defined the early twentieth century. Throughout the novel, Wells repeatedly uses Raven's diary to underscore the paucity of social psychological development. Raven records from the future that, "[r]esearch in social psychology is still only beginning to unravel the obscure processes by which faith in 'democracy' became for the better part of a century the ruling cant of practically all America and the greater part of

---

[60] Bell, "Pragmatic Utopianism and Race," 15. Duncan Bell sees the "dream book" as a model for Wells's sociological thought, as sociologists can use the comparative mode of past and future to "motivate them to act" and "educate people" about possible futures.

[61] Wells, *The Shape of Things to Come*, p. 41.

[62] Wells, *The Shape of Things to Come*, pp. 41–2.

[63] Wells, *The Shape of Things to Come*, p. 42.

Europe."[64] Wells, speaking through Raven, chastises the stultification of social psychology in the mid-century. Wells was not alone in this critique. Others in the field of sociological analysis, particularly Freud's nephew Edward Bernays, considered social psychology underdeveloped, writing in 1926 that the field was "as yet far from being an exact science."[65] But as Wells reflects on the past from the perspective of Raven's proleptic synthesis, the cosmopolitan state's institution could be realized only through the advancement of such sciences. Just as Edward Bernays argued for a "leadership democracy administered by the intelligent minority," Wells understands the advancement of social psychology as the handmaiden to a new form of political and social order. It was what he called, in *The New Machiavelli*, "an aristocracy—not of privilege, but of understanding and purpose."[66]

Wells's aristocracy of understanding, harnessing as it does a sociological noblesse oblige, also ushers in the reestablishment of social order. Symbolizing this transformation is the "Central Observation Bureau," which Wells defines as a "complex organization of discussion, calculation, criticism and forecast" which was "undreamt of" in the early part of the twentieth century; Raven places the origination of such sociological awareness as occurring between 2010 and 2030.[67] Similar theories of psychographic institutional revolution also featured in Wells's non-fiction. In his 1937 lecture "The Brain Organization of the Modern World," Wells outlined that his World Encyclopedia would be the home of "every survey, every statistical bureau in the world."[68] In *The Shape of Things to Come*, no such book exists, but a zeitgeist of sociological-mindedness brings with it a second wave of intellectual and scientific advancement that heralds in Wells's sociological utopia. While technological advancement may have altered the means of material production, it had never properly recognized the mind itself as material. And even if Freud had made the mind more material via his topographical analogies, collective consciousness remained unaltered by the studies of the group that would be so important to Wells's vision of the future. This recalibration of society toward psychographic consciousness, fueled by a properly institutionalized sociology, promised to break the back of beastly capital and provincial nationalism. It would change the collective mind as we understood it.

[64] Wells, *The Shape of Things to Come*, p. 125.
[65] Edward Bernays, *Propaganda* (1928; repr. New York: IG Publishing, [1928] 2005), p. 71.
[66] Bernays, *Propaganda*, p. 127; Wells, *The New Machiavelli*, p. 311.
[67] Wells, *The Shape of Things to Come*, p. 43.   [68] Wells, *World Brain*, p. 69.

It is vital to see the imagining of a new psychographic society as pivotal for Wells's thought. As a foundational part of the British Sociological Society, Wells had long struggled to position sociology as central to the institutional changes he wanted to imagine. Certainly, in his science fiction, technologies lie at the core of any transformation. But more often than not, these technologies were specific to the individual, with enduring natural forces maintaining responsibility for comprehensive social change. As just one example, we can look at the comet in *In the Days of the Comet*, which Michael Sherborne credits with producing "a spiritual change *not* an institutional one."[69] But the revivification of social psychology in *The Shape of Things to Come* manifests the sort of institutional revolution Wells had long sought. Statistics lurks in every corner of the novel, rearing up in times of social unrest. Its domination is assured, Wells tells us, by the time that the "Modern State" is properly established in the 1970s. Until this point of revolution, Wells traces the fall and rise of statistical sociological data in the novel, marking its stops and starts as part of a slow evolution that would eventually rid the world of its affinity for charismatic dictators and blustering tyrants. While Wells maintains his early arguments, theorized in *Mankind in the Making* and posthumously misremembered, that early twentieth-century sociology was a failed state of data analytics, he does not maintain in the 1930s that the study of sociology or psychology is forever doomed to fail under unsubstantiated theories. Rather, Wells revises his vision of *Mankind in the Making* to allow for the evolution and improvement of sociology as a science. In *The Shape of Things to Come* Wells outlines, for the first time, how statistics, sociology, and psychology can practically inform a new age of political and social leadership, a cosmopolitan utopia, free from the fascistic threat breathing down the neck of the world in the 1930s. Wells would find intellectual sympathy with Freud's nephew Bernays, imagining an "invisible government" that could expand globally and lead to the dissolution of the traditional nation-state altogether.[70] The devastation of the plague devolves society into hyper-regional factions; Wells describes "towns, cities, rural districts" that "discovered themselves obliged to 'carry on' by themselves."[71] The plague resets national and geographic boundaries. And when the disease mysteriously disappears in 1960, a new stage is set for the world order: "the Age of European

---

[69] Sherborne, *H.G. Wells: Another Kind of Life*, p. 172, emphasis added.
[70] Bernays, *Propaganda*, p. 371.
[71] Wells, *The Shape of Things to Come*, p. 233.

Predominance lost its defining lines, lost its contrasted cultures and its elaborated traditions [...] It crumpled up, it broke down; its forms melted together and disappeared."[72] Wells's reprisal of contagion rhetoric to denigrate academic sociology sets the stage for his new, post-national, sociological world-state.

If democracy had failed, and the stultified development of social psychology was its cause, the post-plague revolution in the field paved the way for Wells's utopian world-state. Early Wells imagined a world where human devolution was an inevitable consequence of folly, but by 1933 Wells constructs a world saved from the brink of self-destruction by a critical scientific evolution. But Wells was quite specific about the type of science that would salvage mankind; it was not solely technological or mechanical advancement. Rather, it was the advancement of sciences in the field of politics and psychology. In other words, Wells theorized that social psychology had come into its own as a proper science. In *The Shape of Things to Come*, Wells elaborates: "it was no great moral impulse turned mankind from its drift towards chaos. It was intellectual recovery. Essentially what happened was this: social and political science overtook the march of catastrophe."[73] In fact, sociology, group psychology, and political science are framed in *The Shape of Things to Come* as the crucial fields that reinvigorate humanity toward a brighter and better future, fueled by institutional apparatuses like the Central Observation Bureau. Wells frames the revolution as one forged by technocrats, whose contributions changed the political ecosystem of the world.[74] Wells follows the history of group psychology in its infancy in the novel, marking its early failures as precursors to its eventual triumph. Plucky scientists renew the discredited science of "group psychology," which had "been disregarded almost entirely" by the time the pandemic decimated the globe.[75] The fields are officially reestablished after the 1955 pandemic, saving humanity from the brink of destruction. To mark the difference between social psychology as it was known to his readers and the new version of utopian sociology, Wells compares a world familiar to the reader, the world of 1925, to that of the burgeoning world-state: "If you had interrogated

---

[72] Wells, *The Shape of Things to Come*, p. 229.

[73] Wells, *The Shape of Things to Come*, p. 259.

[74] R.D. Haynes would contend that this was a theme throughout Wells's utopianism, writing that "...in nearly all his plans for a utopia, he depends for leadership chiefly on the scientists of society. They, because of their training, are considered sufficiently impartial and morally reliable to remain uncorrupted by the mantle of authority." Haynes, *H.G. Wells, Discoverer of the Future*, p. 37.

[75] Wells, *The Shape of Things to Come*, p. 260.

an ordinary European of the year 1925 about the motives for his political activities and associations and his general social behaviour, he would probably have betrayed a feeling that your enquiry was slightly indelicate."[76] Recognizing that tools of sociological analysis were at one time verboten, Wells then articulates the history of social psychology through this imaginary interrogation. The interviewee, the narrator claims, would have cited the family, kin systems, or even the social contract as an explanation for his behaviors. But, like the Trotterians Wells abhorred, such individuals would have been dead wrong. Rather, the evolution of social psychology would provide a global society with new structures of social cohesion and radical new forms of identification.

Wells provides a chronology for how social psychology developed as a necessary prerequisite for the Modern World-State, the end point of which is a global structure that dissolves localized government entirely, supplanting it with the art of sociology. The catastrophe of the plague would usher in the establishment of *legitimate* social psychology, including the Central Observation Bureau. This, in turn, would instantiate a new society in *The Shape of Things to Come*, led by sociological technocrats, who used the tools of air superiority to transform the world through a global education campaign. This body of social psychologists and their associates became a great critical and disciplinary organism, working side by side with the World Council which, ultimately, it superseded.[77] The dissolution of the World Council—the dissolution of any form of government whatsoever, including the Air Dictatorship that helped secure the Modern State—is the evolutionary endpoint of the utopian society Wells envisioned. But even as the governmental apparatuses, including the Air Dictatorship, fade away, the social psychologists maintain their pride of place in world affairs, despite all other parts of the state being dispersed in a less hierarchical manner:

> Most of the faculties of the Modern State Movement dissolved into technical organizations under these Controls, with the one exception of that former department of the science faculty the department of social psychology, which by 2106 had become, so to speak, the whole literature, philosophy and general thought of the world. It was the surviving vital faculty of the Modern State movement, the reasoning soul in the body of the race.[78]

[76] Wells, *The Shape of Things to Come*, p. 260.
[77] Wells, *The Shape of Things to Come*, p. 370.
[78] Wells, *The Shape of Things to Come*, p. 370.

In this passage, Wells presents the surprising nexus of his utopian world-state. While other organizations or groups are proctored through the expectedly Wellsian system of technocratic organization by the scientists, social psychology maintains a privileged status above all other fields of study. In a highly ironic gesture, the contagion that social psychology had falsely attributed to the group mind would pave the way for the instantiation of authentic institutional sociology.

Social psychology's supremacy in *The Shape of Things to Come* emerges from its ability to focus on micro and macro level concerns simultaneously. The Central Observation Bureau maintains its calculations and forecasts with a meticulous eye, while the larger concerns of social psychology are maintained within the ethereal spheres of "literature, philosophy and general thought."[79] This structure seems strikingly similar to the practical endeavors of Mass-Observation, a group founded only a few years after Wells published the novel. Like Mass-Observation, the fictional Central Observation Bureau simultaneously observed the world through the collection of data while also producing a larger image of the social body as a whole. If Wells had provided a bit more detail on the operation of this fictional Observation Bureau, it might have been seen that he was attempting to design an "anthropology of ourselves," the phrase used by Mass-Observation to define its aims, years before its time. Such detailed descriptions of the Bureau are, however, lacking. It seems that Wells, like Mass-Observation that followed, had a difficult time outlining a practice that would mirror public response, help to contain it, while also leaving room for free and democratic rule.

The Modern World-State: Renucleation and the Technocratic Utopia

Wells was not satisfied in alluding to early sociology solely through his cunning reprisal of the contagion metaphor. The novel still needed a thought-leader, different from the autocrats of old, who could verbalize Wells's author's philosophies for societal restructuring. After unveiling the salvation of the world at the hands of the sociological elites, Wells outlines the story of a psychologist named Gustave De Windt, whose philosophy paved

---

[79] Wells, *The Shape of Things to Come*, p. 370.

the path for the Modern World State's centralization of public opinion and global governance; De Windt's thesis lays the groundwork for a Wellsian philosophy that reprises the foundational theories of social psychology from the likes of Le Bon and Trotter. In Wells's future history, De Windt's groundbreaking treatise, *Social Nucleation*, was foundational to the establishment of the Modern World State; it was a theory of psychology that completely unified social psychology with the society's political and social structure. The narrator frames it as the "first exhaustive study of the psychological laws underlying team play and *esprit de corps*," further arguing that "[i]t did for the first time correlate effectively the increasing understanding of individual psychology, with new educational methods and new concepts of political life."[80] Rather than arguing that group psychology is a result of collective instinct or contagion, De Windt's theory recognizes the foundational role of institutions in the production of both individual and group identity: "He insisted with an irrefutable rigidity upon the entirely artificial nature of the content of the social side of a human being. Men are born but citizens are made [...] before De Windt's time this was not obvious."[81] It is difficult to understate how totally this vision repudiates the early history of social psychology. Not only does Gustave De Windt's name suggest this history, as an ironical homage to Gustave Le Bon, but the theory that De Windt espouses contradicts the claims about human psychology's instinctual basis put forward by Le Bon and Trotter. Wells's De Windt was a true contradiction to early social psychology. While Wilfred Trotter argued for human cruelty as a keystone of group psychology, and Le Bon suggested group mentality was violent and unchangeable, for Wells, the situation is reversed. Humanity lacks innate characteristics. In fact, Wells *directly* undermines the contagion thesis that he had covertly borrowed earlier in his career; De Windtianism allowed society "to begin again at the beginning with *uninfected* minds."[82] Wells, through the esteemed social psychologist De Windt, repudiates the theory of humanity's underlying cruelty and incivility. He instead reframes misguided institutions as responsible for injecting humanity with senseless cruelty through social mores and cultural limitations.

Wells did not limit himself to undermining the predominant theories of group psychology; if group identification was, indeed, socially constructed, De Windtianism gave him the space to theorize completely new methods

[80] Wells, *The Shape of Things to Come*, p. 264.
[81] Wells, *The Shape of Things to Come*, p. 264.
[82] Wells, *The Shape of Things to Come*, p. 265, emphasis added.

for organizing society—a process he calls "renucleation." Renucleation, as the name suggests, involves producing new nuclei for social organization and collectivity. Unmoored from the bonds of nuclear families, peer groups, or religious assemblies, the new world-state can produce new nodes of group identification.[83] Wells dismisses, through his proxy De Windt, a whole history of group formation as had been traditionally discussed in the literature about group psychology to this point. Wells replaces this heterodoxy with De Windt's theories as he continues to repurpose Le Bon's biological metaphors to invent a new utopian sociology. But to "re-nucleate" the world, as De Windt hoped to do, required another version of education and training. De Windt still saw society as "an educational product."[84] Typical of Wells's propensity for technocratic organization, the groups that would replace family, friends, or nations, would be best described in terms of expertise and skill-sets, born of study and natural inclination: "[W]hen De Windt was writing, multitudes of well-meaning people were attempting to assemble 'movements' for social reconstruction and world revolution out of the raw, unprepared miscellany of the contemporary crowd."[85] These groups, comprised of identifiable collectives of protesters and reformers, were unsuited to the mission of the new world-state. These recalcitrant clusters needed to be pulled away from the "impossible *coups d'etat* and pronunciamentos" and towards the "necessary systematic preliminary renucleation of the world."[86] But while Le Bon's crowds might never have made that turn, Wells's could, and did.

The best way to describe the De Windtian re-nucleation project is as a proto-Deleuzian vision of a rhizomatic social organization. The structure, as described in the novel, is purportedly non-hierarchical, with each "nucleus" being "an educational and disciplinary unit" formed through "intensive study circles and associations for moral and physical training."[87] The structure was organized through skill set, in distinction from former eras. "In the past," the narrator describes, "men could live and live fully within their patriotism and their business enterprises, because they knew

---

[83] R.D. Haynes notes that this is an underlying tension in Wells's works: "In designing his utopian world-state, Wells was clearly torn between two divergent ideals—the desire for order and efficiency on the one hand and the desire to foster individual initiative on the other." Haynes, *H.G. Wells, Discoverer of the Future*, p. 118.
[84] Wells, *The Shape of Things to Come*, p. 268.
[85] Wells, *The Shape of Things to Come*, p. 268.
[86] Wells, *The Shape of Things to Come*, pp. 268–9.
[87] Wells, *The Shape of Things to Come*, p. 269.

no better. But now they knew better."[88] The organization and leadership of these nuclei, like the Deleuzian rhizome, suggests the organization of cells as a metaphor for rhizomatic deterritorialization, "ceaselessly establish[ing] connections" between groups.[89] De Windt's further discussion of renucleation makes the Deleuzian metaphor even more undeniable: "if you cannot start nucleation everywhere, then at least you can start it close at hand. 'Get the nuclei going. Be yourself a nucleus.' From the beginning of life, nuclei have begotten nuclei. The Modern State, which had to be evoked everywhere, could be begun anywhere."[90] But curtailing the expansionism of Deleuze and Guattari's rhizome, Wells's renucleation ceases to expand prolifically; he clearly renounces the notion of recalcitrant political uprisings. "Criticize," De Windt writes, "yes, but do not obstruct."[91] Poor ideas would eventually be "[broken] up," but without the necessary shifts in power dynamics that arise as a result of dismissing or delegitimizing certain leaders. Wells sees the inevitable problems that arise with a culture that encourages obstructionism, and the narrator emphasizes that the historical practice of De Windt's model of politics was, at first, incapable of completely ousting the tendency towards reactionary oppositional politics. "In practice," he records, "it was found that criticism and suggestion passed by insensible degrees into incitement and insurrectionary propaganda."[92] But eschewing the violent repression of opponents, the captivating prose of De Windt eventually succeeds in convincing everyone of the value of a new model of living that is utterly divorced from the past fetishization of businesses, families, and nations. "[H]e put all the main structural factors in the establishment of the Modern State so plainly and convincingly before his fellow men that soon thousands and presently millions were living for that vision."[93] The elision of political protest in Wells's utopia is deeply conspicuous, somehow dissipating upon the pronouncements of De Windt without any rancor. Written by an author nearing his seventies, it is difficult to read the quieting impact of De Windt's theories as anything other than Wellsian wish-fulfillment. It was a dream that finally, at last, Wells's radical theories might be seamlessly integrated into modern culture.

[88] Wells, *The Shape of Things to Come*, p. 270.
[89] Gilles Deleuze and Félix Guattari, *A Thousand Plateaus: Capitalism and Schizophrenia*, translated by Brian Massumi (Minneapolis, MN: University of Minnesota Press, 1987), p. 7.
[90] Wells, *The Shape of Things to Come*, p. 269.
[91] Wells, *The Shape of Things to Come*, p. 270.
[92] Wells, *The Shape of Things to Come*, p. 271.
[93] Wells, *The Shape of Things to Come*, p. 272.

And so, with shockingly little difficulty, De Windt's renucleation is the *deus ex machina* that wrests from humanity an entire history of social organization and replaces it with something radically different. But, as is often the case with Wells, the leadership of this new social organization is just as inexplicable as the placating impact of De Windt's words. Social reorganization is conducted in a highly voluntary manner, with groups of "nuclei" recognizing the necessity of reorganization and taking it upon themselves to abandon every urge to see social structure as built on inherent continuity. But Wells's reorganization of the world is fundamentally an elitist one. He describes the most beneficial participants in the nucleation projects as "a number of writers, 'pure' scientific workers, young sociologists, economists and the like and 'intellectuals' from the working-class movement."[94] The emergence of an intellectual elite, and particularly the allusion to an elite with working-class origins, is a Wellsian trope, emergent in early books like *Tono Bungay* and *The New Machiavelli*.[95] But the citation of *young* sociologists was perhaps not incidental; with Wilfred Trotter the age of 61 at the time of publication, Wells seemed dedicated to the notion that sociology must experience a radical reformation in order to realize a world outside of kinship models. It was perhaps also a self-abnegation of Wells's own role in this revolutionary future.

In *The Shape of Things to Come*, Wells's renucleation, while suggesting a Deleuzian deterritorialization—a movement away from traditional systems of organization around class, gender, or religion—embraces a technocratic elite. Symbolizing this encroaching hierarchization, the novel incorporates another well-worn trope in the oeuvre of Wellsian futurology, the airplane, as a means of symbolizing this new brand of hierarchical rule.[96] While the Central Observation Bureau and modernized group psychology are utilized to study and interpolate public opinion, airplanes become the totem of universality, as their transcontinental travels metonymize a unified world. Just as the advancement of sociology allows for the production of a psychological cognitive mapping, the convergence of this intellectual revolution is astutely symbolized through the aerial dominance of the plane, collectivized in the form of what Wells calls "the Air Dictatorship."[97] Like the process of

---

[94] Wells, *The Shape of Things to Come*, p. 275.
[95] Michael Sherborne notes that, almost throughout his career, Wells "believed in inevitable progress to a Utopia run by a scientific elite" Sherborne, *Another Kind of Life*, p. 19.
[96] Wells, *The Shape of Things to Come*, p. 281.
[97] Fredric Jameson describes the working of the cognitive map as the "representation of social totality." Fredric Jameson, "Cognitive Mapping," in *Marxism and the Interpretation of Culture*, edited by Cary Nelson and Lawrence Grossberg (Chicago, IL: University of Illinois Press, 1988), p. 350.

renucleation, the rise of the Air Dictatorship is accomplished without violent revolution or resistance. In fact, the planes in the novel represent global peace but do not achieve it through wartime strategies or tactics. Rather than dropping bombs, planes in the novel act as a communications network, allowing the transfer of ideas across the globe.

The Air Dictatorship comes about with direct inspiration from De Windt, but the power it wields alludes to more authoritarian forms of control, which are conveniently elided in the novel.[98] Wells as narrator interjects in Raven's dream-diary to assert that the Air Dictatorship "had been shaped from the beginning in the aggressive bright new schools of Modern State nuclei, they had fed on a new literature, they looked out upon fresh horizons, and their ideology had been determined more than anything by the social psychologist."[99] Much of the work of the Air Dictatorship is ideological, not militaristic; for example, they only "fined or exiled" members of religious organizations. But the Air Dictatorship first struggles with an "underdeveloped science of social psychology," as well.[100] As a result, they came "upon one of the obscurest and most debatable of all educational problems, the variability of mental resistance to direction and the limits set by nature to the ideal of an acquiescent cooperative world."[101] The narrator admits that, in order to organize the world-state, some methods of "persecution" were inevitable. Casting those methods to the imagination, the novel lauds that the methods of this persecution were interpersonal, that resistance "between teacher and learner" were welcomed, and that it was this dialectical tension, not violent intervention, that led to the ideological convergence of the world.[102] The novel is less interested in Air Dictatorship as a practical tool than it is as a topographical allegory to suggest the advancement of social psychology. Planes in the novel are never mentioned, other than in passing. Rather, the Air Dictatorship is an organizing body, first and foremost. In fact, the Dictatorship is, notably, not aerial in nature; it is seldom depicted as a mobile body. Rather, it symbolizes the act of capturing an "aerial view" of individual behaviors and desires within the world, tacitly in order to reorganize and restructure such heterogeneous belief systems in accordance with one ideological system. But as fleeting allusions to militaristic persecution suggest, the elitist underpinning of Wells's pseudo-utopia bring with them troubling ramifications for how a sociological

---

[98] Wells, *The Shape of Things to Come*, p. 330.
[99] Wells, *The Shape of Things to Come*, p. 361.
[100] Wells, *The Shape of Things to Come*, p. 364.
[101] Wells, *The Shape of Things to Come*, p. 364.
[102] Wells, *The Shape of Things to Come*, p. 366.

elite could practically emerge without fully succumbing to the trappings of autocracy.[103]

Things to Come: On (Not) Filming a Sociological Utopia

When Wells partnered with Alexander Korda to transform *The Shape of Things to Come* into a film he was, according to biographers, disappointed in the result.[104] And, despite the film's exorbitant budget, which surpassed any film produced to date, the film failed, too, with audiences.[105] Struggles between Korda and Wells dominated the film's production, with Korda feeling put out by Wells's presence and Wells inconvenienced by Korda's directorial control.[106] Wells wrote two failed scripts before settling on a final version, with the two aborted scripts described as "apparently unfilmable."[107] But while the behind-the-scenes conflicts visualizing his sociological utopia in script form haunted the film, the final result of the collaboration is visually stunning; as Keith Williams argues, *Things to Come* offered a convincing aesthetic rejoinder to Lang's modernist futurism of *Metropolis*.[108] But lacking an accompanying pamphlet explaining the complex sociological and psychological advancements Wells stages in his novel, the film is devoid of much of the theoretical content of the original text; as "one of the least ekphrastic of Wells's fictions," *Things to Come* had to invent a more comprehensive fictional landscape in which to stage his philosophical vision.[109] Absent the essential philosophical core, Wells's film reveals the shortcomings of his original vision. The film is, at best, ideologically muddled. It features the rise of a benevolent military dictatorship, but concludes with the staging of a justified mass-coup against these leaders, for whom the viewers continue to maintain sympathy. In concluding with a popular uprising, the

---

[103] Haynes notes: "...in nearly all [Wells's] plans for a utopia, he depends for leadership chiefly on the scientists of society. They, because of their training, are considered sufficiently impartial and morally reliable to remain uncorrupted by the mantle of authority." Haynes, *H.G. Wells, Discoverer of the Future*, p. 37.

[104] Keith Williams notes that, publicly at least, Wells argued that the film was "spiritually correct," but he notes that Wells's diary provides a "less sanguine" account of the production. Williams, *H.G. Wells, Modernity and the Movies*, p. 107.

[105] H.G. Wells, *Things to Come: A Critical Text of the 1935 London First Edition, with an Introduction and Appendices*, edited by Leon Stover (Jefferson, NC: McFarland, 2012), p. 3.

[106] Williams, *H.G. Wells, Modernity and the Movies*, p. 207.

[107] Karol Kulik, *Alexander Korda: The Man Who Could Work Miracles* (New Rochelle, NY: Arlington House Publishers, 1975), p. 147.

[108] Kulik, *Alexander Korda*, p. 109.   [109] Kulik, *Alexander Korda*, p. 106.

film alludes to an underlying tension throughout the oeuvre of Wells's scientific utopias: while he purports a skepticism over authoritarianism, he maintains a faith in the technocratic, intellectual elites who might transform the world into something better. When the novel is translated onto the screen, these underlying tensions are exacerbated: elaborate costuming, complex set design, and the depiction of novel technologies likewise underscore the inherent authoritarianism in the sociological revolution Wells touts in *The Shape of Things to Come*. While the film differs greatly from many of the key historical aspects of the novel, I assert that these contradictions in *Things to Come* highlight the inherent, though well-intentioned, limitations of Wells's sociological vision. While Wells's oeuvre repeatedly harkens to the emergence of a benevolent technocratic force that will collate, incorporate, and enlighten public opinion, the inability to actualize this vision on the screen without authoritarian undertones highlights the gaps in his concept of a sociological elite.

Ironically, the breakdown of Wells's sociological utopia in the film *Things to Come* begins with the integration of character-driven conflict. Of course, being a future-history, Wells's novel has no direct protagonist. For the staging of the novel this would, obviously, not do. To demonstrate the conversion of the world from an anarchic, sectarian, provincial grouping of communities to a global world-state, *Things to Come* develops two characters as contrasting leaders who represent the two sides of this world in conflict. On the one side is a man known as the "Boss," a backward dictator of a struggling town called Everytown, whose airpower has been entirely decimated by decades of cultural and technological stagnation. On the other is a man named Cabal (played by Raymond Massey), the figurehead for "Wings Over the World," a pithily-titled rendition of the Air Dictatorship in *The Shape of Things to Come*. After the start of another world war which, in Wells's vision, lasts until the year 1970, and an illness ravages half the population (both of which feature in *The Shape of Things to Come*), Everytown has devolved into a pre-modern agrarian society. The Boss wishes to revive airplane technology, yet lacks the resources to do so. But one day the citizens spot a plane, a supposed impossibility. After the pilot, John Cabal, lands back in the town from which he came, he looks for the leader in order to proffer peace. Despite the Boss demanding Cabal's arrest, Cabal refuses to recognize the validity of the local authorities, instead walking to meet the Boss himself. And though Cabal extends an offer of peace in his role as the "air dictator," he is held hostage all the same, provoking a conflict between the nascent world-governing body and the small parish of Everytown.

The dramatization of these regional struggles, symbolized through aerial combat, leads to several dramatic revisions of Wells's novel in the film version, all of which indicate the troubling proximity of his fictional version of aerial intelligence to a violent version of aerial power and domination. The automatic association between planes and war even emerges in the first minutes of the film, with a scene capturing the aerial bombardment of Everytown in 1940. This bombing, prefiguring the London Blitz, begins a global war. And while the Air Dictatorship in *The Shape of Things to Come* is less of a literal military force than it is a topographical representation of social psychological advancement, the film inevitably must make the Air Dictatorship a forceable feature of the utopia as its plot progresses. As a result, the metonymy of the plane as a hermeneutic tool loses its representative quality altogether. Instead, the plane becomes a literal symbol for global dominance. *Things to Come*'s rendition of the Air Dictatorship testifies to the Foucauldian line, suggesting that knowledge of a population is but a way station on the path to the exercise of power. After Cabal is imprisoned by the Boss, Wings Over the World (WotW) has no choice but to come to his rescue. In a pivotal scene, WotW bombs Everytown with what they call the "gas of peace." And while the peace-gas does not kill most of the citizens of Everytown, it targets the ideologically intractable Boss, whose last acts as he falls into unconsciousness are the ringing of the war-bell and the shooting of a pistol, impotently, into the air, recalling, to some extent, the haphazard blasting of William Leadford's gun decades earlier in *In the Days of the Comet*. After bombing the town, WotW soldiers parachute in and Cabal, now liberated from his prison, stands over the Boss domineeringly, stating in eulogy: "Dead and his world dead with him, and a new world beginning. Poor old boss, he and his flags and his follies. And now for the rule of the airmen, and a new life for mankind."[110] The film zooms out, showing the drugged citizens emerging from their slumber, with the sole exception of the Boss, whose final resting place is under a town bulletin proclaiming "Long Live the Chief."[111] In Wells's novel, the necessity of aerial military power is obviated by the persuasive philosophies of Gustave De Windt, who brings the world into alignment peaceably through intellectual argument. Absent this theoretical framework, the film must supplant De Windtianism with the more familiar and accessible trope of military domination, wielded

---

[110] *Things to Come*, directed by William Cameron Menzies, produced by Alexander Korda, written by H.G. Wells (United Artists, 1936).
[111] *Things to Come*.

as a persuasive tool. In fact, when Cabal returns to the World State's governing body, he indicates that the violent destruction of those who resist is the precursor to any utopian global order: He states, "First a roundup of brigands [...] Then settle, organize and advance."[112] Arguably, the emergence of the aerial war that marks the center-point of *Things to Come* suggests the inevitable violence implicit in Wells's sociological utopia, a feature made opaque in the novel itself. Notably, by the end of *The Shape of Things to Come*, the benchmark of society's transformation into a fully utopian culture lies in the dissolution of the Air Dictatorship; the redundancy of military power comes to represent the supremacy of scientific and sociological reason. But in the film, the aerial military body of WotW not only continues, but it grows increasingly prominent. In the final act of the film, Cabal is determined to send his child and her boyfriend off to space, shooting them off in a space gun in hopes of occupying the moon.

But the Wellsian film is not without its discontents and, unlike in *The Shape of Things to Come*, there is no philosopher De Windt to assuage public dissatisfaction with the new order. This challenge to the new technocratic utopia comes from Theotocopulos, who worries that the acceleration of progress has divorced man from pleasure and art. A sculptor, whose work recalls the Stalinist art of the interwar period, wants to stand in for the leader of the resistance. After a montage of the new world-state's redevelopment—the establishment of subterranean cities with complex, futurist aesthetics—Theotocopulos complains, "What has this progress, this world civlisation, done for us? Machines and marvels [...] Is it any jollier than the world used to be in the good old days when life was short and hot and merry and the devil took the hindmost?"[113] He turns this private complaint into a public creed, targeting the planned space gun mission and declaring on video screens across the world-state: "What is the good of all this progress, onward and onward? We demand a halt. We demand a rest. The object of life is happy living. We will not have human life sacrificed to experiment. Progress is not living. It should only be a preparation for living. They stage the old Greek tragedy again. And a father offers up his daughter to his evil god..."[114] Despite an emotional appeal, the screed is notably absent of any sort of rational appeal that counters the work of WoTW. And this continuation of irrational appeal, marking a failure of the DeWindtian

---

[112] *Things to Come.*   [113] *Things to Come.*   [114] *Things to Come.*

philosophical core to truly manifest itself in Wells's film, underscores the innate challenge in imagining a psychographic utopia.

The reactionary nature of Theotocopulos's claims spreads to the crowd, virus-like, and the space-gun launch leads to mass hysteria and revolt. The scene of the crowd looking to dismantle the massive space gun parallels the first scene of aerial bombardment in the film, which captures the chaos of the crowds during the air raids. An innumerable crowd hustles to try to beat the ship into submission with metal rods before it takes off, despite warnings of the concussive blow of the massive space gun as it eventually rockets the youngsters into the ether. The restoration of a Trotterian vision of group psychology seems to arrest any hope that the film will end with the establishment of a peaceful utopian state like in the novel. But despite the angry mob, the space-gun explodes, shooting the capsule holding the young lovers into the sky. The film does not conclude with the victory of the masses. Rather, the last scene confirms the dominance of technocratic institutions over contrarian public sentiment. The final dialogue between Cabal and his friend Passworthy epitomizes the renewal of Trotterian fears over the animalistic nature of humanity. Passworthy takes up a milder version of Theotocopulos's critique, asking: "Is there never to be any rest?" Cabal's rousing monologue of interstellar colonization suggests the contrary:

> Rest enough for the individual man too much and too soon, and we call it death. But for man, no rest and no ending. He must go on, conquest beyond conquest. First, this little planet with its whims and ways, and then all the laws of mind and matter that restrain him. Then the planets about him and at last, out across immensity to the stars. And when he has conquered all the deeps of space and all the mysteries of time, still he will be beginning.[115]

Alongside the suppression of the masses, this expansionist vision brings with it a tinge of the dictatorial. Where the mastery of public opinion in *The Shape of Things to Come* assures the coherence and cooperation of society, as Cabal and his government set aside the will of the people, the film unveils the deep underbelly of Wellsianism, made most manifest when the complex psychographic underpinnings of his worldview cannot be staged.

And, as if the concluding mob scene did not revive early visions of Trotterian or Le Bonian social psychology sufficiently, Passworthy's final

---

[115] *Things to Come.*

line—"But we are such little creatures…little animals" captures the full reprisal of a pre-psychographic social psychology, fully invested in a knee-jerk instinctual group dynamic.[116] Despite his ambitious vision for mankind, Cabal concedes the point that humanity is overwhelmingly fueled by animal instincts, and only by surpassing such instincts through organization can we truly embrace the future:

> Little animals. And if we're no more than animals we must snatch each little scrap of happiness and live and suffer and pass, mattering no more than all other animals do or have done. It is this or that. All the universe or nothing! Which shall it be, Passworthy? Which shall it be?[117]

The final shot of the film, a silhouette of Cabal's face against the night sky after he proffers this final rhetorical question, provides us with a clear answer (see Figure 1.1). In opposition to aerial shots of the panicking masses, the film's final shot rests on Cabal's face, centered and dominating over the whole of the night's sky. In comparison to global and interstellar dominance, public will is but a piddling interference, hardly to be taken seriously, and certainly to be vetoed by a government of altruistic techno-cratic leaders. Offering no intellectual program to assure psychological cohesion, the film passes back over a psychographic rubicon. As it does, it produces a highly ambivalent utopia, with the world-state leadership taking on the whiff of authoritarianism that Wellsian sociology was meant to abol-ish. "Cabal," as Korda biographer and actor Karol Kulik writes in his analy-sis of the film, "never publicly responds to his critics; and the space gun shot goes ahead not because Cabal has at the last minute 'reasoned' with the malcontents, but simply because he has reached the spacegun first. A sci-ence which so disregards the honest questioning of people *should* perhaps be feared."[118] This ambivalent ending has led some scholars to challenge if Wells's own vision was truly captured here. It is more than probable it was not. But that is precisely my point. It was Wells's inability to dramatize a psychographic worldview that inevitably hamstrung the clarity of his vision.

In his last years, Wells wrote of many autocrats who, depicted with a sense of humor and derision, evinced the author's reticence about the rising authoritarianism across the globe. Even early political leaders like *The New Machiavelli's* Dick Remington are not meant to be sympathetic characters,

---

[116] *Things to Come.*   [117] *Things to Come.*
[118] Kulik, *Alexander Korda*, p. 151, emphasis in original.

Figure 1.1   Cabal looks into space in the last dramatic shot of *Things to Come*. Still from *Things to Come*, directed by William Cameron Menzies, produced by Alexander Korda, written by H.G. Wells (United Artists, 1936).

even if the protagonist's elopement with Isabel Rivers at the novel's end follows a bit too closely Wells's own love affairs. Along these lines, Mr. Parnham's efforts to conquer the world in the 1930 novel *The Autocracy of Mr. Parnham* are futile and pathetic. One of Wells's final novels, *The Holy Terror*, suggests the potential of the totalitarian leader Rud Whitlow, only to have him undercut by his own paranoias and obsessions, leading to his death. This series of failed autocrats makes the conclusion of *Things to Come* a truly shocking one. Unable to massage the nuances of the political revolution as he does in the original novel, what comes of the pseudo-benevolent military force in the film is nothing short of a dictatorship by the academic elite, cast in an unconvincing, though optimistic, light. Giving Cabal, and not the citizens, the final word, the film recognizes that the sociological utopia Wells seeks will always be infected by authoritarian tendencies in its realization, reinforced by military power, and sustained by public suppression. The tools of sociological knowledge Wells so extolled in his novel are but a means to express military supremacy in the film, as it translates statistical knowledge into increasingly advanced war planes.

My aim of looking at the discontinuity of Wells's vision in *Things to Come* is not to claim Wells was disingenuous in his portrayal of a sociological utopia in his previous novel. Wells was a true believer in the psychographically informed vision he put forward. But his case is an instructive one because of, and not in spite of, its failure in its cinematic rendition. It is vital to recognize the difficulty in imagining the materialization of the psyche and, furthermore, the challenge in visualizing the ramifications to a society that managed to institutionalize the collective unconscious. Looking at both Wells's *The Shape of Things to Come* and *Things to Come* emphasizes the potentiality in, and threats of, the mastery of public opinion and polling methodologies, which were emergent at the same time Wells was transforming his book into a film. The disjointedness of the book from the film prefigures the same debates that would saturate the works of psychographically minded writers throughout the mid-century, as hopes for collective unification offered by polling jousted with fears of the technocratic overreach and autocratic control promised in the mass-assessment of public polling by powerful institutions. In her book *Inventing Tomorrow*, Sarah Cole proffers Wells as a figure neglected for his failure to conform to the archetypes that have haunted literary modernism. She suggests that Wells's approach, informed by his work in the sciences, turns away from the "dramatization of partial vision" aestheticized in modernism and, instead, attempts a "view of the whole, a totalizing vision that might be suggested of an entirely alternative set of literary responses."[119] As we will see in exploring the works of other psychographic writers, Wells's works present themselves as urtexts. Writers like Cecil Day-Lewis, Celia Fremlin, Evelyn Waugh, and Olaf Stapledon present variations on this alternative response to modernity, influenced as they were by the emergent field of social psychology and its institutionalization in the practice of modern public opinion polling.

---

[119] Cole, *Inventing Tomorrow*, p. 43.

2
Polling for Peace
Journalism and Activist Polling between the Wars

The Ballot of Blood

Storm Jameson's novel about the 1926 General Strike, *None Turn Back* (1936), emphasizes the newspaper industry as a pivotal force in the coordination and formation of public opinion in the interwar period. In the novel, Hervey Russell, a fledgling author in support of the strikers, enters into a professional relationship with newspaper entrepreneur Marcel Cohen to help her husband, who runs a flagging furniture business. Cohen froths with condemnation for the strikers, unaware of Hervey's sympathy for them, and shares his hope that the failure of the strike "finally finishes socialism in our time."[1] Cohen hopes to expand his capitalist empire by forming a joint furniture store with Hervey's husband Nicholas, but Jameson follows Cohen beyond this business negotiation, surveying his contribution to anti-Socialist propaganda as he hires men to write scathing articles about the miners. In discussing the furniture trade with Nicholas and Hervey, Cohen's propensity for stretching the truth migrates fluidly between his two business ventures, as he suggests that selling inauthentic furniture is a perfectly acceptable business practice. To justify his deception, Cohen cites his work in the newspaper industry. While playfully evading the accusation of manipulating public opinion through his newspaper, he admits to harnessing the power of the press to cement public disenchantment with the political process: "I don't waste my strength trying to form opinion. I give way to it, I use it. Don't you read either of my newspapers? When there's cynicism in the world, and more cynicism than hope, I'm at hand to provide it—I'll provide honest sentiment if it's wanted—only what's wanted—served up sizzling."[2] Cohen's admission—that he has no qualms in reinforcing the

---

[1] Storm Jameson, *None Turn Back* (London: Virago, [1936] 1984), p. 27.
[2] Jameson, *None Turn Back*, p. 31.

Public Opinion Polling in Mid-Century British Literature: The Psychographic Turn. Megan Faragher, Oxford University Press. © Megan Faragher 2021. DOI: 10.1093/oso/9780192898975.003.0003

toxic cynicism of the public—is mirrored in the historical relationship between newspapers and strikers in 1926.

That the press would have been politicized was certainly no surprise at the time of the General Strike. But while the popular press in Britain had boomed in the First World War, the General Strike forcefully unveiled the press as a commodity industry with ideological content as its commodity. Patrick Collier notes that the "newly expanded, diversified press" led to two definitions of the public, as both a "potential audience for printed material" and participants in a "politically active citizenry."[3] Simultaneously, the press's power "shattered the illusion of equal exchange" between consumers and producers, as critics feared the public could be led to want anything newspaper owners desired.[4] So when the Trades Union Congress (TUC) successfully staged an effort to include printers in the strike, the resulting press stoppage highlighted the significance of the news as a medium of public opinion formation. While some presses stopped entirely, others went to print only after editors ceded to demands of workers, who seized the press as a means of production, recognizing the newspaper's product not just as information, but belief.[5] The public, recognizing the press as an ideological machine, also identified what Cohen admits in *None Turn Back*: that the role of newspapers was to manufacture public opinion. And while newspapers claimed to solely reflect the views of its readers, their patronizing embrace of a "top-down model of a passive public" led many to view the newspaper as a morally bankrupt institution abusing its power for its own profit-driven ends.[6] Just as Jameson's portrayal of Cohen intimates the troubling commingling of the press and politics, newspaper magnates like Lord Beaverbrook and Viscount Northcliffe never shied from using their presses as political platforms.

But the overtly opinionated nature of the press would cause trouble in the burgeoning field of public opinion surveys—and vice versa. Polls presented a new potential for a scientific representation of public opinion, unmooring public sentiment from press editorialization. But as polling met its public via print mediation, it also inspired a transformation of the relationship between newspapers and their publics. As *News Chronicle* argued when it published the first public opinion polls in its pages, polling might "give its

---

[3] Patrick Collier, *Modernism on Fleet Street* (Burlington, VT: Ashgate: 2006), pp. 18, 19.
[4] Collier, *Modernism on Fleet Street*, pp. 19, 7.
[5] Gerald Crompton, "'Sheer Humbug': The Freedom of the Press and the General Strike," *Twentieth Century British History* 12, no. 1 (2001), pp. 46–68.
[6] Collier, *Modernism on Fleet Street*, p. 166.

readers an authoritative interpretation of the state of public opinion in Great Britain from moment to moment."[7] Rather than the press claiming to instinctively understand and represent the state of public opinion based on subjective editorialization and selective anecdotes, the publication of polling results promised readers an objective method to assess what their fellow citizens were thinking about current affairs, unmediated by the politicized press. Ironically, the newspapers would be the first medium by which the British reading public learned of this new, exciting methodology of assessing the minds of the masses. Polling's scientific patina meant that newspapers could enthusiastically market polling results in their pages as exclusive features; it was a successful stunt to draw in an enthusiastic readership. And yet, while polls were a sensation, the publication of polling data was a clear threat to the role newspapers had established for themselves as the dominant opinion panderers of the public sphere, a role that Jürgen Habermas dates to the nineteenth century.[8] The publication of polling threatened to wrest the discourse of public opinion away from newspaper owners and partisan stakeholders and return it to the people those discourses purportedly described. Pollsters thus threatened to usurp the press's role vis-à-vis its public. However, the promise of a neutrally established public opinion was not so easily delivered. If newspapers benefited from the credibility of scientific polling, polling was less fortunate, marred by the partisan reputation of the newspaper industry. So while optimism about polls arose from the promise of neutrality, the staging of polling data in the pages of newspapers—a medium so long derided for political biases and ideological leanings—also challenged the reputation of polling as a science. As social scientists worked with newspaper editors, the former constantly fought back against accusations of bias that came of working with the latter. The troubled, symbiotic relationship between polling and the press (so familiar to readers today) begins, I argue, at the very inception of polling itself. In much of the chapter that follows, I trace the origins of this conflict, whereby social science came to partially usurp the role the press had long taken up in relation to its public.

We can trace the British public consciousness of polling to one highly publicized survey: the Peace Ballot of 1934. Historians call the Peace Ballot

---

[7] "What Britain Thinks," *The News Chronicle*, October 17, 1938.

[8] Jürgen Habermas, *The Structural Transformation of the Public Sphere: An Inquiry into the Category of a Bourgeois Society*, translated by Thomas Burger (Cambridge: MIT Press, 1991), pp. 181–93. Habermas likewise suggests the way that polling methodologies alter the landscape of the postwar newspaper industry (p. 194).

the "first British referendum," and those at the time referred to it as "the most remarkable popular referendum ever initiated and carried through by private enterprise."[9] The Ballot was not conducted through the government or a polling institute, but through the League of Nations' National Declaration Committee (NDC). The poll asked participants to assess the platform of the League of Nations, including whether or not England should remain part of the League. The results of this ballot, overwhelmingly in favor of England maintaining its League support, were reported to both Parliament and the press.[10] Historian Maurice Cowling argues that the prevalence of the Peace Ballot in public debate even altered the Liberal party platform in the interwar period to include more focus on foreign policy.[11] Diplomat and novelist Harold Nicolson agreed, using an essay in the inaugural issue of *Public Opinion Quarterly* to argue that the Peace Ballot was one of the three nodal points in the evolution of public opinion throughout the 1930s and a key contributor to the public awareness of foreign policy as a significant political issue.[12] But the survey did more than influence Liberal policy in the interwar. Peace Ballot campaigners were politically savvy, exploiting newspapers to garner profuse public attention. Given that no full-scale surveys of public opinion had been conducted nationally by 1934, the scope of the Peace Ballot was unprecedented. Eleven *million* citizens participated in the survey—nearly a quarter of the population. Based on the massive number of participants, it is fair to say it would have been impossible to be ignorant of the survey if you lived in England in 1934.[13] The survey was a cultural milestone and, as we will see, emerged in fascinating ways in the literature of the period. It established the prominence of political polling in British culture and, due to its ubiquity, ushered in a new vision for polling's future; for the first time, polling was understood as a means of promoting liberal democracy and its values against the rise of fascist and totalitarian forces. The British public was becoming, as it were, "poll-minded."

By tracing the rise of this public "poll-mindedness"—a critical facet of the psychographic turn—this chapter tracks the contours of early beliefs

---

[9] Martin Ceadel, "The First British Referendum: The Peace Ballot, 1934–5," *The English Historical Review* 95, no. 377 (Oct 1980), 810–39; *New Statesman and Nation*, cited in J.A. Thompson, "The 'Peace Ballot' and the 'Rainbow' Controversy," *Journal of British Studies* 20, no. 2, 1981, p. 150.

[10] Adelaide Livingstone, *The Peace Ballot: The Official History* (London: Gollancz, 1935), p. 15.

[11] Maurice Cowling, *The Impact of Hitler* (Cambridge: Cambridge University Press, 2009), p. 10.

[12] Harold Nicolson, "British Public Opinion and Foreign Policy," *Public Opinion Quarterly* 1, no. 1(January 1937), pp. 53–63.

[13] Ceadel, "The First British Referendum," p. 828.

about the role of polls in public and civic life, which were both complex and, at times, contradictory. As in the example of the Peace Ballot, which I will describe in more detail, early polling was not an entirely neutral enterprise. While the Peace Ballot inspired a burgeoning "poll-mindedness," it was not without its biases. That a poll by the League of Nations—and about the League of Nations—set the path for public discourse about polls posed, at best, a problematic precedent in the discourse around polling, particularly when the poll and results were highly mediated by press coverage from both the left and right. From its start, the Peace Ballot suggested to the public a troubling partisan propensity in the institutionalization of polling, prefig-ured by the mediation of public opinion through the press. The divisive and partisan nature of the Peace Ballot stirred troubled waters for polling efforts that followed. This would be particularly evident in later polling efforts, principally in public response to the British Institute of Public Opinion's polls published in *News Chronicle*, which prided itself on neutrality and objectivity. As newspapers had so long been an expected source of bias and pandering, readers and politicians struggled to assess this new form of political data. American investigative journalist George Seldes lambasted newspapers during the war for taking "honest" Gallup polls and marring them through use of "fake" headlines or misleading reporting on the results.[14] Even if polls were meant to take the pulse of the nation, could the newspapers be trusted as a mediating force to properly educate the public as to their meaning? The sketchy history of newspapers in this field threatened to taint the interpretation of polling in its first years and added to increased confusion over the role of polling in a partisan environment.

As the public responded to this ambivalence over polling, walking a slow path towards a time when psychographic data would become a cornerstone of both private and public life, so did writers, who had to assess the role of the newspaper industry at a time when political tensions were on the rise. Despite polling's imbrication in, and mediation through, the press, some remained optimistic about polling's consequences for democracy. Science fiction writer Olaf Stapledon, for example, found such inspiration in the Peace Ballot that he theorized wide distribution of a declaration in support of peace to be signed by every luminary of the 1930s. Similarly, the emer-gence of Wells's editorials in the pages of *News Chronicle*, which prognosti-cated the political crises of the late 1930s and separated by mere pages from

---

[14] George Seldes, "Who Fakes Gallup Polls?" *In Fact* 1, no. 12 (October 21, 1940), pp. 1–2.

the latest polling data, suggests the co-evolution of political prognostication by cultural pundits alongside the institution of polling. But early polling optimists were also challenged by skeptical voices like that of Evelyn Waugh, who became increasingly cynical about the role of sociological analysis as a tool of collective good. Waugh's novel *Scoop*, which I will address in detail in the second half of this chapter, paints a skeptical portrait of public opinion and the papers during the Abyssinian crisis at the same time as the papers themselves attempted to shed the weight of their partiality in the publishing of objective polling data. This, alongside Waugh's ambivalence about the Peace Ballot and the Mass-Observation (M-O) movement, emphasizes Waugh's fears that sociological analysis could only serve to arm the powerful. Balancing these oppositional perspectives, this chapter claims that these varied responses to journalism, corresponding with the rise of the public's awareness of polling as a new field of political science, led to early ambivalence about polling and its role in civic life. But, despite this ambivalence, the popularity of polls increased exponentially in the last years of the 1930s and into the 1940s, bringing with it an increased reliance on this new sociopolitical praxis.

The Peace Ballot on and against Fleet Street

As has been suggested, the Peace Ballot—the first of the major polling initiatives in the 1930s—garnered immense public attention. Responses to the Peace Ballot project were reliably partisan, particularly since the effort was designed to bolster support for the League of Nations—the very organization that designed the ballot. But even these responses spoke to the complexity of emergent discourses over the role public opinion surveys would occupy in civic life. The survey met with some resistance by anti-Leaguers, who thought it a waste of time. This sentiment emerged most vehemently from one-time Minister of Information, newspaper publisher, and isolationist Lord Beaverbrook—the model for Storm Jameson's Cohen in *None Turn Back*—who called the ballot "a wicked and dangerous device."[15] In opposition to the survey, Beaverbrook, whose workers had threatened print stoppage during the 1926 General Strike, used the pages of his *Daily Express* to spread cynicism about the League and its survey, telling readers not to

---

[15] Beaverbrook cited in William Arnold-Forster, "Britain's National Peace Ballot," *World Affairs* 97, no. 4 (December 1934), p. 227.

answer the five multi-part questions presented to interviewees.[16] Throughout November 1934, Beaverbrook's *Daily Express* labeled the survey the "Ballot of Blood," a phrase that suggested a provocative view of the relationship between public opinion and political action.[17] The "ballot of blood" label implied that surveys were not just impotent suggestions of sentiment. The label insinuated that the survey somehow proactively contributed to the implementation of foreign policy positions; filling out a simple survey could have gory results. The "ballot of blood" rhetoric dovetailed with an emergent theory about public opinion at the dawn of the polling age: assessing the will of the people was tantamount to political action and, therefore, the creation of public opinion surveys was equivalent to forming a marching army.

Against this cynicism, though aligned with the underlying impression about the importance of polling, liberal-leaning papers disposed towards the League of Nations diligently promoted the survey and its results. Such papers gave the Peace Ballot a significant signal-boost, and consequently constructed a framework for public discourse about the role of polling in civic life for decades to come. Contemporaneous histories of the Peace Ballot lay bare the extent to which newspapers worked to make the initiative successful and wide-ranging. In her official history of the Peace Ballot, Adelaide Livingstone credits the "generous and almost daily hospitality" of news outfits like *News Chronicle, Daily Herald, Manchester Guardian*, and *Star* for the public enthusiasm around the ballot.[18] With both liberal and conservative papers weighing in, public awareness of political polling in the first half of the 1930s became intimately intertwined with newspapers, each of which continued to have its particular axe to grind. The first British referendum, therefore, was a partisan newspaper affair from start to finish. Adding to the commingling of press and poll was the fact that the League's inspiration for their ballot came from a small-scale newspaper questionnaire in the *Ilford Recorder* in 1934, which had similar questions to the final Peace Ballot. The sizable number of responses, approximately 25,000, inspired the League of Nations's National Declaration Committee to expand the ballot, generalize some of the questions, and present it in a nation-wide forum.[19] The League continued to fine-tune questions, then recruited a half-million volunteers to collect data on a large scale. Aside from the

---

[16]   Crompton, "'Sheer Humbug,'" p. 227.
[17]   Ceadel, "The First British Referendum," pp. 825–6.
[18]   Livingstone, *The Peace Ballot*, p. 24.   [19]   Livingstone, *The Peace Ballot*, p. 7.

discursive transformation around polling ushered in by the ballot, the process itself provided a playbook for future pollsters for how to conduct effective, wide-ranging surveys.

For the liberals who supported the ballot, a public opinion survey like this one was certainly not a "ballot of blood," or a weapon of war. Rather, papers marketed polling as an emergent cornerstone of liberal democracies everywhere. Livingstone's historical assessment of the Peace Ballot characterizes the process as inspiring a Phoenix-like restoration of democratic fervor: "The public response [went] extraordinarily well all over the country. The Ballot was a new thing, and therefore a queer thing [...] on the whole the Ballot was a notable *vindication of British democracy.*"[20] This sentiment, that polling was a technology metonymizing democracy, would only become more pronounced during the war. In a broadcast on public opinion research in 1942, George Gallup stated that "belief in the common man," demonstrated through public opinion polling, was "the fundamental promise of democracy" at threat under the rise of fascism.[21] Though the war was still years away when the League sent out its ballot, the discursive framework for polling as a democratic media was already being primed and prepared as a strategy of war. In a letter to *The Times* supporting participation in the Ballot, *Winnie-the-Pooh* author A.A. Milne shared this belief about polling, citing the Peace Ballot as a political mechanism to empower the disenfranchised voter. For Milne and others, the collection of opinion was not an idle practice; the declaration of collective will was a project of the highest order, akin to voting itself. "No doubt most of us prefer peace to war; Hatfield to Hell," Milne wrote. He continues:

> But we do not get to Hatfield by sitting down at Hendon and waiting for Hatfield to arrive. The great men who have been writing to you all talk of "wanting peace" as if this were all that is to be said for it. What remains to be said is how much (if anything) a man, or a country, is prepared to sacrifice for it. I suggest to the ordinary man that he begins by sacrificing a little of his time in answering the questions "Yes," "No," or "See below," and amplifying his answers. After all, what else can he do?[22]

---

[20] Livingstone, *The Peace Ballot*, p. 19, emphasis added.
[21] George Gallup, "Democracy and the Common Man." *Vital Speeches of the Day* 8, iss. 22 (September 1942) p. 687.
[22] A.A. Milne, "Peace Ballot." *The Times* (November 16, 1934), p. 10.

Meeting the futility of a geopolitical context exacerbated by the prospect of a new war, Milne's interpretation of polling as a brand of activism provides a solution to the threat of political impotence. In his reading, polls amount to a political action towards peace. Writing to Americans, Labour political figure and League member William Arnold-Forster wrote that the ballot "will prove to be a useful development in the technique of democratic 'government by persuasion' [...] founded on a free and informed public opinion."[23]

Both the enthusiastic embrace of polling, typified by Milne and Arnold-Forster, and Beaverbrook's contesting claim that the poll was a "ballot of blood," suggest a parallel between debates over polling and debates over aesthetics in the interwar period. If, as both Beaverbrook and Milne seem to accede, polling acted as a political sign, what was the power of its signification? To some extent, such a debate mirrors those staged around aesthetic realism. By providing a snapshot of the zeitgeist, did polling's self-reflexivity aid in the transformation or elevation of activist political discourse? Was it an opportunity for reform? Or, rather, by mimetically reflecting present conditions, did polling reify the status quo, whose tractability was masked by the scientific veneer of the polls themselves? Milne's argument about polling's utopian potentiality might easily be paralleled to Lukács's argument that realism "captures tendencies [...] that only exist incipiently and so have not yet had the opportunity to unfold their entire human and social potential."[24] But did polling, promising an honest view of public discourse, give us an avenue to grasp onto greater social potential? As I have demonstrated in the discussion of Wells in the previous chapter, the alienation of psychographic aesthetics from the canon comes as a direct result of sociology's inherent ties to discourses of aesthetic realism, born of an interest in the kinds of insights polling proffers. To reaffirm polling's impact on mid-century literature is also to perhaps relitigate the realism debate on different terms.

Whether or not polling was considered a revolutionary exposure of the people's will or a propagandistic reification of society's flawed opinions, it is noteworthy how many perceived the Peace Ballot through the lens of the former, seeing the collection of public opinion data not only as a means of expressing opinion, but also a profound new method of civic engagement, for better or ill. Just like those critics who saw the survey as a "ballot of blood," Milne's plea that the "ordinary man" "sacrific[e] a little of his time"

---

[23] Arnold-Forster, "Britain's National Peace Ballot," p. 229.
[24] Georg Lukács, "Realism in the Balance," in *Aesthetics and Politics* (London: Verso, 1980), p. 48.

to take the survey as a means of proactively working towards peace suggests the first shift in the general attitude towards political polling in the interwar period—a small step in the evolution of the psychographic turn. And despite the fact that the Peace Ballot began at the impetus of politicos who aimed to prove that the League of Nations maintained wide popular support, many continued to be enthusiastic about its potential. The Peace Ballot took on a life of its own, representing far more than a political stance in relationship to war or even the League of Nations. As reflected in the attitudes of Livingstone and Milne, the answering of the pollster's questions was not just a performance of opinion—it was a performative utterance. By stating "Yes," "No," or "See below," a citizen was declaring themselves agents in the maintenance of an upstanding, vibrant democratic order. Even before the results of the survey were born out in the real-world scenario of foreign policy decisions and their repercussions, the Peace Ballot was a massive achievement; it was one of the first moments when polling was put on national display as a new form of democratic expression.

Like the defenders of literary realism who saw such work as pursuing a mission of social reform, the first major political referendum also had a political intent: to reaffirm the importance of pacifism after World War I. Aside from the role that the Peace Ballot played in spreading awareness of public opinion surveys, the results of the survey bolstered the public image of the League. The survey was undertaken under the suspicion that results would be favorable for the League, and the NDC's expectations were certainly not disappointed. Of the over eleven million participants in the survey, 91 percent answered that they wished to remain in the League of Nations.[25] This result alone was enough to justify the survey for the League, which simply wanted a poll that would prove that its aims were in line with the country's will. In order to assess this, there were additional questions that asked about political positions vis-à-vis military intervention abroad, aimed at better identifying how the English public felt about the political grumblings across the continent. There were only five questions in the survey and most of those dealt with the international political turmoil in Europe, asking how the English would perceive its relationship with the League if it were under duress of Italian and German aggression. The final question of the five asked what the League of Nations should do if one nation insisted on attacking another; notably, the survey never really

---

[25] Livingstone, *The Peace Ballot*, p. 15.

identified *which* nation was attacking. All the same, of the nearly eleven million respondents who addressed this question, 95 percent favored "economic and non-military measures."[26] This was not particularly surprising. But a markedly large number—74 percent—also favored "if necessary, military measures."[27] Thus, in the abstract, the English public favored the intervention into territorial expansion by fascist countries. But as the League presented the situations in the abstract, without identifying any particular nation, the survey engaged in a little propaganda work as well. Even in asking these questions which express broad suggestions about territorial aggression, once someone was forced to provide a staid answer to the situation presented in the abstract, it might have been hoped that such an answer would be as relevant for German intervention as it would be for an Italian one. In other words, by anonymizing the possible list of aggressors, the survey rendered abstract what would end up becoming a concrete reality—a reality that, when it materialized, led to much more hesitant responses from the public on possible intervention.

Aside from the pacifist activism inherent in the poll itself, writers found other means by which to take the sociological work of the Peace Ballot and transform it into new aesthetic and political projects. Science fiction novelist Olaf Stapledon was one such writer. Stapledon had spent the first World War as a conscientious objector but found himself increasingly concerned over the rise of fascism and would eventually support a more aggressive stance towards German expansionism. As a young man, he spent time working with the Workers' Educational Association (WEA), a group that eventually would be a lynchpin for the British Institute of Public Opinion's (BIPO) survey infrastructure; BIPO would eventually hire WEA workers to collect survey information *en masse* in England.[28] Stapledon saw the focus on education as crucial for the creation of a better world. And when he observed the breadth and scope of the Peace Ballot, he was inspired by the potentiality of such a tool for the transmission of a political message. If A.A. Milne saw participation in the Peace Ballot as a means of engaging in political activism, Stapledon viewed the survey's methods as a roadmap for changing public opinion on war, possibly leading to global peace.

The transformation of public opinion from a device of collection to one of propagandizing began, for Stapledon, as Hitler brought his forces into the

---

[26] Walter Ashley, "The First Million Votes," *Headway: A Monthly Review of the League of Nations* 17, no. 2 (February 1935), p. 26.

[27] Ashley, "The First Million Votes," p. 26. [28] Durant, "Proceedings," pp. 107–11.

Rhineland, a clear signal of aggression against the League of Nations and the Versailles Treaty. Stapledon joined the Peace Pledge Union, considering an additional signatory campaign inspired by the Peace Ballot, asking for co-signers on the statement: "I renounce War and never again will I support or sanction another, and I will do all in my power to persuade others to do the same."[29] Had Stapledon's signatory campaign taken off, it is possible scholars would give it the same attention now garnered by the infamous Nancy Cunard campaign a year later, *Authors Take Sides on the Spanish Civil War*. When he was considering the campaign, Olaf Stapledon sent a letter to H.G. Wells in March 1936, asking him about the potential pledge cards, which he hoped would signal a collective artistic denunciation of empire and armament, ambitiously titled "Open Letter to All the Peoples of the Earth."[30] In it, he buoyed the prospect of the League of Nations as a force that might realize the highest of his lofty ideals, but Wells's response was lukewarm at best: "Do for God's sake forget about the League of Nations."[31] Peace was Stapledon's real inspiration in the writing of the letter, but the prospect of its influence over the great mass of public opinion derived from the original Peace Ballot effort. Stapledon personally asked Viscount Cecil, draftsman of the League's survey, if he might use the extensive contact list obtained by the survey to spread his letter. Given Stapledon's support of the League, the recorded support from Cecil comes as little surprise, though Stapledon never completed his effort.[32] This desire to transform the use of the Peace Ballot process—from a device of collection to one of persuasion—suggests the continued transformation of the polling apparatus from a tool of sociological reflection to one that additionally transforms the sociological landscape it purports to reflect. Though Stapledon's "Open Letter" foundered, the notion of political activism, bolstered by data and group-mindedness, arose in the plot and vignettes of *Star Maker*, which Stapledon was writing amidst his contemplation of his "Open Letter." While Stapledon was attempting to unite the world under the banner of a unified peace, he was also attempting to finish his novel about intergalactic exploration that systematically categorizes a series of alien communities across the galaxies. But the Abyssinian crisis moved him to distraction. He was fully involved in the movement for peace, giving speeches against Mussolini's

---

[29] Robert Crossley, *Olaf Stapledon: Speaking for the Future* (Liverpool: Liverpool University Press, 1994), p. 236.
[30] Crossley, *Olaf Stapledon*, p. 236.   [31] Quoted in Crossley, *Olaf Stapledon*, p. 236.
[32] Crossley, *Olaf Stapledon*, p. 236.

invasion, and was only able to steal time to work on his novel when he wasn't engaged in protest, causing the whole project to be delayed a year. "Lately I have been extremely busy, chiefly with speaking at peace meetings and carrying out an interminable correspondence in the local press," Stapledon wrote when he told Aage Marcus that *Star Maker* was delayed.[33]

The blurry line between scientific polling and activism was further muddled by an addenda pamphlet, suggestively titled "Peace or War?" which the National Declaration Committee suggested "be circulated with the Ballot Paper."[34] In it, the ballot is explained to polling respondents, with guiding language to help formulate their verdicts. A representative sampling of the pamphlet's commentary confirms its role as a propaganda tool. It asks, "Can you think of a better way of building up a peacefully ordered world than through the League of Nations?" It states, "people feel more and more that it is not right or safe that weapons of war should be made and sold for private profit."[35] The inherent synergy between polling and activism here was equally emergent in Stapledon's fiction, where simply by observing the experiences and views of others, his intergalactic travelers find their own positions irrevocably changed. Both the ballot's methods and Stapledon's fiction (of which there will be more discussion in the next chapter), attest to what we now call the Hawthorne effect: the notion that simply by observation the observer changes the actions of the observed. In a debate with Leo Crespi in 1945, British Institute for Public Opinion's Henry Durant admits to one concern: the notion that the surveyors inadvertently altered their results by simple interactions with the interviewees. Durant notes that in Conservative districts, Labour pollsters collected data far more amenable to Labour results than would eventually be accurate. Arguably, this kind of inevitable interviewer bias had some role to play in the missed Labour wave in 1945.[36] The Peace Ballot was an early, and exaggerated, exemplar of Durant's concerns, as it primed its participants towards results favorable to the League, all the while touting itself as a neutral arbiter of public opinion writ large.

When the Peace Ballot results were widely distributed and touted in liberal newspapers throughout 1934 and 1935, the curated results were deployed as

---

[33] Quoted in Crossley, *Olaf Stapledon*, p. 233.
[34] National Declaration Committee, "Peace or War? A National Declaration on the League of Nations and Armaments," 1934.
[35] National Declaration Committee, "Peace or War?"
[36] Henry Durant, "The Cheater Problem," *The Public Opinion Quarterly* 10, no. 2 (1946), pp. 288–91.

a tool to justify and strengthen the League's position. Dozens of articles in *The Times* reference the Peace Ballot, and even more references are spread throughout other newspapers. The more coverage the ballot and its results received, the more the poll became not a means of registering opinion, but of manufacturing it. The established position of the group mind increasingly became a motivating factor for political and social change; the much-feared herding effect became evident. The very fact that so many supported the League was all the more reason to support the league oneself: to become part of the collective mind that was so trumpeted in the local press accounts. Identifying this dialectic model of influence, it thus came as no surprise when Stapledon saw the 1934 Peace Ballot as a way of changing and manipulating public opinion.

Evelyn Waugh's "An Englishman's Home": Peace Ballot Polling in Practice

Olaf Stapledon was not the only one who saw potential in the methods put forward by the 1934 Peace Ballot. Less than a month before the English declaration of war against Germany, and five years after the Peace Ballot was conducted, novelist and journalist Evelyn Waugh saw fit to revisit the trope of the Peace Ballot in his short story "An Englishman's Home," published in *Good Housekeeping* in August 1939. However, Waugh's view of the Ballot's potentiality to bolster democracy was far more mixed than Stapledon's, particularly in a story allegorizing German territorial aggression. The story takes place in the village of Much Malock, where an outside developer—a German—has unexpectedly purchased a piece of property adjacent to the wealthy Beverley Metcalfe. This interloper and self-described scientist, Mr. Hargood-Hood, intends to use the land to build an unsightly and dangerous industrial laboratory in the middle of the village. Having been caught unawares about the sale, the community panics. The villagers quickly turn on one another; there is deep concern they will be unable to wrest the land from the new owner. They must, as Waugh states in a tongue-in-cheek allusion to Neville Chamberlain's German policy, find a way to achieve "appeasement and peace-in-our-time."[37] Waugh transforms this parable about a small village's internecine struggles into a referendum on the widespread

---

[37] Evelyn Waugh, "An Englishman's Home," in *The Complete Stories* (New York: Little, Brown, 2012), p. 235.

discourse on the Peace Ballot and its capacity to weaponize collective intention in times of international conflict. To defeat the "lot of jerry builders," the villagers must find a way to work as a community.[38] They first lay the responsibility for the re-purchasing of the land, now exorbitantly priced, at the feet of the wealthy Metcalfe, who everyone believes should have already purchased the land to prevent just this kind of incursion. Metcalfe bristles at first, threatening to sell his own property to developers and move away, leaving the rest of the middle and lower-class villagers stuck in an untenable situation.

What saves the community from destruction is a spirit of collectivism, alluded to early in the short story through Waugh's description of the Hornbeams: "a childless, middle-aged couple who devoted themselves in craftsmanship."[39] The Hornbeams, and their active involvement in the Peace Ballot, stand as a symbol of an unflappable community spirit; Mrs. Hornbeam was said to have "canvassed every cottage in bicycling distance" for the Peace Ballot initiative, though she maintains her independence—a trait the contrarian Waugh espouses; her refusal to join the Women's Institute leads to a rift between herself and fellow villagers.[40] But in the end, Mrs. Hornbeam's spirit of independently minded collective action is what saves the community from Mr. Hargood-Hood. Waugh describes that, no one "took the crisis harder than the Hornbeams," and he further ventriloquizes his admiration for their spirited provincial autonomy in the reflections of Mr. Hornbeam: "We ask nothing of their brutish civilization except to be left alone, to be given one little corner of land, an inch or two of sky where we can live at peace and occupy ourselves with making seemly and beautiful things. You wouldn't think it was too much to ask. We give them the entire globe for their machines. But it is not enough."[41] It is this sentiment that drives the community to cohesion; they decide on a project that would do for the property: a new hut for the Scouts. Coming to unified belief as to the future the village should pursue, they work together to raise the money, and those efforts push the rest to put skin in the game, including Metcalfe who, in a bit of Waughian irony, spends even more on the project than he would have had he simply purchased the land outright. The story applauds the plucky villagers who, despite their foibles and peccadillos,

---

[38] Waugh, "An Englishman's Home," p. 226.
[39] Waugh, "An Englishman's Home," p. 220.
[40] Waugh, "An Englishman's Home," p. 221.
[41] Waugh, "An Englishman's Home," p. 228.

unite to defeat an interloper, using the "canvassing" ethos to inspire collective action. The story is also undergirded by a strong critique of the deleterious impersonality of industrial capitalism in favor of a holistic heterogeneous social spirit. To that extent, Waugh's story encapsulates what he saw as the possible benefits of such a survey of the population: the production of civic pride and social empowerment.

However, even in this story, we find some conservative skepticism over the ability of social science to truly fix the political and social divisions that Waugh diligently believed were endemic to the British experience. While the story frames the Harwood-Hood factory as a harbinger for the regimented and dehumanizing force later connected to Nazi science, the story also recognizes other forms of such detrimental science in the British context, as the wealthy Metcalfe argues with his working-class gardener Bogget over the forecast. Metcalfe, "really fascinated by mechanical gadgets," comments benignly on the barometer as a signal of rain to his gardener.[42] But Bogget challenges the findings of the prognosticating weather apparatus, noting that looking at a nearby steeple is far more likely to detect rain than the readings of the barometer. Metcalfe has a moment of recognition: "These old fellows know a thing or two that scientists don't."[43] As it reveres resourceful community members over and above wealthy landowners and technocrats, the introduction to the story concretizes Waugh's preference for provincial knowledge over that garnered by any externally imposed order derived from science. Such a lesson is equally applicable to the Peace Ballot. The benefits of the Peace Ballot are valuable solely as a catalyst for parochial pride; to the extent that scientific analysis like the barometer should be superseded by more parochial knowledge, Waugh critiques the large-scale social science marketed by the Peace Ballot. In a regional context, Mrs. Hornbeam's cycling to canvass activates a public spirit. But when nationalized and executed on an impersonal scale, Waugh expressed deep concern over the ramification of social science. This concern was reflected in his apprehension over Mass-Observation, as he argued their methods might provide means of "discover[ing] the controls" of democracy which might "be dangerous in the wrong hands."[44]

---

[42] Waugh, "An Englishman's Home," p. 217.
[43] Waugh, "An Englishman's Home," p. 218.
[44] Evelyn Waugh, "The Habits of the English," in *The Essays, Articles and Reviews of Evelyn Waugh*, edited by Gallagher Donat (Harmondsworth: Penguin, 1986), pp. 226–7.

It is fairly obvious why Waugh would be thinking back on the 1934 Peace Ballot at the dawn of the declaration of war when he published "An Englishman's Home." Such a time necessarily recalled the years of preliminary conflicts that challenged the British public as to their dedication to peace or their support of military intervention in Europe. There was some reason to have concerns about presuming public consensus on these points. While the 1934 Peace Ballot suggested an overwhelming support for the League of Nations, the earlier, provincial version of the Peace Ballot was a harbinger of what Harold Nicolson called a public opinion "revolt."[45] Before the Peace Ballot was distributed across the country, the smaller version was produced in Ilford, with more pointed questions than what would be sent to the over eleven million participants in the final survey. In the provincial version of the survey, the questioners asked respondents, directly, whether or not they would support intervention if Germany invaded France. While later, in response to the more broadly worded League survey, whether people supported military intervention for unnamed countries invading other unnamed countries, the Ilford results were far more nuanced. A vast majority of Ilford respondents said, as Harold Nicolson records, that if asked to intervene in the case of German aggression "they would do nothing of the sort."[46] The Ilford respondents, it would turn out, were the canary in the polling coalmine, as the purposefully broad wording of the League's nationwide survey would undergo significant pressure testing. When Mussolini secured concessions in Abyssinia in December 1935, it seemed at first as if the Peace Ballot may have been accurate after all. According to Harold Nicolson, the public was livid. He records this moment of potential recuperation for the Peace Ballot's findings: "It was felt that this remarkable explosion of public opinion, this direct exercise of democratic control over foreign policy, proved that the Peace Ballot had been a clear indication of the national will and that the electorate were in fact ready to risk war on behalf of the League Covenant."[47] But this vindication of the Peace Ballot was short-lived. Germany invaded the Rhineland in March 1936. And in this instance, public opinion retreated from the Ballot's predictions. Remembering back to the first world war, Nicolson suggests, the British public were more hesitant about picking a fight with Germany than it had in the case of Italy. This affirmed the validity of the earlier Ilford survey, where

---

[45] Nicolson, "British Public Opinion and Foreign Policy," p. 60.
[46] Nicolson, "British Public Opinion and Foreign Policy," p. 58.
[47] Nicolson, "British Public Opinion and Foreign Policy," p. 60.

the public indicated its unwillingness to fight Germany were it to put England in the position to hold to its Locarno obligations. At the same time, British resistance to intervention against Germany suggested that the Peace Ballot's purposefully abstract language about military intervention led to misleading results.

But during the brief time between the Italian and German invasions, it seemed as if there were broad confirmation of the early findings of the national Peace Ballot survey. Anti-fascist sentiment across the country buoyed the public stance against Italy and its invasion into Abyssinia. So, when Evelyn Waugh wrote a novel about the incursion, focusing intently on how this affair played in the press and with the British public, it appears in the context of the highly publicized results of the Peace Ballot that he would revisit on the eve of the declaration of war. But while Mrs. Hornbeam's volunteerism with the Peace Ballot in "An Englishman's Home" highlighted the underlying solidarity within the village, Waugh does not stray from his skepticism over the power of the elite to mask or overwhelm the intelligence of the provincial villagers. While the villagers are able to save their community from incursions, they do so only under threat of both the foreign land developer and the more local aristocracy, who are both completely oblivious to the vulnerabilities of the village. Waugh's fiction embraces this trend, seeing those with privilege as innately inimical to policies supported by most citizens. It is for this reason that we find in, for example, *Put Out More Flags*, the aristocrat Basil Seal grifting the government through the evacuee relocation scheme. Such moments of political vulnerability expose the power of extant social hierarchies. As polling would increasingly come to enter public discourse, mediated primarily by newspapers, this concern about polling's political ramifications would only intensify.

"Britain Thinks": *News Chronicle* and the Popularization of the Polls

In late October 1938, a few weeks after *News Chronicle* began its reproduction of modern public opinion polls—it was the first newspaper in England to do so—it published a provocative article entitled "Britain Thinks," which foregrounded a compelling question that captured the ambivalent and contradictory views around political polling in the 1930s: "Public opinion (say the hopeful) is the strongest and most vital social force in the world today. Public opinion (say the cynics) is the weakest and most vulnerable social force in the world today. Who is right?"[48] While *News Chronicle* staged this as an open question, the newspaper's first announcement of the polling project, titled "A GREAT NEW VENTURE BEGINS NEXT WEEK," forcibly primed audience response.[49] *News Chronicle* hoped to convert the English public to the practice of polling and justify the claim that public opinion was a strong vital force that would, as A.A. Milne suggested in his Peace Ballot editorial, strengthen democracy in a time of great challenge. As the first newspaper to begin publication and replication of statistical polling analysis in England, *News Chronicle* clearly believed in the value of public opinion data and its distribution. A year after George Gallup set up shop in America with his popular Gallup survey, Henry Durant had begun conducting polls in England using Gallup's new methods, including statistical sampling and weighted polling averages, which differed greatly from the type of self-selected surveys that had preceded it. A year later, *News Chronicle* began its "great new venture," billing it as "one of the most important developments in journalism" which signified that "*News Chronicle* can discover, with accuracy and without bias, what Britain thinks."[50] The language of the announcement similarly emphasized the role of public opinion polls in reinforcing the pillars of the democratic process: "It means that the people of England, 'who never have spoken yet,' will speak at last [...] It means that we shall find out what that inarticulate, baffling object, 'the British public' (and that includes us all) really thinks about questions of the day."[51] Though *News Chronicle* paid lip service to the insecurities the public had over polling and its ramifications, their rhetorical evocation of inclusive democratic principles underscores the optimistic, and even utopian, promise that the outlet hoped to tap in its publication of BIPO's surveys.

In "Britain Thinks," *News Chronicle* editors reaffirmed polling's position as a form of unbiased political engagement. Aside from the grand question about the role of public opinion in modern life, the grandiosity of the article's opening language is marked for its drama:

You are one of the forty-eight million people in the British Isles. You're one of two thousand million people who live on this earth.

In the welter of words you read in the Press and heard by radio and rumor during the Crisis, what were your thoughts—do you think that you as a

---

[48] *News Chronicle*, "Britain Thinks," (October 17, 1938), p. 10.
[49] *News Chronicle*, "A Great New Venture Begins Next Week," (October 15, 1938), p. 1.
[50] *News Chronicle*, "A Great New Venture Begins Next Week," p. 1.
[51] *News Chronicle*, "Britain Thinks," p. 10.

one-two-thousand-millionth part of the world had any effects on the
course of events?

You heard of other men—as infinitesimal parts of mankind as yourself—
Chamberlain, Hitler, Benes, Roosevelt. You knew that they were juggling
with your life.

Do you believe that your thoughts were of any account in their deliberations? Do you believe that your opinions were able to deflect or augment
their actions by one jot?[52]

A few prevalent contemporaneous sentiments about public opinion polling
are worth registering in this passage. First, the rise of public opinion and its
popularity is marketed by *News Chronicle* as a necessary corrective for a
political environment that ignores the everyday citizen. The infinitesimal
singular human of "two thousand million" inevitably feels powerless and
completely at sea less than a month after the Treaty of Munich ushered in
the annexation of Sudetenland. As the geopolitical tensions increased, the
need for people to brandish some kind of control, however fleeting, was an
emotional need *News Chronicle* was desperate to meet. Polling, which could
theoretically weaponize public opinion, was depicted as "the strongest and
most vital social force."[53] In arguing for the value of public opinion as a new
social force, the paper presents polling as a possible way of making insular
and powerless voices more influential in the foreign policy decisions of
the day.

Outside of the publication of self-selected, unscientific readership surveys, newspapers like *News Chronicle* had long demonstrated their commitment to public opinion through the publication of readers' letters. But in
early October, *News Chronicle* cited the "overwhelming" amount of correspondence, further stating that "[it] will, unfortunately, not be possible to
continue to print them in large numbers, owing to the exceptional pressure
on space."[54] In so doing, the paper was highlighting an inherent failure of
traditional journalistic practices to appropriately reflect the views of the
public. Even as late as 1938, when many of the methodological advancements in polling had been established, the newspaper understood that, to
most, the notion of the public opinion *en masse* continued to be both baffling and opaque. This belief was abetted by the equally opaque discourses of

---

[52] "Britain Thinks," p. 10.
[53] "Britain Thinks," p. 10.
[54] *News Chronicle*, "More Letters to the Editor," (October 5, 1938).

group psychology common in early academic social psychology (as discussed in Chapter 1). The "great new venture" sought to demystify the will *of* the public, *for* the public, for perhaps the first time in England's history. But for the British public to fully understand itself, *News Chronicle* felt obliged to explain polling methodologies. It became clear that readers needed recurrent, and often tedious, explanations of polling practices. Known as a left-leaning paper in the 1930s, many *News Chronicle* readers remained unsure whether or not the paper biased the data it presented; the looming ghosts of Beaverbrook and his guild undermined their credibility in the promotion of more scientific polling practices. In the article introducing the public to BIPO polling, *News Chronicle* outlined the methods of "quota sampling" that Gallup used in America, citing that the American Institute of Public Opinion correctly forecasted Roosevelt's victory and touting the accuracy of Gallup's methods.[55] The reliance on these purportedly scientific practices is repeatedly linked to the democratic process. "It is of the deepest necessity, if a democracy is to succeed, that the voice of the people, when it speaks, should make itself not only heard but understood, plainly and without ambiguity [...] Hitherto, public opinion has only been able to make itself known in vague and ambiguous ways."[56] Alongside "Britain Thinks" sits an image of two groups of men and women, each standing on the opposite side of a scale (see Figure 2.1). The image's visual symbolism is striking: standing on two sides of the scale, the public represents both a means to a form of justice, a measurable countable quantity, and the conjunction of scientific discourse and sociological study.

The publication of BIPO results was meant to succeed on two fronts. First, they would inform others about how their fellow citizens and voters viewed an issue in an objective, clear way. Second, as the introductory explication of Gallup's methods indicates, *News Chronicle* hoped to educate their readers on the process of public opinion methodologies and let them know exactly how and why these methods were so impactful and effective. But it seems that the publication of these statistics in a left-leaning newspaper did cause some confusion, which needed to be repeatedly corrected by editors and writers for the paper. On October 18, 1938, *News Chronicle* teased out the first results of the first BIPO survey, to be printed the following day. When they did so, they also repeated some of the warnings about the division between the newspaper enterprise itself and BIPO, who were distinct

[55] *News Chronicle*, "Britain Thinks," p. 10.   [56] "Britain Thinks," p. 10.

Figure 2.1 "Britain Thinks" *News Chronicle* (October 17, 1938), p. 10.

entities. They quickly explained, again, the process of sampling, but also gave readers another warning about interpreting the data as biased in any way: "Remember, the *News Chronicle*, although it has the exclusive right to publish the findings, has no connection with the British Institute of Public Opinion, and the survey is in no way a reflection of what *News Chronicle* readers think. It is What Britain Thinks."[57] The first results of BIPO's *News Chronicle* surveys were touted with aplomb on the first page of the October 19th issue. The leader read: "Widespread Demand for National Register in Public Opinion Test."[58] The first results responded to only two questions: (1) Are you satisfied with Mr. Neville Chamberlain as Prime Minister (57 percent said "Yes" while 43 percent said "No"); and (2) A National Register could be made listing everybody available for civilian or military

---

[57] *News Chronicle*, "A Great New Venture Begins Next Week," p. 1.
[58] *News Chronicle*. "Widespread Demand for Register in Public Opinion," (October 19, 1938), p. 1.

duty in wartime. Should this be done immediately? (78 percent said "Yes" while 22 percent said "No"). But in bold towards the end of the front page, *News Chronicle* again had to register that the survey was "not a referendum of *News Chronicle* readers."[59] This first volley of questions was followed by others. On October 28th, the front page "Britain Thinks" survey brought in more results, on matters both political and personal, including German aggression and the ideal weekly family income.[60] But again, *News Chronicle* is made to reinforce that the facts in the surveys are "[not] solely the views of *News Chronicle* readers," "[not] necessarily the editorial opinions of the *News Chronicle*" and "[not] published as propaganda for or against any particular policy, party or personality."[61] This last stipulation differs in nature from earlier stipulations that simply sought to remind readers that the survey was not of *them* as readers. Rather, the final stipulation in the "Britain Thinks" results suggests early concerns about the way that public opinion polls might lead to herding of opinion. Polling might act not as a form of information or even empowerment, but as a form of persuasion in itself, as people wished to identify their own views in line with, and not counter to, the prevailing wisdom of the crowd. Circumstantial evidence suggests that the partnership between BIPO and *News Chronicle* bore fruit. In January 1939, *News Chronicle* touted a strong rise in sales in the month of October, with a year-high sales number of 1,336,094 papers sold.[62]

Scoop and the Manipulation of Public Opinion

Despite the outlet's optimism, *News Chronicle*'s repeated efforts to explain and justify the British Institute of Public Opinion polls to readers suggests the inherent and perhaps intractable skepticism that met audiences looking to newspapers as a means of objectively assessing public opinion. As suggested, the biased history of *News Chronicle* and relationship to the Peace Ballot might have been one reason for this. Evelyn Waugh himself certainly had no admiration for what he considered the "radical" paper (*News Chronicle*). In recalling *News Chronicle* reporter Stuart Emeny, Waugh writes

---

[59] *News Chronicle*, "Widespread Demand for Register in Public Opinion," p. 1.
[60] *News Chronicle*, "Views on Family Needs and Motoring Penalties," (October 28, 1938), p. 1.
[61] *News Chronicle*, "The Why and the How of 'Britain Thinks,'" (October 28, 1938), p. 12.
[62] *News Chronicle*, "Net Sales in 1938," (January 16, 1939), p. 1.

that "[e]ven his private opinions were those of his paper."[63] W.F. Deedes, a reporter for the *Daily Telegraph* who covered the Abyssinian crisis alongside Waugh, frames his experience as highly influenced by the role of public opinion research in both politics and public discourse. In his recollections, *At War with Waugh*, Deedes recognizes the dramatic influence of the Peace Ballot at the time, which "had an impact on ministers" and acted as a foil against British interests, which were soundly divided in the Abyssinian conflict.[64] Regarding the rather dubious scientific validity of the ballot, Deedes admits that "[s]ome charitably saw the Peace Ballot figures as underlining Great Britain's attachment to the League of Nations; others regarded it as part of a pacifist campaign"; whichever was true, Deedes argues that "in 1935 the desire for peace had a most powerful hold on the country."[65] For Deedes, the Peace Ballot bolstered the peace movement, but this only further complicated British involvement in Abyssinia. The Anglo-German naval treaty abetted German expansionism. At the same time, the public was split between its desire to avoid war and its compulsion to defend Abyssinia as a League of Nations member.[66] It was a sentiment Evelyn Waugh captures in *Scoop* where, in the words of newspaper magnate Lord Copper: "The British public has no interest in a war which drags on indecisively."[67]

Into this public opinion muddle, Evelyn Waugh found himself enmeshed, disentangling the threads of press pressures and political propaganda. While his time as a reporter for the *Daily Mail* is best remembered for his failure to identify a large oil concession organized right under his nose, the dissatisfying experience led Waugh to produce a scathing satire of the journalism industry in *Scoop* (1938). From the start, Waugh lambasted those he worked for, all the while identifying the troubling influence of public taste on the papers, and vice versa. In the novel, Lord Copper, the owner of the Megalopolitan Newspaper Corporation, discusses with a group the publication of a poem deemed the most lucrative and praised work of a poet

[63] Evelyn Waugh, *Waugh in Abyssinia* (London: Methuen, [1936] 1984), 52; W.F. Deedes, among others, notes that the "radical" outlined in *Waugh in Abyssinia* is most assuredly based on Stuart Emeny. W.F. Deedes, *At War with Waugh* (London: Pan Books, 2004), p. 106.
[64] Deedes, *At War with Waugh*, p. 11.
[65] Deedes, *At War with Waugh*, p. 12; in support of the public sentiment, Deedes cites the by-election of 1933 and the General Election of 1935, where a "swing against the government" was "widely interpreted as a triumph for peace and disarmament" (p. 12).
[66] Deedes, *At War with Waugh*, pp. 10–11.
[67] Evelyn Waugh, *Scoop* (New York: Little Brown, [1937] 2012), p. 49.

laureate's career.[68] The poem, commissioned by the editor, was "an ode to the seasonal fluctuation of our net sales."[69] Despite the cynical and self-serving nature of the commissioned work, the author reflected to Copper that it was "the most poetic and highly paid work he had ever done."[70] While it is humorous that the poet seems so ready to treat readerly praise as a mark of aesthetic value, the true satire of Waugh's anecdote rests on the way that the content of the poetry speaks to the other dialectical relationship in the mix: that between news consumer and the content of the work of art itself; the poet laureate has not just produced a poem that seeks to please the readership of the newspaper, but one that preens the audience for their membership in a collective readership. The small aside by Lord Copper is thus a metanarrative conceit, demanding even Waugh's readers to recognize that his own satiric response to the press is born of a historical necessity to grapple with the increasingly codependent relationship between writers and readers.

In Waugh's novel, the newspaper perpetually exists within a system of economic exchange, but even more so in dialectic relationship to its audience's feedback and response, always with an eye towards mocking both the audience and the institution in which he once took a part as a wartime correspondent in Abyssinia. The mockery of the papers, and particularly of the inefficient and fraudulent practice of wartime journalism, is epitomized by the mix-up that sets the plot in motion. William Boot, the protagonist of the novel, is a small-time journalist primarily responsible for the nature column "Lush Places." A natural admirer of beauty, he prides himself on his love of nature-writing, wishing to write of "wild flowers and birdsong," and puzzles over the aesthetic quality of his phrasing, as he repeatedly chants to himself, "*Feather-footed though the plashy fen passes the questing vole*," a preview of his next "Lush Places" article.[71] But when readers first encounter William Boot at his rustic estate of Boot Magna, he is in a heap of nerves. He receives a notice that he is to appear at *The Daily Beast* by request of Lord Copper personally. He expects he is to be given the boot himself, after he was the victim of a prank that led to a highly inaccurate and humorous column being published under his byline. Having written a "lyrical but wholly accurate account of the habits of the badger," his sister Priscilla playfully replaced every instance of "badger" in the copy with "crested grebe," a transliteration

[68] Selina Hastings, *Evelyn Waugh: A Biography* (London, Capuchin Classics, 2013), p. 369.
[69] Waugh, *Scoop*, p. 4.   [70] Waugh, *Scoop*, p. 14.   [71] Waugh, *Scoop*, p. 24.

that makes for some very inaccurate and humorous reporting on the little-considered bird.[72] So, when the editor calls up Boot, the latter expects a high level of reprimand, but also plans to stand defiantly in support of the inaccurate depiction of the grebe. "The great crested grebe *does* hibernate," he lectures to himself in hopes that he can save his position, which he holds onto as a textual vestige of the receding class of landed gentry to which he belongs.[73]

The grebe fiasco speaks directly to the relationship between the press and the readers. When considering his call to London, William recalls responses of readers who responded to his piece with shock and horror. "His mail had been prodigious. One lady wrote to ask whether she read him aright in thinking he condoned the practice of baiting these rare and beautiful birds with terriers and deliberately destroying their earthly homes [...] A major in Wales challenged him categorically to produce a single authenticated case of a great crested grebe attacking young rabbits."[74] Boot is called into the office, expecting to be seen to the door. Instead, he is offered a promotion of epic proportions as a wartime correspondent with an almost bottomless salary, a job he is so ill-prepared for that in his first discussion with Corker, a journalist with *Universal News*, he must ask the question, "And what, please...is a news agency?"[75] It is obvious to every reader that William Boot is highly unequipped for the duties of a foreign correspondent in Ishmaelia. And, unsurprisingly, the reason William won this coveted position lies, again, in the ignorance and incapability of the aristocracy that manages the newspaper industry. That Boot ends up receiving fame and accolades for his efforts by the novel's end simply attends to the way that "sentiment," not "evidence," ends up being the basis of much public opinion on international affairs—a point that Waugh makes in *Waugh in Abyssinia*.[76] As argued by Otis Harrison, "[t]o Waugh, the newspapers and their Byzantine façades are not the only ones trapped in apathy: the British public is also mired. All of society is implicated in one bleak picture of pride and passivity."[77] Waugh doubles down on his vision of the public and the journalists who influence them as filled with equal parts pride and passivity

[72] Waugh, *Scoop*, p. 23.   [73] Waugh, *Scoop*, p. 26.
[74] Waugh, *Waugh in Abyssinia*, p. 23.   [75] Waugh, *Scoop*, p. 79.
[76] Waugh, *Waugh in Abyssinia*, p. 32.
[77] Otis Harrison, "Finding the Lush Place: Waugh's Moral Vision in *Scoop*," *Evelyn Waugh Studies* 46, no. 3 (2013) p. 16.

when he writes to Katharine Asquith in September 1935 that most "journalists are lousy competitive and hysterical lying."[78]

Of course, the placement of William Boot to cover the Ishmaelia crisis is nothing more than a tragic mistake, but one that reveals the insular nature by which the wealthy elite make decisions and delude one another into sharing opinions that have direct impact on public opinion. Before William Boot arrives at the Megalopolitan building to receive his Ishmaelia assignment, the novelist John Boot visits Mrs. Julia Stitch, a Minister's wife with endless social capital. Reading the news placards declaring "Ishmaelite Crisis and Strong League Note," the novelist is hoping for a position as a spy in the Ishmaelia contest, but would find himself satisfied with the role of foreign correspondent, recommended by his reputation as the author of *Waste of Time*, "a studiously modest description of some harrowing months among the Patagonian Indians," "read by the people whose opinion John Boot respected."[79] Stitch takes up John Boot's cause in a luncheon with magnate Lord Copper, wherein Julia's social capital assures that others of the upper classes will audibly mirror her own opinion. Bringing John Boot into the conversation, she reports, "[The Prime Minister] always sleeps with a Boot by his bed."[80] Others sycophantically mirror Stitch's assertion: "*[S]o clever and amusing*," says Lady Metroland; "Such a divine style," reports Lady Cockpurse.[81] Having convinced Copper of Boot's value as a correspondent, Lady Stitch considers her mission accomplished. When Copper demands his foreign editor to hire "Boot," a man who he's never even read, the editor has only the vaguest idea of who the famed writer might be. Scanning through the papers they come across *William* Boot's "Lush Places." Assuming this to be the man he seeks, two editors puzzle over the choice, but seek desperately to justify the tastes of both Lord Copper and the Prime Minister. Reading over his fragment on the "questing vole," the Managing Editor claims, "That must be good style. At least it doesn't sound like anything else to me."[82] And such is Waugh's depiction of the relationship between the newspaper and its audience. Far removed from the angry letters about grebes and the opaque public that it seeks to serve, the decisions of newspapers are fueled primarily by an insular and bourgeoise culture, with only vague notions of its obligations to a wider public, whose views are

---

[78] Evelyn Waugh, *The Letters of Evelyn Waugh*, edited by Mark Amory (London: Phoenix, 2009), p. 98.
[79] Waugh, *Scoop*, p. 5.   [80] Waugh, *Scoop*, p. 12.
[81] Waugh, *Scoop*, p. 12.   [82] Waugh, *Scoop*, p. 17.

contorted by the corruption of the elite. "What the British Public wants first, last and all the time is News," says Copper to the befuddled nature-writer William Boot; it is the only vague sense of the public that Copper has.[83] But what becomes of the innocent outsider, William Boot, and what can he add to Waugh's argument about the dialectic between audiences and media?

A deeper examination of the origins of the William Boot character reveals that perhaps not even the benevolent outsider can succeed in limiting this apathetic trajectory, as his articles will only succeed in sending his "sensational message into two million apathetic homes."[84] Many have attributed the profile of William Boot to *The Daily Telegraph* reporter W.F. Deedes, whose "half-ton" of luggage, matching Boot's own haul into Abyssinia, bolsters the comparison.[85] Deedes himself contests this claim, stating that, aside from the luggage, "I am no more the William Boot of Scoop than I am the Man in the Moon."[86] While Deedes admits elsewhere that his inexperience might have led to Boot, he also forwards a reading of Boot as an amalgamation of several figures, with himself mirrored in but some of Boot's features.[87] I want to suggest that the humorous story of the grebe article in *Scoop* unexpectedly opens up another avenue for inquiry into Boot's origins. While biographer Selina Hastings suggests that the allusion to the grebe comes from a time when Waugh was made to look out for the bird, only to observe how ugly it was, there may be yet another source for this allusion to the grebe in the case of Boot.[88] Tom Harrisson was, of course, famous for his work in the organization that hoped to produce an honest autoethnography of Britain: Mass-Observation. But before Bolton and the Worktown project, Harrisson was an anthropologist. And, bringing us to Waugh's allusion, the Mass-Observation founder's greatest achievement in this realm was his study of one bird: the great crested grebe. In a preview of how we would use the apparatus of mass surveying to unveil English sentiment about everything from wartime rationing to air raid precautions, Harrisson's early interest in ornithology led him to produce the first nationwide census of the species: a hundred page report, written in 1931, titled "The Great Crested Grebe Inquiry."

---

[83] Waugh, *Scoop*, p. 49.   [84] Waugh, *Scoop*, p. 192.

[85] Philip Eade, *Evelyn Waugh: A Life Revisited* (London: Henry Holt and Company, 2017), p. 195.

[86] W.F. Deedes, "The Real Scoop: Who Was Who in Waugh's Cast List and Why," *The Telegraph* (May 28, 2003).

[87] Deedes, *At War with Waugh*, pp. 102–3.

[88] Hastings, *Evelyn Waugh: A Biography*, n369.

More than just the grebe allusion solidifies Harrisson as a target of Waugh's satire. As Waugh was composing *Scoop*, he was also publishing reviews of Mass-Observation's work, which had just entered the public discourse. His 1937 *Night and Day* essay "The Strange Rites of the Islanders" targets Mass-Observation for a rather scathing critique, arguing that mass observers "differ from other keyhole-observers and envelope-steamers in the show they make of their work. I cannot help feeling that there must be countless provincial tea-tables at which it is whispered 'She is so clever and so dangerous—a mass observer, you know.'"[89] For Waugh, sociological studies like those of M-O, which aimed to understand the views and positions of the nation as a whole, instead reified a notion of the individual as a monad of its class, unable to distinguish itself from the choices of his fellow citizen. Waugh contended that the "first major work of the group is the persistent denial of individuality to individuals."[90] Waugh implicitly omits the persistence of individual agency here, suggesting that grouping individuals statistically divests them of their agency. Such observations align with the underlying critique in "An Englishman's Home," which touted a quirky provincialism, not a systematized and aggregated vision of national subjectivity, as the key to preserving order; such a contention was fitting for a man who argued in *Robbery Under the Law* that we should reconceive nationalism as but a geographic provincialism. He writes, "mankind inevitably organizes itself into communities" and "by sharing a common history [communities] develop common characteristics and inspire a local loyalty."[91] Concerned with the ramifications of such widespread sociological inquiry, Waugh's early review of Mass-Observation's *First Year's Work* condemns the role of the pollster, whose tools might fall into the wrong hands. According to Waugh, Mass-Observation "might easily provide a Devil's Handbook for the demagogue," as the individual relinquishes the sanctity of their thought to an outside agency.[92] Waugh, after his Catholic conversion, identifies inherent spiritual violence at the heart of wide-scale sociological study. And this esoteric theme continues throughout this review. Waugh echoes the spiritualist roots of psychographic study, even as he condemns them: "From the position of divinely inspired oracle," he argues, "the lout with the ballot-paper has suddenly been deposed and his place taken by an

[89]   Evelyn Waugh, "The Strange Rites of the Islanders," *Night and Day* (October 14, 1937), p. 28.
[90]   Waugh, "The Strange Rites of the Islanders," p. 28.
[91]   Cited in Hastings, *Evelyn Waugh: A Biography*, p. 378.
[92]   Waugh, "The Habits of the English," pp. 226–7.

automaton for whom the key has got into the wrong hands and the manufacturer's book of instructions mislaid."[93] The lout with the ballot-paper—
the very image of the Hornbeams of the world—has been displaced by a
large-scale, industrialized mechanism for public opinion research. In such a
transition, Waugh sees the oracular power of polling falling into the wrong
hands, abetted by the development of a more professional and nationalized
sociological apparatus symbolized by M-O.

Further supporting the notion that M-O acts as a source, even if just an
unconscious one, in the composition of *Scoop*, the title of his review,
"Strange Rites of the Islanders," sets up a dynamic familiar in many of
Waugh's novels between the subject and object of study. Like the amateur
anthropologist, William Boot is yet another underprepared rube whose
own ineptitude causes him to look at both the newspaper industry and the
international crisis from a position of pure naivety. Boot, like any other
observer, considers himself an outsider thrust into a foreign cultural ecosystem he must record and eventually master. As Selina Hasting characterizes
it, Waugh's novels specialize in the "innocent and passive hero [...] cata-
pulted into chaos."[94] In *Scoop*, the relatively benign Boot's utter incompe-
tence as a correspondent gives him a unique ability to anthropologically
observe the practices and traditions of a field of journalism marred by
immense corruption and ineptitude. So, Mass-Observation's novice observers, writing down bits of overheard conversation to paint the canvass of May
12, 1938 were, to some extent, right up Waugh's alley, though it should come
as little surprise that the socialist leanings of the project would find a way to
rankle the notoriously conservative writer. It is for this reason that Waugh
observed, in a more magnanimous tone, that Mass-Observation's project
had an uncanny ability to capture the reality of the Coronation day festivi-
ties. He argued that Mass-Observation's perspectives of the crowd were
"incomparably better than anything that was published in the press. No
doubt many novels are in preparation for the autumn season with
Coronation scenes. I suspect they will seem pretty flat."[95] While Waugh was
actively reflecting on the work of Mass-Observation, there are other minor
suggestions of M-O co-founder Harrisson throughout the novel, including
allusion to the work of journalists attempting to embed themselves amongst
cannibals. In the novel, the reporters were eaten by the cannibals, and the

[93] Waugh, "The Strange Rites of the Islanders," p. 28.
[94] Hastings, *Evelyn Waugh: A Biography*, p. 367.
[95] Waugh, "The Strange Rites of the Islanders," p. 30.

reporting scoop abandoned; the same year as *Scoop*'s publication, Harrisson published *Borneo Jungle*, an accounting of his own expedition. And, to some extent, his depiction of Harrisson is not necessarily disparaging. Framing Boot as an anthropologist of reporters is fitting; as Boot himself has no knowledge of the intricacies of being a wartime correspondent, he is able to defamiliarize all the asinine and strange practices of the journalists. He approaches reportage as a true outsider, adopting and learning the ways of reporters from the reporters themselves. In doing so, the eccentric practices of journalism are laid bare for the reader, and defamiliarized from any context that would justify them as part of a cohesive cultural practice. To see even a little of Harrisson's work reflected in Boot's backstory is to also liken the type of reporting done in Abyssinia to a sort of psychological observational work.

To suggest the influence of Mass-Observation on *Scoop* leads our attention to other facets of the novel bound up in the quagmire of public opinion politics. The model for Lady Stitch, who recommends John Boot for the job accidentally given to William Boot, was none other than Lady Diana Cooper, wife of Duff Cooper. In 1935, Cooper had emerged as the Secretary of State of War. By 1940, Cooper would be the head of the Ministry of Information, the pivotal propaganda arm of the British government during the war. Waugh would maintain a very close relationship with Diana Cooper from the time of her first pregnancy onwards. When John Boot arrives to see Julia Stitch to ask for a recommendation, much as Waugh had done with Cooper, he briefly encounters Algernon Stitch, looking "fully the English cabinet minister."[96] But Waugh suggests that even English government policies are duly impacted by the work of the papers, as Stitch's morning routine is troubled by the newspaper, which he cannot seem to manage holding whilst also putting on his coat. Algernon holds the paper between his teeth; John takes the newspaper from Stitch's mouth as a means of assistance, complementing him on the quality of his speech as presented in the very paper Stitch was on the cusp of consuming in his morning ritual: "Your speech reads very well this morning," states John as he holds the paper for Stitch.[97] Algernon leaves for the Ministry of Imperial Defense, and Boot goes up to see Julia Stitch, who agrees to meet with Lord Copper to get Boot a position as a foreign correspondent. But the awkward scene between Algernon Stitch and Boot underscores the dialectic relationship that the

---

[96] Waugh, *Scoop*, p. 6.   [97] Waugh, *Scoop*, p. 6.

novel unveils between governmental policy and the news itself. The policy positions Stitch argues in parliament are consistently mediated through the paper's delivery of them. The speech must "read well" in the morning to be of any value. Furthermore, even Algernon has to acquiesce to the power of newsprint; his clumsy morning routine suggests the paper as a consumable object for bureaucrats like the cabinet minister. He must inevitably "eat" the paper on a daily basis, reading himself through the medium of print and falsely consuming the biased reporting on his own performance as a true estimate of public opinion.

Waugh suggests the inner workings of the paper as an incessant and self-affirming feedback loop; those reported in the pages of the paper consume its contents, provide responses to the publishers, who then respond, in kind, by altering content based on an understanding of the public taste. But troublingly, the "public taste" they record is not that of the public at all, but rather of the bureaucrats and institutions the paper is meant to examine. Waugh emphasizes the point in his usual ironic manner when Lord Copper waxes philosophical on the industry: "The workings of a great newspaper [...] are of a complexity which the public seldom appreciates. The citizen little realizes the vast machinery put into motion of him in exchange for his morning penny."[98] But the "vast machinery" we see in this scene is hardly so vast and certainly not complex. Rather, the direction of the paper is established based on the relationship between aristocrats within the government and those outside of it. But the incompetency of the newspaper is further derided in the implementation of the plan to hire John Boot.

The abysmal muck-up that pushed William Boot to Ishmaelia extends throughout the novel and even marks its conclusion, as Lord Copper wishes to give Boot a knighthood. At 10 Downing street the Prime Minister receives the recommendation to give "Boot" a knighthood under the auspices of his "Services to Literature."[99] Of course, The Prime Minister imagines this to be a recommendation of the *Waste of Time* novelist, John Boot, who seems quite surprised by his honors; finally realizing his profound error in hiring him, Copper satisfies himself giving the honors to the original Boot who was meant to be the Ishmaelia correspondent from the start. It is significant that the farce arises because the editor is more intent on listening to the advice of wealthy political patrons than he is hearing the complaints of his unsatisfied readers, who originally squawked about the unfair

---

[98] Waugh, *Scoop*, p. 14.   [99] Waugh, *Scoop*, p. 224.

maligning of the great crested grebe. Boot, an outsider of institutional journalism, enables Waugh the best possible avenue for critiquing the relationship between audience expectation and news coverage. Boot, constantly at the beck and call of telegrams demanding news, no matter how ill-founded and false it might be, repeatedly fails to meet the expectations of the newspaper and its audience. This was much like Waugh himself who, repeatedly scooped by *The Daily Telegraph*, experienced a souring of his relationship with the *Daily Mail* and eventually resigned.[100] But, of course, in the completion of the comedy in *Scoop*, Boot's ineptitude ends up producing the most newsworthy story of the entire press campaign in Ishmaelia.

Waugh is thus staging two interventions in the pages of *Scoop*. The first is against the institution of journalism, which he sees as truly failing to recognize the desires of its audiences. Waugh argues that, indeed, coverage of a news event (no matter how trivial) will inspire readers to spend money. But, as the angry corrections of the grebe story show, the newspaper is not attentive enough to the actual responses of its readership. Rather, the newspaper engages in a unilateral effort to manage its audience, forming public opinion by fiat, informed only by the elite inner circles in which newspaper magnates circulate. And they are duly unscrupulous about their facts. William Boot, learning the rules of the game as he goes, witnesses blatantly false stories, the correction of those false stories only revealed by rival reporters who wish to advance their own positions, and the failure to report or pursue real stories for reasons of inconvenience. But the novel stages a second critique as well, against the amateur approach to professionalism articulated in the Harrisson stand-in Boot. Waugh sees an ornithologist who delves into anthropology (as Harrisson did) as not dissimilar to a nature-writer taking on a big news story. Of course, Waugh did actually attend to the war in Abyssinia, resulting not only in *Scoop*, but in Waugh's book of wartime journalism, *Waugh in Abyssinia*. What becomes apparent from both is the way in which Waugh began to see the field of journalism as responding in similar ways to the public at large. Certainly, it is clear that getting "scoops" helps to sell papers; readership drives media narratives, even if readership comes at the cost of producing and spreading fake news to meet a seemingly bottomless readerly hunger. But it wasn't just the public that was possessed by a mania for news. The fetish for scoops also led journalists to truly convince themselves that, despite a dirge in actual news

---

[100] Eade, *Evelyn Waugh: A Life Revisited*, pp. 196–7.

or information, there was a meaningful scoop to be had. More often than not, this was not the case, either in the real case of Abyssinia or in its fictionalization in *Scoop*. There was, it turns out, a real scandal going on in Abyssinia. The entrepreneur Francis Rickett, British but acting on behalf of American companies Socony Vacuum Oil Company and Standard Oil, had made an agreement with emperor Haile Selassie to appropriate the right to Abyssinian resources. But, as with many of the other news stories in the war, it was more hot air than it was real substance.[101] In *Scoop*, Waugh suggests the Rickett story, noting that there was very little proof that Abyssinia actually contained any of the resources that had been so touted. Again, it seemed the truth of the matter was less important than the craving for a scandalous story.

The tension between public opinion and the newspaper that functions as the catalyst for *Scoop* grew increasingly significant in the 1930s. The cresting tide of political polling in America was beginning to make waves on British shores. In England, the first major readership poll was also produced by *News Chronicle* in 1931 in collaboration with the London Press Exchange, and conducted by Robert Silvey.[102] The survey, never published, consisted of three volumes of data that emerged from interviews of 20 to 30,000 people about their daily newspaper reading habits. The survey tracked which titles caught the eyes of readers, which illustrations they were attracted to, and the choices they made in the articles they read. *News Chronicle*'s goal was to get a firm grasp on their own readership. Building from this commercial research, the Peace Ballot, and the eventual publication of BIPO polling in *The News Chronicle*, promised a new avenue for public sentiment, even if its impact was tainted by the very biases of the papers in which the results were published. And other media were quick to join the polling craze. By the mid-1930s, the mind behind London Press Exchange's "Reader Interest Survey," Robert Silvey, had gone elsewhere: to the BBC, where polling was to become a major force in wireless research.

---

[101] Michael Salwen, "Evelyn Waugh's *Scoop*: The Facts Behind the Fiction," *Journalism and Mass Communication Quarterly* 78, no. 1 (2001), pp. 150–71.
[102] Robert Silvey, *Who's Listening? The Story of BBC Audience Research* (London: Allen & Unwin, 1974).

3

What the Listeners Want

Public Opinion on the Wireless

Introduction: The Peace Ballot and the BBC

"With the exception of nine days in September when the work was dislocated by the necessity for immediate evacuation from London, returns of listening have appeared every day since 3rd December, 1939. Between its beginning and 31st December 1940, some 300,000 people have been interviewed—not far from one in every hundred of the population."[1] This passage, published in a British Broadcasting Corporation (BBC) internal Listener Research Report over a year after the institutionalization of its Listener Research Department (LRD) on 3 December 1939, understatedly commemorated the belated anniversary of the corporation's internal efforts to track listener opinions on the BBC's favorability and programming. These fledgling efforts to record listener satisfaction, tabulated by Hollerith machines churning out data amalgamated by countless interviewers borrowed from the British Institute of Public Opinion, were remarkable for their time. The BBC professed its accomplishments proudly, applauding its singular, pioneering role in radio listener research and noting that "[e]ven in the United States there is no comparable Continuous Survey available to broadcasters."[2] And yet, the timing of this celebration corresponded with a crisis at the BBC, which illuminated the tension wrought by these new, revolutionary listener surveys. Just days before the publication of this report, a political controversy had erupted at the BBC. Sir Hugh Robertson, an extremely popular Scottish composer and founder of the Glasgow Orpheus

---

[1] "Listener Research Report," January 11, 1941, BBC Written Archives Centre (hereafter BBC WAC), R9 9/1, No 18.
[2] "Listener Research Report," January 11, 1941, BBC WAC, R9/1, No 18; Asa Briggs notes that while American listener research originated from market research, pressure in Britain first "came from people who wanted to develop professional programmes." Asa Briggs, *The History of Broadcasting in the United Kingdom: The Golden Age of Wireless* (Oxford: Oxford University Press, 1995), p. 257.

Public Opinion Polling in Mid-Century British Literature: The Psychographic Turn. Megan Faragher, Oxford University Press. © Megan Faragher 2021. DOI: 10.1093/oso/9780192898975.003.0004

Choir, had been banned from the BBC for his membership in the Peace Pledge Union (PPU). While similar bans and blacklisting of pacifist speakers led many significant broadcasters, including E.M. Forster and Rose Macaulay, to boycott broadcasting for the BBC, the general high regard for Hugh Robertson led to a surge in public protest.[3] Ironically, on the same day that the BBC's Listener Research Report touted the success of its revolutionary research methods, the body of the report records extensive listener objection over the PPU ban, with 450 angry letters from listeners excoriating the BBC for its treatment of Robertson. The new statistical methods of listener research reinforced this anecdotal data; while the BBC marked a relatively high level of listener satisfaction at that moment, with 80.6 percent approval, this was down from 82 percent the week prior, and would fall to 74 percent by the end of January. Previously, such low approval numbers had only been associated with technical difficulties, including poor reception during the night bombing campaigns in October.[4] Similar BBC policies regarding the Communist Party's People's Convention later in 1941 brought letters accusing the BBC of incorporating "Nazi methods."[5]

Despite extolling its Listener Research efforts, the BBC refused to reverse its policy on pacifist speakers in response to either protest by the public or boycotting by broadcasters. Though the corporation internally touted its innovations in mastering and responding to public opinion, the Robertson affair demonstrated a sustained hesitation in allowing public opinion to drive the BBC's broadcasting policies. As the first part of this chapter will demonstrate, the hierarchical Reithian ideological inheritance of the BBC often stood in direct and irreconcilable conflict with any efforts to elevate the role of public opinion in internal operations, particularly during wartime. Adding further to the irony of the BBC's position on the peace movement and its representatives was the fact that the peace movement, and the

---

[3] Sarah Le Fanu, *Rose Macaulay: A Biography* (New York: Time Warner Books, 2003); Mary Lago, "E.M. Forster and the BBC," *The Yearbook of English Studies* 20 (1990), pp. 132–51; Richard Rempel, "The Dilemmas of British Pacifists During World War II," *The Journal of Modern History* 50, no. 4 (1978), D1213–29; "Listener Research Report," January 4, 1941, BBC WAC R9/1, No 17; Richard Rempel argues that the banning of Peace Pledge Union speakers from the BBC was "[t]he most effective government measure against pacifists" during the war (D1218).

[4] Several reports, including that of October 26, 1940, record bad reception as the cause of decreased listener satisfaction. "Listener Research Report," October 26, 1940, BBC WAC R9/1, No. 10. But, at the time of this survey, which was over a month after the initial Robertson controversy, the BBC was still receiving complaint letters about the affair. "Listener Research Report," January 25, 1941, BBC WAC R9/1, No. 20.

[5] "Listener Research Report," March 1941, BBC WAC R9/1, No. 25.

publicity around the Peace Ballot it incited (discussed in Chapter 2), played a crucial part in inspiring the BBC to institutionalize listener research in the first place. In August of 1935, less than five years before the BBC Listener Research reports began internal publication, Foreign Director C.F. Atkinson noted that the impressive results of the Peace Ballot might serve as methodological inspiration for the BBC to develop its own public opinion infrastructure; that same year, former BBC Talks Director Hilda Matheson's essay "Listener Research in Broadcasting" cited the Peace Ballot directors as a resource that "might be tapped for purposes of listener research."[6] But while the League of Nations' Peace Ballot was held in high esteem by many in 1934, the politics of the peace movement in the subsequent years shifted dramatically; by 1940 those who maintained dedication to peace during the war stood out as, at best, enemies of the nation's self-defense and, at worst, "too sympathetic to the demands of fascist governments."[7] Tensions between interventionists and pacifists were high, as suggested by the PPU's publication of Aldous Huxley's *What are You Going to Do About It: The Case for Constructive Peace* (1936) and Cecil Day-Lewis's corresponding publication *We're Not Going to Do Nothing*, published by the New Left Review the same year. In the latter, Day-Lewis captured this common critique of pacifism in the lead-up to the war, accusing Huxley of "failing to face the threat of fascism."[8] Further demonstrating just how far out of favor the peace movement had fallen in esteem, Home Intelligence director Mary Adams even inquired about active alliances between pacifists and fascists in a letter to actress and suffragist Cicely Hamilton: "we hear that the P.P.U. and the British Union of Fascists join forces occasionally. Have you ever seen that?"[9] And so, the BBC's relationship with the peace movement had achieved a radical about-face; where once the pacifist movement inspired the BBC to take listener opinion into account, the political allegiances of the BBC in the winter of 1940–41, bolstered by a tight connection to the Ministry

---

[6] Briggs, *The History of Broadcasting*, p. 245; Hilda Matheson, "Listener Research in Broadcasting," *The Sociological Review* 27, no. 4 (1935), p. 420.

[7] David Lukowitz, "British Pacifists and Appeasement: The Peace Pledge Union," *Journal of Contemporary History* 9, no. 1 (1974), p. 125.

[8] Richard Overy, *The Morbid Age: Britain Between the Wars* (Bristol: Allen Lane, 2009), p. 248.

[9] Mary Adams to Cicely Hamilton, February 23, 1940, Mass-Observation Archives, SxMOA4/2/4/1, University of Sussex Special Collections. Overy also discusses the waning enrollment of peace organizations; the League of Nations Union declined from 4,000,000 in 1931 to 264,000 by 1938. Overy, *The Morbid Age*, p. 251.

of Information, led it to resist the clear public backlash to its silencing of the PPU.[10]

Though the Hugh Robertson episode dramatized the BBC's reluctance to adjust its policies in response to listener research, this is not to imply that tension over listener research had only begun after the wave of pacifist blacklisting. Rather, the BBC's conservative response to its own public reception predated the institutionalization of statistical listener research. In 1932, the BBC Year-Book published an article entitled "Studying Listeners' Tastes." This article, which discussed the fledgling efforts at listener research to that point and projected possible advancements in the field, also gave glimpses into the underlying conflict at the BBC between its desire to satisfy its audience and the organization's ideological commitments. In recording the methods of assessing listener opinion, the article cites the most traditional methods of unsystematically and casually recording "[c]orrespondence and conversation with listeners."[11] In addition to the age-old reliance on post, the pre-LRD BBC also traced audience response by resorting to the only other type of data they collected on their listeners: the number of license-holders. Despite the obvious limitations with such an assessment, as owning a license did not necessarily mean approving of any individual BBC program, the corporation interpreted an increase in licenses as confirmation of a broad boon in the BBC's popularity. While recognizing the problems with the aforementioned methods, the BBC's Year-Book defended its ability to satisfy its audiences without any data that assessed listener response. By taking seriously its "responsibility to the country as a whole which is the central conception of British broadcasting" and pursuing a "policy of impartiality which has never seriously been challenged," the article suggested that an underlying dedication to nationalism and first principles supplanted any need for concrete assessment of the audience it served.[12] In lieu of information about its audience, the BBC relied on a common ideological framework as a rudder to steer programming selection at the BBC.

---

[10] Concerns over Nazi infiltration into pacifist groups was noted by pacifists themselves. Rose Macaulay's biography notes her concerns over the Peace News "coming under the influence of Nazi propagandists." Constance Babington Smith, Rose Macaulay (Stroud: Sutton [1975] 2005), p. 145.
[11] British Broadcasting Commission (BBC). The BBC Year-Book, 1932 (London: The British Broadcasting Corporation, 1932), p. 105.
[12] BBC, The BBC Year-Book, 1932, p. 108.

The ethical aims of the BBC under John Reith, described by Todd Avery as the production of "religious and moral benefit, to the nation first, and then to humanity in general," never truly addressed the paucity of research as to what BBC audiences actually wanted.[13] Likewise, by reinforcing the Reithian "categorical imperative" of contributing to the "national good," the *Year-Book* simply enabled those with institutional power to set an agenda within the framework of the BBC's high-minded creed.[14] The *Year-Book's* disparaging attitude towards the future development of scientific listener research underscored the BBC's early fetish for its own ideologically founded methods for vetting programming choices. In "Studying Listeners' Tastes" the BBC reinforced this position, arguing that the imposition of mathematical certitude on matters of aesthetic judgment inevitably stripped individual nuance from any study of popular opinion. The essay skeptically noted that "[n]o system of counting votes can give any final or equitable result where minorities are themselves so large that they cannot possibly be ignored."[15] Practically speaking, this lack of objective data about listener expectations meant that the BBC responded only to the views and perspectives of fringe listeners, motivated and eager enough to share their opinions via post. Listener research enthusiasts eventually gained a victory at the BBC, bringing to the organization the methodology of the Peace Ballot in establishing the Listener Research Department in December 1939. But as the tenuous relationship with the peace movement demonstrates, internal ambivalence over listener research was never entirely allayed. On the one hand, in maintaining its self-professed position as an arbiter of taste and a curator of proper national subjectivity, the BBC proposed itself capable of forming the mind, soul, and spirit of the proper citizen-subject. On the other, in using the radio's power over its audience in an effort to form public taste, the BBC overrode the voices of those very listeners who formed the national body.

This tension is substantiated by internal debates at the BBC over the possible adaptation of statistical listener research. Some opposed listener research having any significant role at the BBC because, as Stobart argued, "broadcasting is not and should not be democratic."[16] Charles Siepmann, who followed the legendary Hilda Matheson, filling the role of Talks Director, at times intermittently fell to this Reithian line of argument, declaring in an

---

[13]   Todd Avery, *Radio Modernism* (New York: Routledge, 2006), p. 19.
[14]   Avery, *Radio Modernism*, p. 207.   [15]   BBC, *The BBC Year-Book, 1932*, p. 105.
[16]   Cited in Briggs, *The History of Broadcasting*, p. 242.

internal memo that "our policy and programme building should be based first and last upon our own conviction as to what should and should not be broadcast."[17] But this traditionalist position often conflicted with concerns over meeting the demands of a growing audience. Despite his initial hesitance, Siepmann eventually supported the establishment of listener research. In so doing, he joined the BBC's Drama Producer Val Gielgud, who was one of the staunchest promoters of listener research at its inception, justifying its value through an appeal to the radio's fragile relationship with its audience. Gielgud asserted that "there is no other entertainment in the world which is so much at the mercy of every single member of its audience as is broadcasting."[18] This concern over the tenuous connection between listener and broadcaster remained a significant feature of wartime depictions of the BBC. And it would be none other than Val Gielgud who dramatized these tensions when he took to pen as an author, informed by his work in broadcasting. In co-writing a series of plays set in BBC studios during the war, with American author John Dickson Carr, Gielgud used the intimate medium of the stage to theorize the more troubled relationship between the radio and its public, with radio positioning itself, in the words of Andrew Crisell, as both a "long-distance mode of communication" as well as "an inward, *intimate* medium."[19]

The first half of this chapter will trace Val Gielgud's co-authored BBC-based wartime dramas alongside the internal debates over listener research at the BBC. In Gielgud's detective plays, he dramatizes the bureaucratic tension between the BBC's insular Riethianism and the democratic possibilities proffered by its listener research program. These plays, including *Inspector Silence Takes the Air* and *Thirteen to the Gallows*, repeatedly reference the frangible relationship between broadcaster and audience during the war. In exploring the BBC's views of its relationship to its audience, this chapter traces the conflicted institutional response to public opinion research. The second half of this chapter escapes the insular study of the BBC's self-conception, instead looking to authors Olaf Stapledon and Virginia Woolf, who both imagined the radio's "potential for helping in the

---

[17] Siepmann, cited in Briggs, *The History of Broadcasting*, p. 242.

[18] Briggs, *The History of Broadcasting*, p. 242. Briggs notes that both Siepmann and Gielgud "stressed the necessity for some sort of systematic research into the social psychology of regular listening" (p. 238). Robert Silvey cites Siepmann as one who "pressed for systematic inquiry" of listener habits; Robert Silvey, *Who's Listening? The Story of BBC Audience Research* (London: George Allen & Unwin, 1974), p. 14.

[19] Andrew Crissell, *Understanding Radio* (London: Methuen, 1986), p. 11, emphasis in original.

creation of an informed and enlightened democracy," aestheticizing wireless technologies as both a metaphoric and literal medium for actualizing poll-consciousness.[20] Looking at both the institutional and cultural impact of public opinion on the work of radio, this chapter emphasizes that "public opinion was [...] of crucial importance to the whole history of broadcasting's role in the politics of twentieth-century society."[21]

Fearing Dead Air: Val Gielgud's BBC Dramas

In 1942, reviewers in the small Welsh town of Llandudno praised the debut of the BBC-based crime drama *Inspector Silence Takes the Air* as "the best play of its kind" during the war.[22] Audiences to the play were wowed by the climactic presentation of a murder staged within a faux BBC recording studio; Val Gielgud's experience in proper BBC production and John Dickson Carr's experience writing for the BBC led to an increased verisimilitude between the staging of the BBC studio and the real McCoy. Carr and Gielgud met via the Detection Club and, together, wrote two BBC-based murder mysteries—*Inspector Silence* and *Thirteen to the Gallows*—both of which had brief wartime theatrical runs like the well-received one in Llandudno.[23] And while these little-known wartime BBC murder dramas may seem unrelated to questions about public opinion and group psychology, both *Thirteen to the Gallows* and *Inspector Silence Takes the Air* dramatize the anxieties of the BBC regarding its ability to connect to its audience during the war. This theme gained increased significance at a time when Gielgud's BBC work forced him to confront the tension between the institution's conservative approach to its audience and the possibilities opened up by scientifically acquired listener research.[24]

As an introduction to the BBC's internal dynamics during the dawn of quantitative listener research, I want to take up the first of the two

---

[20] Paddy Scannell and David Cardiff, *A Social History of British Broadcasting: Volume One 1922–1939* (London: Basil Blackwell, 1991), p. 7.

[21] Tony Medawar, "Suspense on Stage," in *13 to the Gallows*, edited by Tony Medawar (Norfolk, VA: Crippen & Landru, 2008), p. 7.

[22] Medawar, "Suspense on Stage," p. 7.   [23] Medawar, "Suspense on Stage," pp. 10–11.

[24] The oath of the Detection Club mirrors the preference for scientific over intuitive investigations. Members like Carr and Gielgud swore to the following: "Do you promise that your detectives shall well and truly detect the crimes presented to them using those wits which it may please you to bestow upon them and not placing reliance on nor making use of Divine Revelation, Feminine Intuition, Mumbo Jumbo, Jiggery-Pokery, Coincidence, or Act of God?" James Brabazon, *Dorothy L. Sayers* (New York: Scribner's Sons, 1981), p. 144.

Carr-Gielgud dramas, *Inspector Silence Takes the Air*, and argue that the play allegorizes, through its murder plot, a conflict between two contending forces within the BBC in the 1940s. On the one hand, the advent of the Listener Research Department in late 1939 meant that producers were able to more concretely decide programming based on audience demands, changing content and scheduling to adjust to the tastes of listeners. But this new force of audience research pushed against the calcified self-image of the BBC as an entity designed to *lead* its listeners and shape them into national subjects, fueled by a broadly constructed moral dedication to the country in a time of war. Through the unlikely dramatization of a murder at a BBC studio, Gielgud's *Inspector Silence Takes the Air* expresses the necessity of using listener research to understand radio audiences. But while Gielgud hopes to maintain the tenuous tie between listener and broadcaster, his play continues to covertly defend elements of the BBC's conservative approach to programming by suggesting that, in the absence of the ability to assess its audience, BBC orthodoxy protects creators from their most dangerous, and unpopular, impulses.

In the opening scene of Gielgud and Carr's *Inspector Silence*, BBC producer Antony Barran hears he is being made redundant. His final radio production is a drama, wherein a husband murders his wife's lover. As curtains open on *Inspector Silence*, Gielgud and Carr situate foley effects at the center of the action. Stage directions describe "a miscellaneous collection of 'Effects': a tin bath, a roller skate, a cushioned chair, water carafe and glasses, and other appropriate gadgets," lying in front of the staged BBC Listening Room.[25] As the curtain rises, the junior program engineer George Sloane is featured, "his right hand in the air holding a cane with which he has been beating the seat of a chair," which is the traditional way the effects artist simulates a gunshot in the sound studio.[26] But using his imminent departure as an excuse to cast off the constraints of the BBC's conservative culture, Barran decides to end his career by incorporating more avant-garde approaches to sound design. He radically alters the production directions with the aim of generating a hyper-realistic radio performance. First, to make the voice actor playing the murderer feel more psychologically prepared, Barran demands him to carry a real, though unloaded, weapon, quite

---

[25] John Dickson Carr and Val Gielgud, *Inspector Silence Takes the Air*. In *13 to the Gallows*, edited by Tony Medawar (Norfolk, VA: Crippen & Landru, 2008), p. 20.

[26] Carr and Gielgud, *Inspector Silence Takes the Air*, p. 20.

against company policy.[27] He then does away with traditional sound effects; instead of George Sloane beating a chair with a cane to replicate the sound of a gun, Barran hands the assistant an actual gun, with blanks, to be shot at the ceiling during recording. To justify his risky decisions, Barran cites the revolutionary potential of radio as an auditory medium. When Sloane warns him of the technical difficulties and mortal dangers of shooting a gun inside the BBC studio, Barran retorts: "All progress is called impossible—until someone has the guts to try it."[28] Providing a weapon to the voice actor and shooting blanks into the ceiling both aim to produce a broadcast more dramatic and realistic than any performed before. Shooting literally into the dark, with no real insight as to how these production changes might impact the broadcast's reception, Barran attempts to awe listeners through embracing danger, lacking any data that might support the notion that these risky moves will wow his audience. It is clear that Gielgud disapproves of Barran's radical approach to production, adopted with no concrete knowledge of what his audience actually wants, and only a vague notion that the more experimental the radio production, the better it will be.

As one might expect, Barran's avant-garde approaches do not lead to resounding success. The scheme to include a fake gunshot and the fake murder in his radio broadcast flops; instead, a real murder takes place, marking the beginning of *Inspector Silence*'s mystery plot. The titular Inspector Silence, who is there to introduce the radio play-within-the-play to the listening audience, then adopts the new role of a detective in search of a killer. During the dramatic scene where the fictional murder turns real, the voice actor meant to be "shot" for having an affair falls dead. At first failing to see that fiction has transformed into reality, the voice actors and actresses perform their lines normally, until it dawns on them that they have witnessed a real death. The tenor then becomes even more dramatic; the death has provided the sense of realism that Barran sought, and more. But by pushing beyond the bounds of traditional protocol and inviting violence onto the set with no real evidence of its efficacy on his presumed audience, Barran's efforts to appease his unseen public backfire spectacularly; the performance cannot go on. It becomes unairable. The program comes to a stop due to "technical difficulties," and the entire crew set

---

[27]   Gielgud states the BBC held a highly conservative view of experimental programs, which they "'tried out' upon a patient, but necessarily uncomprehending public." Val Gielgud, *British Radio Drama, 1922–1956: A Survey* (London: Harrap, 1957), p. 26.

[28]   Carr and Gielgud, *Inspector Silence Takes the Air*, p. 37.

themselves to the task of identifying the murderer at the BBC studio, thus putting the plot of the *Inspector Silence* stage-play into motion.

Barran's rogue production alludes to the historical conflict between the BBC's erudite self-definition and its struggles to both identify and appease its audience. While wireless technology aided audiences in accessing information and entertainment in ways never before imaginable, the newly added burden placed on listening audiences who wanted to provide feedback remained a quandary for BBC administrators; as mentioned, listener response before the establishment of the Listener Research Department was limited to written correspondence, thus presenting a challenge to the BBC due to its very intermediality. As Debra Rae Cohen, Michael Coyle, and Jane Lewty remark, "[d]espite its precise reproduction and breathtaking range, radio opened up into a void. To scatter words abroad in space, either through auditory sign or lonely inscription, serves as a reminder of the absent other, as well as the dissolving of the individual into a massed rank."[29] But how to quantify or even qualify the absent other or massed ranks? A listener might be attentive and excited to respond to a broadcast, but what could they recall of a broadcast when they sat to write a letter? With no script to review, could feedback be relied upon for a fair representation of the listener experience?[30] Could letters by self-selected listeners be used to stand in for broader listener response? Some were certainly skeptical. Gielgud complained, in a 1933 letter, that written responses to the BBC were composed by "ego-maniacs, cranks, axe-grinders or the incorrigibly idle who can find nothing better to do."[31] Social psychologists Hadley Cantril and Gordon Allport similarly asserted that many listener letters come from "neurotics," "character analysts, mystics, and horoscope experts."[32] In response to this skepticism, the first fledgling efforts to introduce statistical listener research began just a few years later.[33] But the BBC's hesitation to materialize a proper listener research program spoke to deep concerns as to how such research would dictate programming. Without the use of such data, producers like the fictional Barran, who wished to cast aside the BBC's

[29] Debra Rae Cohen, Michael Coyle and Jane Lewty, "Introduction, Signing On," in *Broadcasting Modernism* (Gainesville, FL: University Press of Florida, 2013), p. 3.

[30] *The Listener* was meant to obviate such concerns about the gap between listeners and broadcasters. Debra Rae Cohen, "Intermediality and the Problem of *The Listener*," *Modernism/ Modernity* 19, no. 3 (2012), pp. 560–92.

[31] Cited in Briggs, *The History of Broadcasting*, p. 244.

[32] Hadley Cantril and Gordon Allport, *The Psychology of Radio* (New York: Harper & Brothers, 1935), p. 96.

[33] Briggs, *The History of Broadcasting*, p. 250.

self-imposed moral standards with no data to rely on, risked alienating their audience or, as happens in *Inspector Silence*, producing a broadcast that listeners could not "hear."

The fear of being cut off from its audience was dominant at the BBC, particularly during wartime. This emerges in both of Gielgud's plays, set in country houses and disused schoolhouses retrofitted into BBC studios. This geographic displacement mirrored reality at the BBC as many units, including the Listener Research Department, were displaced outside of London for much of the war; the LRD left its Duchess Street location and had to move the operation to Bristol in September 1940.[34] This wartime framework went some distance in realizing Gielgud's worst fear from the 1930s in his role as BBC producer, when he first began to express interest in listener research: that the BBC would be "broadcasting into a void."[35] Listener Research reports during 1940s raids reflect a reduction of listeners as a result of the crisis, particularly for programs after 6:30 p.m.[36] The war, therefore, materializes the feared chasm between the audience and the BBC. But violence on the air, as dramatized in Gielgud's plays, could embody an even more ominous possibility; the annexation of Austrian radio by the Nazis in the failed 1934 putsch would have also been front-of-mind to those cognizant of radio's vulnerability to interruption and intrusion. But it was not only bombing or invasion that could sever the relationship between broadcaster and listener. Barran's experimental foley effects do not just facilitate the actual murder, they are also technically disastrous—likely to "blow a transmitter," as production assistant Sloane tells Barran.[37] Alienation of both setting and technique suggests a symbolic disconnection between the BBC and its audience, which becomes increasingly literalized in the course of the play. The ambitious but wrong-headed special effects lead to a dead body in the middle of the floor, necessitating the cessation of production entirely, and the pun-inspired title of the play, *Silence Takes the Air*, stands in for the death-knell of the broadcasting experience: "dead" air.

Gielgud was, most definitely, concerned about dead air, even before the war made these concerns more pressing. As early as 1930, he noted anxiety at a board meeting about the dearth of listener research: "I cannot help

[34] "Listener Research Report," September 1940, BBC WAC, R9/1, No. 9.
[35] Cited in Briggs, *The History of Broadcasting*, p. 241.
[36] "Listener Research Report," October 26, 1940, BBC WAC R9/1, No. 10.
[37] Carr and Gielgud, *Inspector Silence Takes the Air*, p. 37.

feeling more and more strongly that we are fundamentally ignorant as to how our various programmes are received, and what is their relative popularity."[38] Gielgud's acceptance of radio's subjection to audience response differed from others at the BBC. Some, concerned a shift at the BBC to incorporate listener research would subject it to the same level of commercialization already underway in America, continued to express hesitation at the incursion of public opinion into radio programming decisions. Even Charles Siepmann maintained after the war that "we shall do well to take a broader view of [radio's] function than the mere consideration of our likes and dislikes of programs that we hear."[39] All the same, in the 1930s Siepmann consulted Seebohm Rowntree, the sociologist who had established his credentials by conducting the first demographically fueled sociological survey of British poverty.[40] Unfortunately, the conversation was a non-starter; BBC interest in listener research stalled in early 1930, only to be revived at a critical moment for the continued evolution and progress of audience research in England.

Technocratic Approaches to Listener Satisfaction: *Thirteen to the Gallows*

The dramatic specter of "dead air" haunts Gielgud's *Inspector Silence*, with silence summoning to mind the severance of audience from broadcaster. And while silence threatens to undermine a successful broadcast, it likewise puts into relief the foundational fragility of the broadcaster's relationship with its unseen, unknown listeners. Under pressure to unseat Reith's Arnoldianism, new approaches to program design and listener assessment emerged in the BBC ecosystem. Gielgud's sense of vulnerability as a BBC Director, aestheticized in his dramatic work with Carr, was also shared with other BBC workers, including Directors like Hilda Matheson.[41] Arguably one of the most revolutionary theorists of radio at the BBC, Hilda Matheson resigned as Talks Director in 1931 following a conflict over censorship. While she had wanted to broadcast a favorable review by Harold Nicolson

[38] Briggs, *The History of Broadcasting*, p. 241.
[39] Charles Siepmann, *Radio's Second Chance* (New York: Little Brown, 1946), p. xii.
[40] Rowntree's *Poverty: A Study of Town Life*, alongside Charles Booth's *Life and Labour of the People in London*, influenced a whole generation of sociologically oriented public opinion researchers. Rowntree's work at the BBC never came to fruition, reasons unknown.
[41] Briggs, *The History of Broadcasting*, pp. 241–3.

of the controversial novels *Ulysses* and *Lady Chatterley's Lover*, Reith pushed back, causing an unbridgeable rift between Matheson and the BBC, leading to her resignation.[42] Finding herself on the outside, Matheson published on the relationship between broadcasters and their audiences before her untimely death in 1940.[43] In a 1935 article in *The Sociological Review*, she notes the existence of a "gap [...] between the transmitting process and the listening ends" of broadcasting.[44] For Matheson, this anxiety-producing chasm might be better managed with some basic knowledge of the audience's complexity. To mitigate this threatening gap, radio producers needed to foster an "understanding of the listening audience, not as a bundle of 'average listeners,' but as a public of infinitely varying elements."[45] She further conceded that, to some extent, the BBC "suffer[ed] from the lack of co-ordinated listener research."[46] Sharing Gielgud's preference for a statistical over an Arnoldian approach to programming decisions, Matheson chastised the sanctimonious attitudes that had led to her resignation; she further railed against the "ignorance and dishonesty" that led the BBC to cancel its novel reviews after her departure.[47] According to Todd Avery, Matheson heralded "the arrival of a new spirit" in broadcasting, "opposed to Reithianism."[48] Partly, this was due to her cautious optimism about the role listener research could play in the advancement of broadcasting. "There is no need to fear that [...] statistical methods would tie the hands of broadcasters," she writes, "nor that they must become the slaves of ballots and surveys."[49] For the former Talks Director, what superseded a false sense of moral superiority was a more technocratic leadership, an "understanding of the microphone's possibilities," and a systematic philosophy regarding the radio which might bridge the chasm between listener and broadcaster.[50] In this, Matheson likened radio production to art: "Technique in broadcasting, like style in literature, is not trimming, but the essence of its quality."[51]

---

[42] In his biography on Hilda Matheson, he cites the "pressure on Harold Nicolson to changes his talks" as one of the two main contributors to her resignation Michael Carney, *Stoker: The Life of Hilda Matheson, OBE, 1888–1940* (Llangynog: Michael Carney, 1999), p. 73.

[43] Carney, *Stoker: The Life of Hilda Matheson*, pp. 72–5; Avery, *Radio Modernism*, p. 96.

[44] Matheson, "Listener Research in Broadcasting," p. 408.

[45] Matheson, "Listener Research in Broadcasting," p. 408.

[46] Matheson, "Listener Research in Broadcasting," p. 410.

[47] Hilda Matheson, "The Future of BBC Talks," *The Nineteenth Century and After* 111 (1932), p. 346.

[48] Avery, *Radio Modernism*, p. 41.

[49] Matheson, "Listener Research in Broadcasting," p. 422.

[50] Matheson, "Listener Research in Broadcasting," p. 410.

[51] Briggs, *The History of Broadcasting*, p. 67.

Matheson sought to understand technique's impact on audiences; for her, the mastery of sonic method and auditory form was a precondition for public approval of a particular speaker or program. Matheson thus proposed technical, not moral, guidelines as an accompaniment to listener research, with the intention of making radio more responsive to its audience.

Matheson's discourse of the expert emerges in the corners of Gielgud's play, informed by his own in-depth experience as a drama producer. The technical failures of *Inspector Silence* highlight the importance of skilled, not experimental, technocrats who only succeed when they understand all the intricacies of the business. The technical possibilities, and limitations, of wartime radio production for reaching a wide audience were at the front of Gielgud's mind as he noted that "the technique of production was compelled to be radically simplified" while, at the same time, "thousands of listeners who had never bothered to give serious attention to [radio dramas] [...] found themselves making these necessary contributions to their own enjoyment simply because they had little or no alternative" during the blitz.[52] This convergence of an awareness of audience desire with a technocratic approach to production likewise emerges in the second of the two Gielgud–Carr productions: *Thirteen to the Gallows*. Where Barran fails in *Inspector Silence* because he embraces the avant-garde and exceeds the technical capabilities of the studio, *Thirteen to the Gallows* proposes a technocratically informed alternative to Reithianism, which finds its allegory in listener research.

Thirteen to the Gallows begins with a common enough crisis in radio: the cancelation of a singing guest due to laryngitis. Needing to fill the empty airtime, it is decided that a local handyman will fill the spot of the singing guest. This handyman, Wallace Hatfield, happens to be at the BBC studio completing some manual labor, a pariah accused of his wife's murder; though technically acquitted, the entire community turned against him, assuming he is the murderer. While the station director is biased against Hatfield and believes in his guilt, the producer Barran arrives (the same character featured in *Inspector Silence*) and decides that a detective inspecting the Hatfield murder case over the air would be of considerable local interest. When Hatfield agrees to a studio interview, Barran recognizes the potential convergence between professional experiment and audience

---

52 Gielgud, *British Radio Drama*, p. 84.

response. "The Drama boys will be green with envy," he states.[53] In the interview, Hatfield retraces the day when he heard his wife was dead at the bottom of a local school bell tower, with "an armful of Arum lilies" around her body.[54] A witness to the scene, the former headmaster, also submits to an interview. The interviewee, Whitehead, recounts the discovery of her body after he heard the school bell ringing. The bell had been silenced for the duration of the war (with the exception of its potential use as a warning for German invasion), so its unexpected ringing alarmed Whitehead, who rushed to find Hatfield's wife dead on the ground next to the tower. In retelling his story Whitehead states, "No one can ring [the bell] now." He then "pulls [the key] out of his pocket" to prove the bell is safe from further vandalism.[55] But, just as he states this, the bell rings yet again, throwing the interview into chaos. Whitehead "hurries out through the door," and another guest "slides off the couch in a dead faint."[56] Barran screams, "For God's sake, everybody, pull yourselves together! This pro-gramme's going to hell and Jericho."[57] The interruption of the broadcast unsettles the expected plot of the play as well. When all in attendance rush to the bell to see what has happened, they find yet another corpse surrounded by the selfsame scattered lilies that encircled Hatfield's wife. The original investigation into the Hatfield murder is thus superseded by a fresh murder mystery. This time, however, Hatfield is fully alibied by his presence in the studio. The interruption and seeming innocence of Hatfield force both the play and the broadcast-within-the-play onto an entirely new trajectory. The act break that falls after the discovery of the new body suggests both the upending of the anticipated plot—the re-litigation of the Hatfield murder—and the derailing of the broadcast, which is put in a state of suspended animation as producers decide what to do under the circumstances.

Hatfield expresses relief at finding himself seemingly acquitted of the identical murders. But, much like a broadcaster too smug for his audience, he turns off his love interest, Carol, with his self-assured demeanor. His cockiness over his newly proven innocence makes him unsympathetic. "He was really gloating over poor old Jonas' death, because it proved his

---

[53] Carr and Gielgud, *Thirteen to the Gallows*, in *13 to the Gallows*, edited by Tony Medawar (Norfolk, VA: Crippen & Landru Publishers, 2008), p. 112.
[54] Carr and Gielgud, *Thirteen to the Gallows*, p. 134.
[55] Carr and Gielgud, *Thirteen to the Gallows*, p. 150.
[56] Carr and Gielgud, *Thirteen to the Gallows*, p. 150.
[57] Carr and Gielgud, *Thirteen to the Gallows*, p. 150.

innocence," Carol states. "I didn't like it, and I didn't like *him*."[58] The shift of public opinion against Hatfield in the studio suggests that some qualitative measures might be useful in determining how the BBC might satisfy its audience. But, as always, such expertise must be brought by those well-versed in understanding both the mechanics of radio and the audience's wishes. The suspicion of Hatfield, renewed as a result of his haughty behavior, ends up being precisely the line of inquiry required to solve a case made almost unsolvable through the use of mechanical expertise. Eventually, investigator Bryce narrows in on some key evidence: "a small bruise about the size of a sixpence" on Mrs. Hatfield's body.[59] The broadcast recommences, now tracing the additional crime and transgressing the boundaries of the studio walls to plant a microphone in the belfry. The resolution of the mystery rests, it turns out, in Bryce's technical know-how about the studio's operations. He asks Hatfield to walk the steps of the belfry while, in the studio, he asks Burnside to pull the handle of the emergency ventilation system that Hatfield installed when converting the school into a BBC studio. When Hatfield refuses to walk into the tower, Bryce pushes the ventilator's handle himself, and the bell correspondingly rings. Bryce has thus solved the crime. The ventilation system Hatfield installed was supplemented by the installation of a tube of pneumatically compressed air connecting the studio to the bell. The compressed air, "generating eighty pounds pressure per square inch," was "governed by the turning of [the ventilator's] handle, face out from a pipe set" in the belfry "at an angle which struck anyone crossing its floor like the kick of a mule," making them fly out the belfry to their deaths.[60] Bryce unveils Hatfield as the murderer of both his wife and Jonas after all, despite the fact that he was in the studio all the while. Furthermore, the highly technical means by which Hatfield commits (and Bryce solves) the murders speaks to the importance of technical ability to the successful conclusion of any dramatic plot.

It is worth reflecting on the unique methods by which Gielgud and Carr stage the deaths in both *Inspector Silence* and *Thirteen to the Gallows*. In the former, the crime is facilitated by the over-exuberant, though ill-informed, experimentation at the hands of the departing Barran, who refuses to take his audience into account. In *Thirteen to the Gallows*, the mastery of the means of production, including the intimate knowledge and involvement in

---

[58] Carr and Gielgud, *Thirteen to the Gallows*, p. 164, emphasis in origina.
[59] Carr and Gielgud, *Thirteen to the Gallows*, p. 170.
[60] Carr and Gielgud, *Thirteen to the Gallows*, p. 172.

the studio's construction, allows Hatfield to nearly get away with his crimes, were it not for a man more expert than he. Additionally, Hatfield's technical failures in charming his audience guide it towards his guilt. In both Gielgud–Carr plays, the untangling of the mystery and the satisfaction of the plot require the application of technical mastery. The broadcasting technocrat enables the fulfillment of audience desire. Having been cleverer by half in his efforts to gain the support of witnesses and the inspector, Hatfield's guilt symbolizes the fear of the BBC in underestimating its audience. In a charming, clever metaphor befitting a mystery set in a BBC studio, it should not go without note that while the play's beginning again alludes to the horrifying prospect of "dead air," the air that constitutes the murder weapon, as forceful and assertive as Hatfield's declaration of innocence, was deadlier still. But in the end, the broadcasting expertise of Hatfield is only partially complete. While his construction of the studio lends him a technical mastery over the physical studio space, allowing him to build a pneumatic weapon in its walls, the emotional mechanics of "broadcasting" his innocence remain opaque to him, adding to his continued unpopularity.

When Hilda Matheson looks to her list of facets that broadcasters should have in attempting to master their craft, she cites one in particular that applies to the case of Hatfield: the "psychology of aural impressions."[61] In part, positive "aural impressions" are fostered by the popular and charming personalities of broadcasters like Vernon Bartlett and Harold Nicolson who, as Matheson writes, elicit "correspondence from an almost complete cross-section of public opinion."[62] In other words, popular broadcasters like J.B. Priestley, who composed themselves with an "unpatronizing and simply expressed" attitude, fostered an environment where public opinion could be more acutely assessed and responded to.[63] The Ministry of Information was likewise concerned with the effectiveness of speakers, as Home Intelligence director Mary Adams sent letters to the BBC about who would be effective

---

[61] Matheson, "Listener Research in Broadcasting," p. 417.

[62] Matheson, "Listener Research in Broadcasting," p. 415.

[63] Ian McLaine, *Ministry of Morale: Home Front Morale and the Ministry of Information in World War II* (London: George Allen & Unwin, 1979), p. 99. Ian Whittington attests to the popularity of Priestley's "broadbrow" approach to the medium. Ian Whittington, *Writing the Radio War: Literature, Politics and the BBC, 1939–1945* (Edinburgh: Edinburgh University Press, 2018). The discontinuation of his famous "Postscripts" led a Listener Research Department to report of "the great storm of doubt" in the minds of listeners. "Listener Research Report," November 23, 1940, BBC WAC R9/1, No 14. His return led to the influx of "a thousand letters." "Listener Research Report," February 1941, BBC Written Archives Centre (WAC), ref R9 9/1, No 21.

messengers; in considering women broadcasters for the program "Answering You," she noted that Rose Macaulay, Dorothy L. Sayers and Rebecca West had, as she put it, "poor voice."[64] In the anti-Reithian ethos facilitated by the work of Hilda Matheson, the cordial tone and friendly attitude of speakers became increasingly important. In producing a play where it is the cocky, patronizing demeanor of the suspect that ultimately leads to the revelation of his guilt, Gielgud analyzes the value of this new "intimate broadcast style" to wireless production.[65] Concerns of tone at the BBC were high in the Home Intelligence Department, with internal memos from censors recording disgust at "how cheerful [broadcasters were] there after these raids."[66] Of course, no one would literally die if broadcasters were too patronizing, too forceful, too soft, or too pedantic with the listener. All the same, the symbolic death of the broadcast, which might come without a proper assessment of audience response to speakers, loomed large at the BBC. Hatfield's inability to market himself to his audience of judges is humorously mirrored in the murderous apparatus he creates, which produces such a strong impression over the air as to murder those who receive it. Both Hatfield's braggartism and the assassination-by-ventilator speak to the importance of personality as a means by which the BBC could supersede moral dogma in an effort to better appease its audience.

Peace Over the Wireless: Olaf Stapledon's Mediated Communities

During World War II, the BBC and Ministry of Information (MoI) worked in tandem to finesse and manage morale, with the latter using the former's listener research in its morale assessment, and the former dictating the latter's messaging about wartime efforts over the air; the MoI even forwarded requests for folk music at times to improve morale.[67] But this relationship

[64] Mary Adams to the BBC, September 1, 1941, Mary Adams Papers, SxMOA4/5/3/1, University of Sussex Special Collections.

[65] Todd Avery notes the transformation that occurs under Matheson and Siepmann, writing that it "represented...a potentially serious threat to Reith's efforts to reform public taste" and caused Reith "trepidation." Avery, *Radio Modernism*, p. 45.

[66] "Note on the Affect of Radio taken from Postal Censorship," March 17, 1941, Mary Adams Papers, SxMOA4/5/1/1, University of Sussex Special Collections.

[67] McLaine, *Ministry of Morale*, p. 72; records from the Wartime Social Survey include memos on potential BBC speakers. Mary Adams to the BBC, "List of suggested subjects and speakers, 1939 and 1940," Mary Adams Papers, SxMOA4/5/1/5, University of Sussex Special Collections.

did not always benefit the BBC's popularity; as the opening of this chapter demonstrated, the corporation's adherence to the MoI line on pacifism led to a rift between the public and the BBC. But for many outside the more cynical administrative workings of the BBC, an unfettered utilization of radio could—and should—work in tandem with pacifist causes, facilitated by the revolutionary potential of wireless transmission itself. Cantril and Allport argued in *The Psychology of Radio* (1935) that "[r]eflective souls" knew radio to be "a revolution in communication," "a gigantic tribute to human enterprise," as well as an "agency of incalculable power for controlling the actions of men."[68] The wireless might even harness this revolutionary potential to materialize collective consciousness in what Cantril and Allport called a "consciousness of kind" leading to a "vast social unity."[69] Transmission of information over air had wide-reaching philosophical consequences, particularly when paired with new techniques to amass public opinion. The ephemerality of both technologies—radio and public opinion—lent itself to precisely this sort of symbolic convergence. When Allen Weiss traces the antecedents of radio's metaphysical reception, he might very well be tracing the history of polling, as he cites the " 'animal magnetism' of mesmerism," the "spiritualist manipulation of electric waves in the ether," and the "psychic waves of the departed" facilitated through electricity.[70] Writers even considered the possibility that wireless transmission might provide the institutional means for constructing the long-awaited poll-conscious society. Wells, the most vociferous advocate of the sociologically inflected utopia, insisted that "no branch of applied science has ever exercised such a fascination for the man in the street as radio transmission."[71] And one of the foremost followers of Wells, novelist Olaf Stapledon, also believed radio might bridge the gap between individuals and help manifest collective will. Like the BBC, which saw the Peace Ballot as an inspiration for methods of data collection on a massive scale, Stapledon was likewise inspired by the democratic promise of the 1934 Peace Ballot. As mentioned in Chapter 2, Stapledon even wanted to begin his own pacifist signatory campaign in the years before the war. So, by the time Stapledon wrote the short story "A World of Sound" in 1936, he had long toyed with the possibility that the airwaves could be a medium to

---

[68] Cantril and Allport, *The Psychology of Radio*, p. 3.
[69] Cantril and Allport, *The Psychology of Radio*, p. 18.
[70] Allen Weiss, *Phantasmic Radio* (Durham, NC: Duke University Press, 1995), p. 3.
[71] Cited in Avery, *Radio Modernism*, p. 93.

inspire a collaborative and cooperative national, global, or even intergalactic culture. As an adult educator through the Workers' Educational Association, Stapledon's work made him deeply aware of social stratification by class, and the absolute necessity of a collective reckoning with class struggle.[72] At the same time, Stapledon's love letters to his long-distance cousin Agnes Miller featured the airwaves as a means of bringing distant beings together; in one letter it is music itself which transports the love-struck Stapledon across the planet to meet his beloved.[73] This trope would eventually find a home when Stapledon began to write fiction, with wireless transmission acting as a means of bringing together heterogeneous audiences and manifesting collective will.

A struggling writer, later to become a struggling academic before the publication of *Last and First Men* in 1930 brought him literary success, the young Stapledon had long been interested in the utilization of airwaves to bring together divergent and diverse audiences. Stapledon's new-found popularity in the early 1930s led him to acquire increasingly influential contacts in the literary world, notably Naomi Mitchison and H.G. Wells.[74] Fittingly, he was also invited to give a talk at the BBC—a mark of his emergence in the popular zeitgeist. His April 1931 broadcast "The Remaking of Man" hit on many themes of evolution and change he had addressed in his novel *Last and First Men*. On the one hand, Stapledon was optimistic about the way radio might change the future of humanity. He envisioned in radio a new technology capable of inspiring political engagement, arguing that radio "has contrived to wake up quite a large minority of ordinary men and women to care about the life of their community and to be interested in current problems."[75] However, he was quick to recognize the BBC's monopolistic, and even authoritarian, management of this new engaged citizenry, expressing concern that the "B.B.C. is *making* citizens."[76] In his short story "A World of Sound," the protagonist is confronted by the taste-making power of the BBC. In a music hall, the protagonist finds himself "disgusted"

---

[72] A transport strike and the Bloody Sunday that year forced Stapledon to recognize his privileged lifestyle and the necessity of an external force capable of ushering in a spirit of mutual understanding across classes. Stapledon took a job at the Workers' Educational Association in 1911. Crossley, *Olaf Stapledon*, p. 95.

[73] Crossley records, as early as 1911, prose sketches similar to the essay "A World of Sound," including a sketch "about himself as a dancer swaying to the homely music of a Liverpool dinner party [...] At last he joins Agnes Miller in Australia in a universal waltz that, he fancies, with many feet would smooth and buff the earth's surface, making the planet gleam in the eye of a cosmic beholder." Crossley, *Olaf Stapledon*, pp. 93–4.

[74] Crossley, *Olaf Stapledon*, pp. 191–3.   [75] Cited in Crossley, *Olaf Stapledon*, p. 196.

[76] Cited in Crossley, *Olaf Stapledon*, p. 196, emphasis mine.

when confronted by the "land of 'program music,'" which he claims to be the "whole world that violated the true canons of musical art!"[77] As Pierre Bourdieu notes, the ability to hold fast to a "pure" notion of the aesthetic, as the protagonist does, speaks to his economic privilege; to detach oneself from the enjoyment of art and give deference to the canon belies a life devoid of most economic worry.[78] This is further evinced by his presence at a music hall, revealed at the end of the story, a signal of at least a modicum of economic flexibility. The BBC's control over audiences is materialized in "A World of Sound," as music becomes a physical presence to the protagonist, who confronts the various types of music which approach him as if they were material bodies, formed into "perceptible bodies of living things."[79] As the music becomes alive, the protagonist's "pure" aesthetic stance manifests itself in a physical rejection, like the turning away from a vulgar acquaintance. Just as poll-consciousness is understood as a means to either bolster or dismantle democratic norms, here the rejection or embrace of music stands in for such social and political tensions.

While Stapledon expresses anxiety about the BBC's influence over its audiences, the privileging of bourgeoise and middle-class tastes was often baked into the kind of market research the BBC conducted. When the corporation hired public relations expert Robert Silvey to spearhead listener research, observers recognized how private sector market research worked hand-in-glove with the ideology of cultural uplift typified by organizations like the BBC, aimed at the middle-class consumer. Iconic interwar documentarian John Grierson even mentions Silvey by description, stating that so much of interwar progressive propaganda derived "not from the Ministry of Health but from the Gas, Light, and Coke Association," the organization through which Silvey had made himself famous in the industry.[80] Silvey recalls the first stage of listener research as a limited Variety Listener Barometer, garnering 350 responses from self-identified BBC listeners. More extensive efforts at listener research followed, as the LRD sent out 3,000 surveys to random license-holders. Throughout the process, Silvey was concerned about a "distinctly middle-class bias" in the surveys, but was

[77] Olaf Stapledon, *Far Future Calling: Uncollected Science Fiction and Fantasies of Olaf Stapledon*, edited by Sam Moskowitz and Stephen Fabian (Philadelphia, PA: O. Train, 1979), pp. 160–1.
[78] Pierre Bourdieu, *Distinction: A Social Critique of the Judgement of Taste*, translated by Richard Nice (Cambridge, MA: Harvard University Press, 1984), pp. 4–5.
[79] Olaf Stapledon, *Far Future Calling*, p. 160.
[80] Cited in James Purdon, *Modernist Informatics: Literature, Information, and the State* (Oxford: Oxford University Press, 2016), p. 147.

unable to determine whether or not such a bias mirrored that of the listening public itself.[81] This middle-class bias continued to be represented even as listener research expanded; the Variety Listener Barometer suggested, too, that respondents to BBC surveys were "untypical of the general population."[82] But another discovery was also made: despite the issues around self-selection in some surveys, those in the general population still liked the same programs in proportion to those who were self-selected. This meant that, scaled down, the self-selected listeners surveyed might stand in for the general radio listener.[83] So while, on the one hand, the BBC's early methodologies were clouded by fear of middle-class bias, the eventual expansion of the survey suggested that the radio audience may, in fact, represent a universal sample of the British listening public. While discovering that the purportedly middle-class taste of the BBC was reflective of the wider culture, little sense could be made as to why this was. The BBC may have been, as Stapledon feared, "making citizens." But listener research, far from revealing this influence, only obscured it further, making it easier for the BBC to see itself as preternaturally attuned to the tastes of a supposedly autonomous public consciousness.

Just as BBC research hints at the institution's homogenizing role in public opinion formation, in "A World of Sound" the potential benefits of a unified audience are staged against the homogenizing impact of cultural institutions. The protagonist describes "[reaching] out a musical limb" and "[obtaining] a purchase on the [sound] object," stating that he "could draw [his] whole body towards it."[84] But the relationship between the music and the protagonist, just like between listener research and opinion itself, engages dialectically, forcing an insincere consensus. The dynamics between the music and the protagonist, having become mutual and interdependent, at once become potentially threatening and overwhelming. He describes being "confronted by a crowd of intelligent beings tumbling helter-skelter toward me and jostling one another in their haste."[85] He quickly moves several "octaves" lower to "avoid their frantic course," attempting to find himself unhindered in his journey by the anthropomorphic version of "The Big Bad Wolf."[86] While the protagonist has fought against the popular world of program music, here that same music becomes a means to join a collective

[81] Silvey, *Who's Listening?* p. 63.   [82] Silvey, *Who's Listening?* p. 82.
[83] Silvey, *Who's Listening?* p. 84.   [84] Olaf Stapledon, *Far Future Calling*, p. 164.
[85] Olaf Stapledon, *Far Future Calling*, p. 166.
[86] Olaf Stapledon, *Far Future Calling*, p. 166.

and hide himself from the more threatening influences that alienate him from others. The story ends abruptly, as the audience in the music hall disperses and he leaves. Finally rejecting the alienated state of elite aesthetic judgment, the story of conflict and convergence that the protagonist tells applies itself to the masses who partake in the same cultural experience, all of them joined together by the music, as conscribed by their social positioning and capital. The portrait Stapledon paints is at once fantastic and ominous, alluding to the promise of the airwaves as a symbolic space of freedom while simultaneously reinforcing his fears over the manipulation of this medium to achieve autocratic control over the listening public. But the materialization of thought over air, specifically manifested in the trope of telepathy, would continue to emerge in Stapledon's work, tinged with the selfsame excitement and dread that we find in "A World of Sound."

Olaf Stapledon's Wireless Telepathy

The fascination with telepathy, for Olaf Stapledon, originates in conversations with family and loved ones, but quickly transforms into a central feature of much of his fiction. His persistence in deploying telepathy as a tool of materializing collective consciousness extends from *Last and First Men* (1930), to *Far Future Calling* (1930), *Last Men in London* (1932), and *Star Maker* (1937). While some of these texts drip with anxiety and ambivalence about the wireless as a means of fostering an authentic collective consciousness, Stapledon intermittently ascends into a utopian vision, inspired by the likes of Gerald Heard, who believed telepathy to be the next stage in human psychological evolution.[87] Stapledon achieves this by imagining telepathy as a tool for uniting the collective mind, "dissolv[ing] distance in both space and time and thereby bring[ing] faraway beings into the range of apprehension."[88] And while, as Mark Taylor has argued, telepathy is a critical trope of the Stapledonian oeuvre, I want to add that this centrality is heavily informed by poll-consciousness and the increased cultural prevalence of collective

---

[87] According to Naomi Mitchison, Stapledon thought Heard's *The Ascent of Man* "brilliant and helpful," though he was somewhat skeptical about its "co-consciousness and spiritualism." Naomi Mitchison, *You May Well Ask: A Memoir 1920–1940* (London: Flamingo Press, 1979), p. 138.

[88] Mark Taylor, "Olaf Stapledon and Telepathy in Literature of Cosmic Exploration," *Science Fiction Studies* 47, no. 2 (2020), p. 176.

psychology.[89] Both the promises and perils of collective consciousness are prefigured in *First and Last Men*, which presents readers with a skeptical vision of telepathy as a tool harnessed by an invading and aggressive Martian species. Stapledon describes the Martian species forming into "cloudlets," where individual organisms become a "group of free-moving members dominated by a 'group mind.'"[90] Individually, the Martian organisms become an invasive biological species united by "an immense crowd of mobile 'wireless stations,'" and the Martian cloudlet wreaks havoc on the community of the men they invade. While communication over the air can bring the Martians—like the crowd of music-hall-goers in "A World of Sound"— together, it also facilitates more aggressive acts against outsiders. The Martian cloudlets may be united by the airwaves, but the collective consciousness the species achieves is, as Stapledon notes, a failure: "[f]ar from being superior to the private mind, the public mind which obsessed every Martian [...] remained at heart a military mind."[91] Stapledon's theories over the role of radio in turning the public into a tool of interventionist nationalism continues to haunt him. The success of the Martian species in destroying man suggests the value of collectivity fostered through radio technologies. And yet, the militaristic foundations of the group mind should strike us as a warning from the pacifistic Stapledon who cautions of the susceptibility of group dynamics to aggressive and dangerous impulses. The notion of telepathy as a form of autocratic collective control likewise emerges in *Last Men in London* (1932), where a time-travelling alien abuses telepathy to control the protagonist Paul, even going so far as to make him hallucinate and act aggressively towards women. This dynamic would mirror the anxieties over persuasion and propaganda put forward by early theorists of social psychology, like Cantril and Allport, who, despite their optimism about the medium of radio, feared that the "average consumer" might fall to the propagandist's use of "suggestion."[92] The notion of the authoritarian airwaves not only suggests hierarchical models of public opinion formation, but the integration of radio alludes to the BBC's power and control over public taste via broadcasting. Stapledon repeatedly warns readers that when individuals harness telepathic power to control and dominate others, it leads to dangerous social consequences.

[89] Taylor, "Olaf Stapledon and Telepathy," pp. 176, 178.
[90] Olaf Stapledon, *First and Last Men* (Mineola, NY: Dover, [1930] 2008), p. 117.
[91] Stapledon, *First and Last Men*, p. 126.
[92] Cantril and Allport, *The Psychology of Radio*, p. 242.

Stapledon's skeptical vision of radio-collectivity emerges yet again in *Far Future Calling*, the unproduced radio play for the BBC based on *Last and First Men*, which uncomfortably merges radio and telepathy, using the former to address the nascent power of the latter. The play features four main characters. Two have travelled from two thousand years in the future, denoted as "A Future Man" and "A Future Woman." The others, "An Actor" and "An Actress," are in a radio play of their own. The two sets of time travelers set up a contrast between the world as we imagine it will be—a vision set forth by the two actors—and the radical future that actually awaits us, described by the time travelers. After the actors present this imagined future, where everything is "bigger and faster" than that which exists in 1931, they are paralyzed by the real time travelers, the Future Man and Woman.[93] And though the paralysis of the actors reinforces the authoritarian potentiality of telepathic manipulation, Stapledon's play also highlights a vital contrarian impulse that would run throughout many of his latter works: the emergence of telepathy as one of the constituent features in the utopian future. This revised version of radio-centric telepathy is still embryonic in *Far Future Calling*, as when the Future Man describes the additional senses which will emerge in man's mental evolution: "By means of a special kind of telepathic intercourse, our individual minds can come together to give birth to a single racial mind."[94] Here we find Stapledon's clear invocation of poll-consciousness applied to his utopianism. As private judgment transformed into the popular field of "public opinion," older tropes of telepathy and psychical exploration transform into symbols of the emergent science of group psychology. Telepathy thus comes to represent a positive version of collective consciousness and group identification; in identifying it as such, Stapledon draws from the long history of telepathy's tie with group psychological study.

We owe the concept of "telepathy" to the late Victorians; Society for Psychical Research founder Frederic W.H. Myers coined the term the year after he founded the Society in 1882.[95] Jeffrey Sconce marks the homologous relationship between radio and telepathy historically, citing the "uncanny liberation of the body in time and space" as a feature of radio which led many to theorize that this technology might channel the minds of

---

[93] Stapledon, *Far Future Calling*, pp. 175, 177.
[94] Stapledon, *Far Future Calling*, p. 202.
[95] *Oxford English Dictionary* (2020), s.v. "Telepathy."

the dead and the living.[96] The notion of reading thoughts also emerged nearly concurrently with the notion of "psychography," the latter of which involved the reading of the wishes of the dead through writing and records.[97] It is for this reason that we find Woolf, inspired by a "psycho-graphic" mode of biography associated with Lytton Strachey, arguing in *Three Guineas* that biography presents a medium akin to "blood and mem-ory transfusion."[98] But while psychography promised the unmitigated access to the beliefs of the past, telepathy promised insight into the beliefs and perspectives of the present and future. Advocates of telepathy like Gerald Heard viewed the concept as uniquely tied to evolutionary theory. There is thus little surprise as to why the subject of telepathy returned to the fore of interwar culture with such gusto. Just as telepathy's academic sibling, sociology, became the discipline favored by the Wellsian futurism, the revival of telepathy symbolizes poll-consciousness brought to its terminus. Stapledon suggests in *Far Future Calling* and other works that telepathy might provide the social infrastructure for any future global or interplane-tary utopianism. Telepathy comes to stand in for a world fully consumed by poll-consciousness but, furthermore, the fascination with telepathy in the 1930s is not insubstantially influenced by new radio technology, producing a materialist analogy for just such a practice: the transmission of pure thought over air.

But the revival of telepathy in Stapledon's work is not just the vestige of a residual late-Victorian occultism; rather, it is a reimagining of this spiritual-ism via emergent radio technologies, as witnessed in the radio drama *Far Future Calling*. The symbolic prevalence of the airwaves reactivates residual cultural propensities towards occultism, and while *Far Future Calling* merely uses radio as a means of dramatizing telepathic modes of control and communication, the emergence of radio-centric telepathy in Stapledon's 1937 novel *Star Maker* transforms the wireless medium into a mechanical device facilitating the transmission of opinion into decentralized, airborne clouds of collective consciousness. While more positive visions of radio-telepathy are merely alluded to in *Far Future Calling*, the novel *Star Maker* centralizes radio's role in the rise of species-wide telepathic communication, incorporating far more optimism than in this former theorization of the

[96] Jeremy Sconce, *Haunted Media: Electronic Presence from Telegraphy to Television* (Durham, NC: Duke University Press, 2000), pp. 75–91.
[97] *Oxford English Dictionary* (2020) s.v. "Psychography."
[98] Virginia Woolf, *Three Guineas* (New York: Harcourt, [1939] 2006), p. 9.

practice. Just as early theorists of polling argued that public opinion research would inevitably lead towards more democratic institutions, early theorists of the wireless, like Cantril and Allport, suggested that the wireless "presses always towards [...] universal democracy."[99] In *Star Maker*, Stapledon comes to his own unsettled vision of a wireless collective consciousness.

By the time Stapledon wrote his novel *Star Maker* (1937), he had developed an increasingly complex view of telepathy, suggesting that the threat it presented was countered by the potentiality of its use towards the creation of a harmonious, peaceful collectivity. In his more optimistic version of telepathy, radio arises as a surprising supplement to his telepathic utopias and enables a more cooperative and peaceable world to emerge without the forceful and dangerous propagandizing he describes in *Last Men in London* and *Far Future Calling*. The use of radio as a medium to promote telepathic communication in *Star Maker* suggests Stapledon's rising interest in the way that radio might foster and guide public taste while holding true to the principles of democracy. While early renditions of telepathy mark it as a skill likely to lead to thought control, when fostered and aided by radio, telepathy becomes a facilitator of group opinion and not its master. Of course, many in radio at this time were considering the way that Germany was integrating broadcasts in its most nefarious form; Charles Siepmann feared that German broadcasting sought to "induce throughout the world a slave mentality."[100] In the transition from *Far Future Calling* to *Star Maker*, we find Stapledon working through his ambivalence about radio's potential authoritarianism, in the end recognizing that such technologies might produce "constant radio intercourse" in which people from across the globe could "[exchange] ideas" and "[modify] each other's opinion."[101] In locating this kind of discursive liberty at the heart of the wireless, Stapledon mirrors the views of Cantril and Allport in seeing wireless as a possible "agent of democracy."[102]

Typical Stapledonian anxieties about radio monopoly emerge in the early pages of *Star Maker*, where he first presents radio taking on a familiar, ominous role. The protagonist begins the novel in his yard, wistfully looking amongst the stars. He finds himself able to escape his present reality in his hometown and instead go far into outer space and through time, seeing

[99] Cantril and Allport, *The Psychology of Radio*, p. 22.
[100] Charles Siepmann, *Radio in Wartime* (Oxford: Oxford University Press, 1942), p. 4.
[101] Cited in Crossley, *Olaf Stapledon*, p. 197.
[102] Cantril and Allport, *The Psychology of Radio*, p. 22.

other forms of species throughout the ages, all in an attempt to understand the creator—the "star maker." In the protagonist's adventures, he encounters many future species, but a significant portion of the novel details the first species he encounters: a species he calls "the Other Men." The protagonist is, like in *Last Men in London*, able to use some modified telepathy to understand the feelings and thoughts of foreign species. So, as he encounters the Other Men, he is able to enter the brain of one of its members. He first discovers that the Other Men use radio in a unique way that helps solidify the group psychology of the culture. The Other Men use the wireless to solidify their group identity even beyond the auditory sphere, becoming a medium of "touch, taste, odor, and sound."[103] Bypassing the ears entirely, the radio functions through the "direct stimulation of the appropriate brain-centers."[104] Stapledon's Other Men suggest nascent anxieties about the wireless medium; the lack of a discrete physical housing for radio's ideological content meant that the medium might drive directly into the unconscious mind, superseding any mediation or interrogation. Charles Siepmann noted a similar concern that radio propaganda's "verbal cargoes are shipped to every corner of the globe [...] Radio comes across an undefended frontier in continuous waves of verbal assault."[105] Walking down the street, the susceptibility to broadcasting without consent led to the type of fear shared by both Siepmann and Stapledon; the subsequent anxiety of influence was only befitting for a medium with so much reach and penetration. In Stapledon's re-creation of the radio, he takes on this anxiety and explores its most dreadful consequences. By directly acting on the nerve center, radio achieves a completely unmediated access to the body and mirrors the dynamics of telepathy, but also highlights the use of broadcasting as a means of controlling the population and managing the poor and disenfranchised.

This unmediated access to the physical bodies of "listeners" makes radio an addiction; it constitutes a technologically advanced version of bread and circuses, enabling citizens to remain completely ignorant of their conditions and instead live entirely in a fantasy world of sensations brought to them over the wireless. Subsequently, the radio became a tool of the Right, with "the political Left Wing" opposing "the further development of radio amusements" which "made the Governments and the propertied classes the more ready to accept it."[106] Social unrest is easily managed by "the mere

[103] Olaf Stapledon, *Star Maker* (Middletown, CT: Wesleyan University Press, 2004), p. 41.
[104] Stapledon, *Star Maker*, p. 51.   [105] Siepmann, *Radio in Wartime*, p. 4.
[106] Stapledon, *Star Maker*, p. 42.

threat to close down the broadcasting studios," which all citizens were dependent on and addicted to. Radio becomes a politicized cause, defended by the right and lambasted by the left, who argued that radio amusements were "pure Capitalist dope, calculated to prevent the otherwise inevitable dictatorship of the proletariat."[107] A purging of the radio industry by the right escalates; they rid the wireless of any employee sympathetic to the ideals of pacifism and freedom. In the world of the Other Men, a man can "spend all his time receiving radio programs" with "nourishment and all his bodily functions" "attended to by doctors and nurses attached to the Broadcasting Authority."[108] Stapledon has imagined a type of radio that is the BBC in extremis—where the radio's ability to manage middle brow taste slowly transitions to a form of fascistic control, seizing on the listener's brain and body alike. In this dystopian BBC, the radio becomes the most efficacious form of propaganda, as infants who were susceptible to radio were educated entirely through its programming, as directed by the authoritarian regime. Stapledon's "radio-bliss" is described as the "Other Fascism," as he theorizes a totalitarian state that uses radio as its means of empowerment, producing "a fundamental imbalance in the relationship between individual and community" that ends up destroying the species of Other Men.[109]

This reflection on the authoritarian possibilities of radio certainly has correlatives in discussions about radio during World War II. Again, looking to Charles Siepmann's *Radio in Wartime*, we find allusions to a possible world in which the omnipresence of radio exposes the vulnerability of susceptible minds to fascist ideology. Just as Stapledon's imagination of the radio exposes its power as an ideological weapon to quell working-class protest, Siepmann notes that radio propaganda, distinguishing itself from the objective and discrete instances of leaflet propaganda in World War I, "infects the very air we breathe."[110] In an extended military metaphor, he adds that "radio propaganda drops its verbal parachutes into the internal of our subconscious mind."[111] And while Stapledon deems the process one of "radio-bliss," Siepmann attributes to radio an "almost hypnotic influence."[112] Referencing the mesmerizing effects of radio—"radio-bliss"—Stapledon warns readers of the radio's ability to influence the mind of the public. As previously noted, one of his primary concerns was the BBC's management

---

[107] Stapledon, *Star Maker*, p. 42.   [108] Stapledon, *Star Maker*, p. 43.
[109] Gerry Canavan, "'A Dread Mystery, Compelling Adoration': Olaf Stapledon, *Star Maker*, and Totality," *Science Fiction Studies* 43 (2014), p. 320.
[110] Siepmann, *Radio in Wartime*, p. 4.   [111] Siepmann, *Radio in Wartime*, p. 6.
[112] Siepmann, *Radio in Wartime*, p. 7.

and control of its audience. If Stapledon argued, in linking the BBC's curation of cultural taste to more authoritarian forms of control, that the BBC could "make" citizens, Siepmann's citation of radio propaganda from abroad testifies to the deep-rooted concern that fascist influence over the wireless might undermine British war aims. The quelling of these fears became one of the aims of the BBC's listener research throughout the war. And it could be argued that the unique methods of inquiry at the BBC's LRD allowed the government to better assess the validity of such threats.

Even before the war, the BBC was concerned about the incursion of foreign broadcasts onto the British airwaves and into British minds. Robert Silvey even found himself interested, as a matter of competition, in the extent to which the "British public was turning to Radio Normandy and Radio Luxembourg on Sundays."[113] But at the start of the war, concerns over the popularity of German stations increased profoundly. Charles Siepmann estimated that "5 to 10 percent" of domestic audiences admitted to listening to foreign stations, though he assumed the real number to be far higher.[114] On the surface, these results might have suggested a groundswell for fascist ideology at home. But the interview methods of the BBC's listener barometer allowed further excavation of this data, as interviewers could receive qualitative analyses of listener habits. These interviews revealed that listeners to Haw-Haw also liked the BBC, and even *The Times*; their attention to German radio was generally a means of reaffirming, not upending, their national identity.[115] In a 1941 broadcast, "Answering You," Mass-Observation's Tom Harrisson suggested that "[p]eople listen now [to Haw-Haw] much less than they did. The first curiosity and amusement have worn off—it used to be amusing to hear ourselves insulted—Haw-Haw is now a bore."[116] The purely behavioral tracking promised by either radio licenses or Nielson Audiometers would inevitably have missed this complex explication of listener motivation.[117] The important intelligence the BBC offered to the

---

[113] Siepmann, *Radio in Wartime*, p. 15.   [114] Siepmann, *Radio in Wartime*, p. 7.

[115] Though anti-fascist action like the Battle of Cable Street suggests anti-fascist sentiment, Martin Pugh estimates that by the dawn of war, the British Union of Fascists had between 22,500 and 36,000 members; it was banned in 1940. Martin Pugh, *Hurrah for the Blackshirts! Fascists and Fascism in Britain between the Wars* (London: Pimlico, 2005), p. 285.

[116] "Scrapbook of the Scripts from the BBC Radio Program, 'Answering you,' 1941–42," July 28, 1941. Mary Adams Papers, SxMOA4/5/2/1, University of Sussex Special Collections.

[117] Nielson audiometers were attached to radio receivers and traced which stations the receivers had been tuned to. There were several downsides to this system, including the limitation on people willing to put the meters in their homes. It also did not account for actual listener behavior, blending the listening habits of families as one "listener." Silvey, *Who's Listening?* p. 76.

MoI through such methods allowed for the barometer's continued expansion. In fact, the "Appreciation Index" that resulted from the barometer became more advanced than even American technologies according to Silvey, who was told by one researcher, "We have nothing like this in the USA."[118] In studies on Lord Haw-Haw and the like, the BBC's LRD, maintaining its commitment to the interview survey as their format, was firmly able to understand the relationship between audiences and fascism over the wireless. In part, this quelled anxieties that radio publics might be hypnotized in the way Siepmann feared, or in the way Stapledon described in *Star Maker*'s allusion to "radio-bliss" as just another form of fascism.

But, in a critical shift, Stapledon finds himself casting aside his anxieties over the totalitarian dynamics of the radio in the latter pages of *Star Maker*, instead introducing a world where radio's power is dynamic, multidirectional, and anti-authoritarian. While Stapledon is in the world of the Other Men, many of whom remain subject to "radio-bliss," he meets Bvalltu, with whom he shares a telepathic bond. This shared and dynamic telepathic bond between the protagonist and Bvalltu prefigures the more optimistic version of air-based mind alteration which Stapledon depicts later in the novel. The two escape the dystopian world of the Other Men, and proceed to travel together through space and time to find other species, both more enlightened and more barbaric than their own. As Fredric Jameson argues, the proliferation of alien species in *Star Maker* presents readers with "oppositions which seek (structurally and narratively, which is to say unconsciously) to resolve social contradictions."[119] In terms of wireless transmission, Stapledon's novel does the same. In their travels, the two stargazers uncover a means by which the radio might both promote and encourage democratic social structures. They travel by means of sympathetic telepathy. As they locate other species, they find specimens with whom they share "psychical attraction," experiencing new cultures and environments through these intermediary agents. As the partners gather an increasing number of psychic interlocutors, their network grows rhizomatically: a telepathically facilitated version of Wells's re-nucleation process in *The Shape of Things to Come*. The increasingly heterogeneous group attracts still others into their network, expanding the circle of connection still farther. In reimaging radio as an inherently interactive medium, with waves crossing,

[118] Silvey, *Who's Listening?* p. 119.
[119] Fredric Jameson, *Archaeologies of the Future: The Desire Called Utopia and Other Science Fiction* (London: Verso, 2005), p. 130.

interacting, and collaborating, Stapledon suppresses anxieties around collective and group dynamics that had particular dominance in the interwar years. His network of telepaths maps an infrastructural model for political cohesion at a time when the most successful models for political identification were premised on centralized authoritarian control. Collectively, this ragtag group of interstellar telepaths, in their journey to find species who provide the solutions for a culture plagued by war, create their own utopian society free of internecine strife and violence. In their aims, they shared a great deal with Stapledon, who sought to form his own decentralized networks before and during the war, both in his work as a teacher for the Worker's Educational Association and as a political activist.[120]

While the Other Men section of *Star Maker* presents readers with a model of an authoritarian wireless collectivism, Stapledon's more rhizomatic vision of the wireless arises most acutely when Bvalltu and the protagonist encounter a "swarm of avian creatures" in their interstellar travels, who foster their collective mind through the use of radio devices.[121] Unlike the use of radio amongst the Other Men, the radio here is not controlled through one centralized bureaucracy, but instead collectively owned and cooperatively controlled. The unity of the avian species is "based on the unit of a complex electromagnetic field, in fact on 'radio' waves permeating the whole group."[122] Stapledon describes the process of this communal identification: "Radio, transmitted and received by every individual organism, corresponded to the chemical nerve current which maintains the unity of the human nervous system."[123] Facing an environment of division and controversy, the use of radio for the fostering of a collective mind suggests an alternative means of harvesting public opinion towards higher aims. But Stapledon's vision of the functioning of radio is slightly different than the model that had led to the need for listener research at the BBC. The need for listener research came from the basic fact that while listeners *received* the broadcast, they had limited ways to master the ideological means of production. Stapledon envisions a world where radio is no longer unilateral by design. Radio thus transforms what Cantril and Allport identify as the social situation of radio—from a linear relationship to that of a "congregate assembly" (see Figure 3.1). And while the collective broadcast collates

---

[120] Not only did Stapledon work for the WEA as an educator, he also published in its journal *Highway*. Stapledon viewed broadcasting as a project similar to his work at the WEA: a pedagogical tool to inform a wider public. Crossley, *Olaf Stapledon*, pp. 111–12, 196.
[121] Stapledon, *Star Maker*, p. 111.   [122] Stapledon, *Star Maker*, p. 112.
[123] Stapledon, *Star Maker*, p. 112.

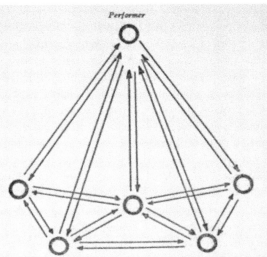

Fɪɢ. I.—The social formation of the *congregate assembly*, showing circular relationship between performer and auditors, as well as the influence of one auditor upon another.

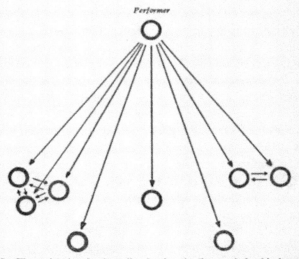

Fɪɢ. II.—The social situation in *radio*, showing the linear relationship between the speaker and his auditors, and, excepting where listeners are grouped in their own homes, a complete absence of social facilitation in the audience.

Figure 3.1 The social situation of radio and the congregate assembly. Figures from *The Psychology of Radio* by Hadley Cantril, Gordon Allport. Copyright 1935 by Harper & Row, Publishers, Inc., renewed (c) 1963 by Hadley Cantril. Used by permission of HarperCollins Publishers.

public opinion into one embodied cloud, it refuses to strip autonomy from the individuals in the bird-species. Stapledon attempts to describe this process, which stages a vibrant, continuous intercourse between the individual and the collective: "[e]ach brain reverberated with the ethereal rhythms of its own environment; and each contributed its own peculiar theme to the complex pattern of the whole."[124] Stapledon paints this collective consciousness as truly beneficial for each member; if one of the creatures left the group, they "degenerated" into "a very simple instinctive animal."[125] Individual agency is not drowned out by the noise of universal opinion, but elevated and enriched by the knowledge that a collective consciousness proffers. Of course, this is what Stapledon hoped to achieve in his activism and teaching. It is what he would call, in his 1942 essay "Sketch-Map of Human Nature," "personality-in-community," a "superhuman" goal of social development that unifies a diverse collective.[126]

Ideographs, Psychometers and Barometers: Technologies of Collective Consciousness

While Stapledon's earlier texts are informed by a unilateral model of wireless communication, we find in *Star Maker* a clear alternative, which reprises the role of radio technologies towards the achievement of social cohesion that avoids authoritarian pitfalls. This vision—of beneficent waves of sentiment traversing the ether—was not just a utopian feature of *Star Maker*, but was also a trope central to his most intimate correspondence. Biographer Robert Crossley records that in his wooing letters to Agnes Miller, Stapledon theorizes an "ideograph," a type of "gramophone of the mind that could transmit thoughts unambiguously."[127] This idyllic vision of aerial thought-transmission, the notion that interiority could transmit from person to person in a process that is simultaneously material and immaterial, was not isolated to Stapledon. And while in June 1937, Virginia Woolf complained of the potentiality of "hearing a gramophone forever braying" in her head, mere weeks later she was writing a letter to Olaf Stapledon about *Star Maker*, a novel that inspired her own representation of wirelessly facilitated collectivity in her two final book-length works, *Three Guineas*

---

[124] Stapledon, *Star Maker*, p. 112.   [125] Stapledon, *Star Maker*, p. 112.
[126] Olaf Stapledon, "Sketch-Map of Human Nature," *Philosophy* 17, no. 67 (1942), p. 223.
[127] Crossley, *Olaf Stapledon*, p. 108.

(1938) and *Between the Acts* (1941).[128] In her letter to Stapledon in early July, she proclaims that *Star Maker* "elated" her, adding that "sometimes it seems to me that you are grasping ideas that I have tried to express, much more fumblingly... [b]ut you have gone much further and I can't help envying you—as one does those who reach what one has aimed at."[129] Woolf's embrace of Stapledon's vision emerges in her subsequent works as she, too, tries to imagine a wireless technology capable of producing and collating collective consciousness.

This is particularly the case in *Three Guineas*, Woolf's pacifist polemic housed in the guise of an epistolary debate on the best way to end war. In engaging with her fictional correspondent, Woolf repeatedly seeks to reclaim the potential of a collective that exists outside the patriarchal, militaristic society of which she is a part, but "in cooperation with [the] aim" of pacifism.[130] In the end, this leads Woolf to theorize her famous "Outsiders' Society," a group of women who achieve pseudo-autonomy from the domination of patriarchy through the careful rejection of capitalist and nationalist incentives.[131] Woolf's efforts to outline the dynamics of a collective without centralized control suggests a series of concerns quite similar to those of Stapledon. Additionally, just as in *Star Maker*, the processes of mediation between the individual and the collective arise as dominant themes in *Three Guineas*. Scholars have long noted the importance of intermediation in the text itself. Even the grammatical quirks of the book denote her struggle to produce a collectivity within a heterogeneous society. In a work structured around epistolary correspondence, Woolf's utilization of ellipses, which emerge at moments when her, and her correspondent's, differences in social status threaten to break their unity entirely, are suggestive of sonic distance. After introducing the goal of the text—answering the question of "How [...] are we to prevent war?" to her educated, male correspondent—Woolf alludes to the chasm between herself and her interlocutor, tinging the textual form of the epistolary with symbolism of the sonic realm: "But...those three dots mark a precipice, a gulf so deeply cut between us that for three years and more I have been sitting on my side of it wondering whether it is any use to *speak* across it."[132] As ellipses threaten to sever the fragile collectivity between the writer and her male interlocutor,

---

[128] Virginia Woolf, *The Letters of Virginia Woolf, Volume 6: 1936-1941*, edited by Nigel Nicolson and Joanne Trautmann (London: Harcourt, 1980), p. 139.

[129] Stanley Kim Robinson, "Why isn't Science Fiction Winning any Literary Awards?" *New Scientist*, no. 203, iss. 2726 (2009).

[130] Woolf, *Three Guineas*, p. 170.   [131] Woolf, *Three Guineas*, p. 126.

[132] Woolf, *Three Guineas*, p. 6, emphasis added.

Woolf reminds us of the violence of patriarchy and nationalism that seek to tear peace-loving peoples from one another. As scholars have long oscillated between seeing *Three Guineas* as a theorization of new collectivity and understanding it as the recognition of irreconcilable difference, understanding the ellipsis as an ambivalent theorization of public opinion's promise and impotence puts both approaches into a different light.

These ellipses, evincing the struggle to transmit sentiment over the air, were so essential to the text that they featured prominently in the notebooks where Woolf first sketched out her planned polemic. It is clear from Woolf's notebooks that two apparatuses—one mechanical and one textual—are foundational to her early thinking on *Three Guineas*. The mechanical is one of the most significant technologies of mental transmission in her book: the atrocity photograph. She calls such photographs a "statement of fact addressed to the eye." Woolf expresses some hope that photographs of war horrors might provide a means to unify public opinion, since "the eye is connected with the brain; the brain with the nervous system."[133] But this lengthy chain of mediation, between photograph, brain, and body, only underscores the significance of the spatio-auditory gap between her and her correspondent, which her notebooks reference directly. In the published version of *Three Guineas*, the photographs, though they partially inspire collectivity, also bring Woolf right back to the same disconnection between the two pacifists. Woolf hopes that her letter can persuade her correspondent without the need to point to "the photographs that are all this time piling up on the table—photographs of more dead bodies, of more ruined houses."[134] But just as the photographs are mentioned, the tell-tale ellipses, the most pertinent textual apparatus of the polemic, emerge to represent the chasm between sender and recipient: "But...it seems that there is some hesitation, some doubt—not certainly that war is horrible, that war is beastly, that war is insupportable and that war is inhuman, as Wilfred Owen said, or that we wish to do all we can to help you to prevent war."[135] A nascent, abbreviated passage of Woolf's *Three Guineas* notebooks suggests the strong association Woolf sees between the impact of photographs and the elliptical relationship between women and men: "but look at the photograph...abhor to me."[136] The notebook's inclusion of the extended ellipses reinforce the critical nature of the elliptical gaps to Woolf's conception of *Three Guineas*.

---

[133] Woolf, *Three Guineas*, p. 14.   [134] Woolf, *Three Guineas*, pp. 50–1.

[135] Wolf, *Three Guineas*, pp. 50–1.

[136] "Notes about Women, War etc," Monks House Papers, SxMs-18/2/B/16/C, University of Sussex Special Collections.

But just as this critical textual gap represents a sonic distance made textual, it also highlights the impossibility for existing technologies to bridge the gap between her and her correspondent. But Woolf finds another way. The ellipses in *Three Guineas* are supplemented in Woolf's polemic by an alternative mediatory device that seeks to counter the prevalence of these social anxieties. Just as *Star Maker* doubly deploys the radio—first as device of social control and then one of collective harmony—wireless technologies in *Three Guineas* are at once a source of social tension and one of social cohesion. While the ellipses of *Three Guineas* are not technological per se, they mirror a kind of physical and acoustic chasm between the author and her correspondent. As a complement to this allusion to severance, *Three Guineas* alludes to another more technological device—the psychometer—which utilizes air to bridge the gaps between people divided by culture, class, or gender. The psychometer's function is to help the individual understand the best ways to become a more enlightened and informed citizen. Woolf describes the dynamics of the device in some detail:

> It is the psychometer that you carry on your wrist, the little instrument upon which you depend in all personal relationships. If it were visible it would look something like a thermometer. It has a vein of quicksilver in it which is affected by any body or soul, house or society in whose presence it is exposed. If you want to find out how much wealth is desirable, expose it in a rich man's presence; how much learning is desirable, expose it in a learned man's presence. So with patriotism, religion and the rest. The conversation need not be interrupted while you consult it; nor its amenity disturbed [...] Go to the public galleries and look at pictures; turn on the wireless and rake down music from the air; enter any of the public libraries which are now free to all. There you will be able to consult the findings of the public psychometer for yourself.[137]

As Todd Avery argues, Woolf's psychometer acts as an invisible barometer of taste and a tacit celebration of radio's unifying potential.[138] Like the BBC's early listening barometers, it aids in the formation of views and opinions of the holder through the acquisition and judgment of others. And, as Stapledon suggests in "A World of Sound" and *Star Maker*, Woolf proposes

---

[137] Woolf, *Three Guineas*, p. 98.   [138] Avery, *Radio Modernism*, p. 36.

the materialization of opinion as a means of producing a more collaborative culture. But the nature of the formation of opinion in this passage remains intensely Woolfian. Opinion, she notes, should be formed on the basis of the best and the most inspired of culture, harnessed not from the knowledge of the crowd but through those sources deemed worthy of mining for information. As Woolf attempts to theorize visions of collectivity in symbols like the "magic tree," which she borrowed from mystic Gerald Heard's *The Emergence of Man* (reprised as the "Mulberry Tree" in Woolf's polemic), the psychometer presents an alternative for the acquisition of public and collective knowledge.[139] Rather than relying on fellow citizens to mediate culture, the psychometer instead takes on the role of curator, deriving inspiration from the select. The public galleries and the learned man are the mediators of public culture, meant to form public taste. While the psychometer turns outwards for its influences, it does so selectively, looking to the paragons of high culture to suggest the types of information and influences the individual should adapt.

Woolf suggests the psychometer "rake[s] down music from the air," using the results to understand the best of music, just as the learned man mediates the most useful knowledge for the psychometer's user; in doing so, Woolf mirrors the materialization of the sonic sphere Stapledon alludes to in "A World of Sound."[140] And despite Woolf's disparagement for the BBC over the years, she continues to look to the institution as a source of cultural enlightenment. Woolf expressed her dismay at what she perceived as the BBC's middlebrow influence. But all the same, Woolf understood the inevitability of the BBC as an influencing force on British sensibility, and even on public opinion; her involvement with the BBC as a broadcaster testifies to this.[141] It thus becomes, like the public galleries and the intelligent men, a resource for determining the highpoint of culture that will produce an intelligent citizenry. For Woolf, the successful maintenance of peace—the underlying mission of *Three Guineas*—rests on the ability to produce a cultural environment that educates and informs, through the curation of a device like the psychometer which can mediate public culture by triangulating it through the views of others: the "rich man" or the "educated" one.

---

[139] Hermione Lee, *Virginia Woolf* (New York: Vintage, 1999), p. 611.
[140] Woolf, *Three Guineas*, p. 98.
[141] Leila Bronson argues that, "Woolf's connection with the BBC demonstrates her contact with spheres of cultural life and cultural production that extend beyond the confines of the 'high art' of the modernist novel." Leila Bronson, *Reading Virginia Woolf's Essays and Journalism: Breaking the Surface of Silence* (Edinburgh: Edinburgh University Press, 1999), p. 164.

The importance of the psychographic turn for Woolf, so clearly demonstrated in her invention of the psychometer and admiration for *Star Maker*,
likewise looms in *Between the Acts*, Woolf's posthumous novel. Just as
Woolf's early *Three Guineas* journals testify to her interest in facilitating collective consciousness, the convergence of private thought and public consciousness again emerges in the sketches for *Between the Acts*, which feature
an enigmatic note: "The private feeling: the public."[142] Such a notation, I
argue, not only suggests interest in the poll-conscious dialectic between
public and private feeling, but it enables Woolf to reverse the dangerous
autocracy of the radio which, as Michele Pridmore-Brown argues, views
listeners as an "aggregate of statistical bodies divested of individual
agency."[143] Like Stapledon, Woolf's ambivalence about the wireless as a
medium of collective unity is palpable. When she schematizes the public as
a private feeling in her notebooks, Woolf actively reverses a phrase from her
diary—"the common feeling covers the public"—a phrase Woolf had used
to describe the radio's malignant impact on consciousness.[144] Despite
Woolf's notorious decimation of H.G. Wells for his sociological aesthetics
and her own reputation as a writer of subjective interiority, Melba Cuddy-
Keane notes that *Between the Acts* reflects the desire for "communal art"
inspired by works like Freud's *Group Psychology* and the communally oriented classicism of Jane Harrison.[145] Many features of the novel, including
the role of the communal chorus, the dialectic relationship between audience and playwright and, perhaps most importantly for my purposes, the
self-reflexive conclusion of the novel which merges the two, attest to the
prominent influence of psychographics in *Between the Acts*.

Just like Stapledon before her, Woolf's utopian vision of community and
collective consciousness is hedged by the prospect of the sonic space as preternaturally designed to impose unilateral force on the audience. As
Mr. Streatfield, the minister and Treasurer, appeals to listeners for funding
to continue the community pageants, his words are "cut in two," a "zoom

---

[142] "Notes for 'Pointz Hall,'" September 19, 1938, Monks House Papers, SxMs-18/2/B/2/B,
University of Sussex Special Collections.
[143] Michele Pridmore-Brown, "Virginia Woolf and the BBC: Public and Private Voices,"
Virginia Woolf Miscellany 56 (2000), p. 4.
[144] Virginia Woolf, *The Diary of Virginia Woolf: Volume Five, 1936–1941*, edited by Anne
Olivier Bell (New York: Harcourt, 1943), p. 231. Michele Pridmore-Brown notes that Woolf
"chaffs at the way the BBC [...] implicate her in mass emotion." Pridmore-Brown, "Virginia
Woolf and the BBC," p. 4.
[145] Melba Cuddy-Keane, "The Politics of Comic Modes in Virginia Woolf's *Between the
Acts*," *PMLA* 105, no. 2 (March 1990), p. 275.

sever[ing]" them, as "[t]welve aeroplanes in perfect formation" cause the audience to "gape" and "gaze."[146] The auditory rendering of governmental force, recalling the same instance of commercial interpellation as the Kreemo Toffee advertisement in *Mrs. Dalloway*, affirms the deleterious role of communality when seized by powerful institutional forces. Along these lines, there are yet more ambivalent allusions to the communality of the air; the "chuff…chuff…chuff" of the gramophone inspires the question, "How long would time hold them together?"[147] That the "tick, tick, tick," playing before the play as the audience anticipates the communal experience, "seemed to hold them together, tranced," presents a promise of communality tinged with anxiety over the tenuous nature of the air as medium for that cohesion. As Matthew Weber argues, the novel dramatizes the ambiguity of community-formation, as "the gramophone […] cuts the audience off from a reimagining of their collective state, even though the play appears to invite the renewal."[148] Countering the ambiguous gramophone, Miss La Trobe's experimental pageant play of English history presents an optimism more akin to Stapledon's rhizomatic swarms.

Obsessed with her audience, whom she fears will "[slip] the noose," and rankling against the "torture of […] interruptions," La Trobe maintains her bravery and pushes her audience towards a moment of communal self-reflection. After the Victorian period, La Trobe's script reads, "try ten mins. of present time. Swallows, cows, etc."[149] Woolf describes, "[s]he wanted to expose them, as it were, to douche them, with present-time reality."[150] The experiment is poorly received, with La Trobe theorizing that "reality" was "too strong," further thinking to herself that "[a]udiences were the devil!"[151] But the purported artistic failure, like Lily Briscoe's painting in *To the Lighthouse*, is a success in its formal innovation even as it fails in its reception. La Trobe, even in this moment of tension, "felt everything they felt," suggesting a more authentic convergence between writer and audience, who think, "So that was her little game! To show us up, as we are, here and how."[152] Despite La Trobe's anxieties, and the obstinate audience response, the playwright pushes the audience towards the production of collective consensus; Woolf's efforts to confront the "hollowness" of both "aesthetic

---

[146] Virginia Woolf, *Between the Acts* (New York: Harcourt, [1941] 2008), p. 131.
[147] Woolf, *Between the Acts*, p. 103.
[148] Matthew Weber, "Those Dots: Suspension and Interruption in Virginia Woolf's Three Guineas and between the Acts," *Journal of Modern Literature* 40, no. 3 (2017), p. 27.
[149] Woolf, *Between the Acts*, p. 122.   [150] Woolf, *Between the Acts*, p. 122.
[151] Woolf, *Between the Acts*, p. 122.   [152] Woolf, *Between the Acts*, p. 126.

sovereignty" and "sovereignty in general" are best understood in the complexity of La Trobe's efforts at inducing group cohesion.[153] Facing the mirrors La Trobe has positioned to make her point clear, the audience "saw themselves, not whole by any means, but at any rate sitting still."[154] Despite her audience's collective confusion and even aggression, La Trobe succeeds in pushing this muddled group of individuals to share their thoughts and feelings, even inching them close to a collective consciousness: " 'That's them,' the back rows were tittering. 'Must we submit passively to this malignant indignity?' the front row demanded. Each turned ostensibly to say—O whatever came handy—to his neighbor. Each tried to shift an inch or two beyond the inquisitive insulting eye. Some made as if to go."[155] La Trobe's self-reflexive final act pushes the audience to come to a "common conclusion," albeit a defiant one. It introduces what Pridmore-Brown calls a "communal enterprise," whereby "members of the audience are players implicated in what they observe."[156] Their failure to recognize their agency before the final speech of the play, far from condemning it a failure, is an embrace of the prospect of a heterogeneous public opinion, one that takes its lead not from the braying of the wireless or the ticking of a gramophone, but from re-centering energy on the individual subject, and giving citizens the agency and empowerment to voluntarily proffer their views to one another, and to themselves.

Between the Acts, like the many texts addressed in this chapter, deploys the elastic symbolism of the wireless to theorize the proper role of public opinion research in institutional discourse. As this chapter has demonstrated, public opinion research was not only a prominent feature within institutions like the BBC, but was also a practice readily theorized using the wireless as sign. The ominous opacity of both the wireless and public opinion facilitated this convenient figurative confluence; the science of wireless transmission, in the works of Stapledon and Woolf, "reintroduces the mystical world of unseen forces."[157] Concerns over public opinion polling, much like those over the radio during the war, centered on the power of this technology in manipulating private thought and harnessing a dangerous, unilateral

---

[153] Andrew John Miller, " 'Our Representative, Our Spokesman': Modernity, Professionalism, and Representation in Virginia Woolf's *Between the Acts*," *Studies in the Novel* 33, no. 1 (2001), p. 36.
[154] Woolf, *Between the Acts*, p. 126.   [155] Woolf, *Between the Acts*, pp. 126–7.
[156] Michele Pridmore-Brown, "1939–40: Of Virginia Woolf, Gramophones, and Fascism," *PMLA* 113, no. 3 (1998), p. 410.
[157] Pridmore-Brown, "1939–40: Of Virginia Woolf," p. 409.

control over publics. But, in what continues to be a dominant theme in this book, the threats posed by public opinion also generated optimistic visions of a new technology capable of uniting the masses, of producing more cohesive communities, and inspiring utopian versions of the collective. The aspirational collective consciousnesses theorized by both Stapledon and Woolf attest to this. This aspirational vision of polling even inspired new interpretations of the practice of polling itself. The material theorization of "ourselves," a recurrent chorus in Woolf's novel that spoke to its utopian impulses, would be the backbone of the most experimental, utopian polling effort of the mid-century: Mass-Observation.

4

The Gender of Public Opinion

Naomi Mitchison, Celia Fremlin, and the Women of Mass-Observation

Introduction: Poll-Consciousness and the Emergence of Mass-Observation

The previous two chapters of this book have traced responses to the rise of quantitative public opinion polling within mid-century writing, mapping the diverse and contradictory reactions to polling as it became increasingly commonplace in English culture before World War II. Aided by the popularity of the Peace Ballot and the publication of British Institute of Public Opinion polls in *News Chronicle*, the interwar witnessed the rapid emergence of "poll-consciousness," a necessary catalyst for the transition to modern psychographics. There are several key aspects of poll-consciousness worthy of emphasis. First, poll-consciousness suggests, in the most obvious sense, the awareness of public opinion polling as an emergent cultural practice. As this practice concretized, poll-consciousness actively synthesized two discursive fields: psychology and politics. Poll-consciousness enabled new interventions into these fields, leading to the construction of new infrastructures responding to each. Psychologically, the poll-conscious individual sees herself as not just an object of study, but as one node within a network of others who also share in the vision of the psychological self as a point of data. She sees her own opinions as discrete objects, marketable products in their own right. As historians such as Sarah Igo and Dan Bouk have suggested, the rise of poll-consciousness in the 1930s marks "a broad shift in consciousness linked to the technologies of social surveying."[1] When Virginia Woolf argues in her 1938 polemic *Three Guineas* that "private judgment is *still* free in private," the phrasing at first seems highly tautological;

---

[1] Igo, *The Averaged American*, p. 21. Dan Bouk presents similar arguments in *How Our Days Became Numbered: Risk and the Rise of the Statistical Individual* (Chicago, IL: University of Chicago, 2015).

Public Opinion Polling in Mid-Century British Literature: The Psychographic Turn. Megan Faragher, Oxford University Press. © Megan Faragher 2021. DOI: 10.1093/oso/9780192898975.003.0005

private judgment is, by self-definition, private.[2] But the inclusion of the word "still" suggests that, for Woolf, the privacy of private judgment is newly under siege in the interwar period. If private judgment is "still" free, it may not be so in the near future; by the time Woolf was writing, such cautious sentiments were an emergent mode of response to the transformation of private belief into a public commodity. Poll-consciousness plumbed the depths of private judgment and brought the results into the public sphere for scrutiny, reinterpreted as both a product and a service. But other thinkers of the period were likewise aware of this cultural transformation. Woolf's subtle dirge for the traditional alliance between privacy and freedom testifies to the emergent "connection between the reification of consciousness and established sociology" which Theodor Adorno diagnosed in his postwar book *Introduction to Sociology*; as Adorno argues, the unfreedom of consciousness and its reification at the hands of a "functioning administrating apparatus" lead it to "congeal into something solid."[3] The bevy of polling institutions that arose in every conceivable field of public life in the mid-century catalyzed the solidity Adorno cites, publicized through the production and distribution of polling in the press. This objectification of private opinion is the first of the two major facets of poll-consciousness.[4]

Another pertinent impact of poll-consciousness consists of the successful marketing of polling as a new, compulsory form of democratic praxis. As I argued in Chapter 2, much of the clamor around polling centered on its potentiality as a new, democratic institutional apparatus. Structurally homologous to casting a ballot, people imagined polling as a means to force increasingly opaque governmental bureaucracies to be responsive to the needs of a public whose private thoughts were now subject to objectification and quantification. Of course, there was no real obligation for the government to listen to polls or to respond to them, but failure to participate nevertheless precluded the dialogic relationship between citizen and government from ever taking place. First sold as a new opportunity for citizens, polling quickly became a new responsibility.

As a result of increasing poll-consciousness, public opinion survey organizations multiplied in the 1930s, their growth best conceptualized as mitotic, with new groups duplicating those which already existed, sometimes

---

[2] Woolf, *Three Guineas*, p. 99, emphasis added.
[3] Theodor Adorno, *Introduction to Sociology* (Stanford, CA: Stanford University Press, [1962] 1999), p. 149.
[4] Aside from Gallup's institution of AIPO in 1935, Elmo Roper began polling in the pages of *Fortune*; BIPO and M-O were founded subsequently.

including the same people and methods and at other times presenting modifications from previous forms. But Mass-Observation (M-O), the famous project of social observation that aimed to produce an "anthropology of ourselves," complicated early visions of polling through the promotion of *qualitative* observation as a crucial tool for assessing public opinion; in so doing, M-O proposed a variant on the statistical models put forth by academic sociology and the British Institute of Public Opinion.[5] Co-founded by Tom Harrisson and Charles Madge, Mass-Observation aimed, as Julian Huxley put it, to "[disclose] ourselves to ourselves by the application of scientific methods of observation and record," including the work of trained interviewers and diligent note-taking on everyday behavior by observers, both expert and novice.[6] In several ways, M-O's mission aligned with the views of sociological utopians like H.G. Wells and Olaf Stapledon; M-O even cited Wells in multiple venues as a key supporter of the project.[7] In particular, M-O co-founder Tom Harrisson saw public opinion research as capable of producing a new cultural self-awareness that would dialectize the relationship between the masses and sociology. He argued that his army of observers would usher in "a band of socially-minded and scientifically-minded people within the community at large."[8] As poll-consciousness emerged as a dominant ideological framework, M-O's mission was to aid the public in adapting to it, bolstering the theory that participation in polling culture would buttress democracy. But M-O remained more cautious than some about the mechanics that formed public opinion to begin with, consistently arguing that learning what people believed was much more difficult than simply asking them. In the operations of Mass-Observation, this inherent contradiction manifested itself in decisions about public opinion research methodology. M-O maintained a complicated relationship with the commodification of public opinion, as it publicly railed against the toxic influence of commercialism on the field of social analysis while simultaneously embracing commission-based work for private companies

---

[5] Tom Harrisson and Charles Madge, *Mass-Observation* (London: Frederick Muller, 1937), p. 10.

[6] Julian Huxley, "Preface," *Mass-Observation* (London: Frederick Muller, 1937), p. 6.

[7] Wells is referenced as providing "general criticism and advice" in the production of *War Begins at Home*. Mary Adams lists Wells as a reference for Mass-Observation's work. See Harrisson and Madge, *Mass-Observation*; Mass-Observation, *War Begins at Home* (London: Faber & Faber, [1940] 2001), p. 24; Mary Adams to Ivison Macadam, March 8, 1940, Mary Adams Papers, SxMOA 4/1/2/2, University of Sussex Special Collections.

[8] Harrisson and Madge, *Mass-Observation*, p. 6.

and government agencies to financially maintain its operations.[9] In other words, M-O embraced the part of poll-consciousness that encouraged a revival of democratic principles while eschewing the concomitant com-modification of the psyche underway in market research, spearheaded by American corporations. Suffice it to say, they were not entirely successful; walking such a tightrope was impossible.

By focusing on the internal tension in Mass-Observation and its public reception, this chapter has two goals. The first is to examine M-O's method-ological approach (or, more accurately, approaches) to public opinion data in light of the institutional and academic pressures that existed in a field overwhelmingly predisposed towards quantitative methodologies, like those of the British Institute of Public Opinion. While the first chapters of this book articulated the aesthetic responses to public opinion research as either highly utopian or uniformly skeptical, this chapter and the following chapter on the Ministry of Information's Home Intelligence Department detail individual cultural institutions grappling with the troubling duality of poll-consciousness I have outlined; as they did so, these institutions contin-ued to elevate the profile of polling practices and ensconced public opinion research as a dominant and essential part of public political life, an ethos that would become further entrenched in the postwar period. M-O's unique methods of research, including not just polling, but also in-person free-form interviews, diaries of self-selected observers, and written recordings of overheard conversations, presented a stark alternative to the supposedly neater quantitative methods of other organizations. By attempting to find a synthesis between the technocratically inflected academic field and the flux of human experience, M-O imagined a fully inclusive method of data col-lection. I will argue that these efforts led to increased cultural reflection on the gender of public opinion science in the 1930s, as revealed in the novels of Naomi Mitchison and Celia Fremlin, both of whom worked for M-O.

The second aim of this chapter is to identify writers who resisted bureau-cratic pressures towards a quantitative approach to public opinion polling. Certainly, Tom Harrisson's writings challenged the fetishization of the sta-tistical "fact" and proclaimed the value of qualitative and humanistic approaches to polling. But Mass-Observation also sought to "recruit from

---

[9] Histories of Mass-Observation, including those of James Hinton and Nick Hubble, further assess the history of M-O's patronage by corporations and government agencies. In the open-ing chapter of *War Begins at Home*, M-O cites a variety of institutional patrons, including the BBC, London Press Exchange, and the Ministry of Information. Mass-Observation, *War Begins at Home*, p. 23.

all classes, from all localities and from every single shade of opinion."[10] In doing so, M-O opened itself to the influence of a diverse and varied group of observers often excluded by both the disciples of academia and the corporate public relations experts who organized traditional surveys. While early academics and researchers, predominantly male, saw the public opinion apparatus as a means of extending a democratic voice to all, the methods and practices to collect that data were inexcusably blind to the interests of many traditionally underserved communities, particularly women. As demonstrated in the fiction of Celia Fremlin and Naomi Mitchison, the quantitative analysis favored by the academic sociological community was particularly inept at collecting data from women and failed to incorporate women in the administrative and bureaucratic positions which might remedy this problem. To some extent, the diversity of Mass-Observation addressed concerns Mitchison raised in her unpublished writings, that "all historians have been men" and the "nearer we get to the human side to truth [...] the more we find that the sex of the seeker or researcher or writer makes a great difference to the result."[11] M-O, though founded by three men, was patronized and influenced by women who attempted to remedy this gender bias in social surveys through a qualitative and inclusive approach. Likewise, the early practices of M-O, which incorporated a variety of methods to gather inclusive data, forged an alternative path for the future development of psychographic study. As Fremlin and Mitchison aided in the collection and publication of data for Mass-Observation, they were likewise identifying, through their fiction, the ways that the administrative and bureaucratic fetish for patriarchal technocracy threatened to limit women's access to the democratic expression of their views, promoting what Donna Haraway calls "situated and embodied knowledges."[12] Fremlin and Mitchison identified what Adorno had also noted after the war: sociology's new "idol," the "concept of fact," was, in fact, "amputating [...] experience."[13] Both authors attempt to reclaim the value of experience as an egalitarian method of wrestling with the patriarchal underpinnings of polling culture.

---

[10] Harrisson and Madge, *Mass-Observation*, p. 52.

[11] Jill Benton, *Naomi Mitchison: A Century of Experiment in Life and Letters* (Kitchener, ON: Pandora Press, 1990), p. 74.

[12] Donna Haraway argues that situated knowledges "require that the object of knowledge be pictured as an actor and agent." Donna Haraway, "Situated Knowledges: The Science Question in Feminism and the Privilege of Partial Perspective," *Feminist Studies* 14, no. 3 (1988), p. 592.

[13] Adorno, *Introduction to Sociology*, pp. 148–9.

The Debate over the Soul of Social Psychology

Aside from Naomi Mitchison and Celia Fremlin, many everyday citizens contributed to M-O's information-gathering efforts through the sharing of private journals and diaries. Such methods of observation, which did not require academic training, were more available and accessible for women who wanted to participate. But such methods were not widely recognized within the burgeoning world of academic sociology. In both academic journals and public discourse, Henry Durant's Gallup-inspired quantitative methods were by far the most popular, cited as the most "scientific" of the available methods of assessing public opinion. While the publication of BIPO's polling in *News Chronicle* attests to this fact, the pages of the journal *Public Opinion Quarterly* demonstrate academia's similar preference for quantitative sociological methods. In the third issue of *POQ*, Walter A. Lurie stated definitively that any questions a manufacturer might have about the wishes of his customers are "basic questions which the *quantitative* methods were developed to answer."[14] But *POQ* did not entirely ignore the work of Mass-Observation, either. The journal's attitude towards M-O in its first years was decidedly mixed, though typically pessimistic. In 1938, Paul Lazarsfeld and Marjorie Fiske looked at M-O with some optimism, but argued that the attitudes of observers tainted their work, making it "more detached and conscious"; they concluded that M-O suffered from a "problem of [...] representativeness."[15] Lazarsfeld had earlier toyed with the idea of detailed interviews as a basis for marketing polls in an article for *The Journal of Marketing* but affirmed that such qualitative data was only credible if "submitted to adequate *statistical* treatment."[16] In 1940, *POQ* followed *News Chronicle* in announcing a "new section featuring measurement of public opinion," reprinting the results of Gallup polling in its pages and

---

[14] Walter A. Lurie, "Statistics and Public Opinion," *The Public Opinion Quarterly* (October 1937), p. 78, emphasis added.
[15] Paul Lazarsfeld and Marjorie Fiske, "The 'Panel' as a New Tool for Measuring Opinion," *The Public Opinion Quarterly* 2, no. 4 (1938), p. 611. Lazarsfeld and Jahoda's study of unemployment, *Mariennthal* (1933) was highly influential to Harrisson in his survey of Yorktown. James Hinton, *The Mass Observers: A History, 1937–1949* (Oxford: Oxford UP, 2013), p. 79. Both Lazarsfeld and, even more so, Marie Jahoda, critiqued M-O's methods harshly; the latter even calls *The War at Home* a "slovenly" book. Marie Jahoda, "Letter," *Tribune*, June 4, 1943, Mary Adams Papers, SxMs12/2/2/5, University of Sussex Special Collections.
[16] Paul Lazarsfeld, "The Use of Detailed Interviews in Market Research," *The Journal of Marketing* 2, no. 1 (1937), p. 3, emphasis added.

indicating a clear endorsement of statistical methodology over that of M-O.[17] The pages of *POQ* testified to the fact that academia viewed quantitative data as more reliable due to its impersonal and mathematical approach; while M-O's methods were intellectually stimulating, they purportedly lacked probative value.

Interwar novels referencing M-O, like Cecil Day-Lewis's pseudony-mously published *The Smiler with the Knife*, underscore not only the public skepticism about M-O's methods, but reveal the cultural assumptions that underwrote processes of observation. In the novel, the detective Nigel Strangeways' wife, Georgia, infiltrates a pro-Nazi English political party to thwart a fascist coup. In an amusing scene, Georgia tries to hide herself from some would-be fascist assassins by borrowing a costume from a group of "four, five, six Father Christmases."[18] She offers to pay for the privilege of becoming a cross-dressing Santa, but the man donning the jolly suit states, "I thought, when you asked me, you wur one of them Mass Observers they writes about in the papers." Georgia retorts with a bit of irony, "No. I'm just one of the mass-observed."[19] The ludicrous notion of an observer taking cover as a benign Father Christmas and watching the oblivious public incites the sort of mockery that sometimes met early incursions of Mass-Observation into the sphere of public scrutiny; after all, what could be more instinctively vile than Saint Nick surreptitiously reporting to the authorities on the behaviors of holiday shoppers? And while this vignette underscores anxieties over the invasive possibility of instituting, as Julian Huxley describes M-O's mission in his preface to *Mass-Observation*, "the observa-tion by everyone of everyone," it also highlights the public's gendered expectations around observation: that any proper sociological observer should at least *appear* male, even if that requires a bit of cross-dressing.[20] When Georgia reverses Santa's hypothesis to argue that *she* is the observed—the victim of the violent gaze of male political rivals—she subtly reinforces this gendered dynamic; observers are meant to be masculine predators, hunters of women and, in this case, they are actually seeking to kill her and install a fascist state in England. The scene, for all its humor, alludes to dire concerns about gender and social observation that emerged with more

---

[17] British Institute of Public Opinion, "Public Opinion Survey," *Public Opinion Quarterly* 4, no. 1 (1940), p. 75.
[18] Nicholas Blake, *The Smiler with the Knife* (New York: Harper & Row, [1939] 1978), p. 216.
[19] Blake, *The Smiler with the Knife*, p. 217.
[20] Harrisson and Madge, *Mass-Observation*, p. 10.

prominence during the war.[21] As I will address in the final chapter of this book, the Ministry of Information's "Silent Column" campaign, discouraging the public sharing of information, only exacerbated these concerns.

Day-Lewis's *The Smiler with the Knife* subtly alludes to an assumption about observation solidified by academic public opinion research: that it is a field dominated by men. The nascent field of academic public opinion research, directed as it was by male academics, viewed Mass-Observation as a bit of an eccentric outsider; in *The War Begins at Home*, M-O even admits it is "regarded as rather a rough customer and outsider by professional sociologists."[22] One anecdote puts this division between M-O's methods and academic sociology clearly in focus: the April 1942 meeting of the British Psychological Association. In this meeting, Tom Harrisson defended M-O's methods against Henry Durant, the head of the British Institute of Public Opinion.[23] The debate was meant to determine which methodology, quantitative or qualitative, was most useful in the collection of public opinion data. Mass-Observation defended a qualitative approach to the question of public opinion over a quantitative one, even if their work had originally sought a "method of co-ordination" between their work and that of academic social scientists and had often incorporated quantitative methods.[24] Durant's work aligned more closely to popular trends of the time, as he promoted use of statistical surveys to quantify public responses to any number of political or social issues of the day.

Durant favorably compared quantitative methods of BIPO to the popular field of psychoanalysis. Taking his audience back to Freud's *Project for a Scientific Psychology*, Durant renewed Freud's reputation within the network of "hard" scientists, arguing that "it is possible to point to quantitative elements in a discipline so 'qualitative' as psychoanalysis," further citing Freud's theory of displaced energy to support his claim.[25] Durant's efforts to claim

---

[21] A reference in Blake's *The Beast Must Die* is equally flippant. "Why is it all generals are kindly...whereas colonels are invariably bores...? A subject 'Mass-Observation' might investigate." Nicholas Blake, *The Beast Must Die* (Ipso Books, [1938] 2017), p. 28.

[22] Mass-Observation, *War Begins at Home*, p. 14. It is important to note that Harrisson's relationship to academia was complicated, as James Hinton observes. He describes the "pleasure of irritating the academic bourgeois" (Hinton, *The Mass Observers*, p. 90).

[23] Durant and Harrisson also occasionally joined forces; in a 1939 memo to Home Intelligence's Mary Adams, Harrisson cites meetings with Durant to plan the co-ordination of social research during the war. Mary Adams to Tom Harrisson, November 6, 1939, Mary Adams Papers, SxMOA 4/4/6/1, University of Sussex Special Collections.

[24] Harrisson and Madge, *Mass-Observation*, p. 33.

[25] "Quantitative and Qualitative Method in Sociological Research," *Nature* 149, no. 3784 (1942), p. 517.

Freud a proper quant are clever; by utilizing the part of Freud's work most quantitative in nature, Durant appropriates the cultural capital of Freud, a thinker M-O often cited as a key methodological influence.[26] If Durant insisted that all qualitative work (like that of M-O) be validated only if met with a "vigorous insistence upon exact statistical measurement," Harrisson expectedly argued against the foundations of this assessment. He "reject[ed] the conception that such research must be predominantly quantitative," arguing that it should "be *secondarily* quantitative."[27] The practical goal of quantitative analysis, for Harrisson, had always been the evaluation of humanity from a qualitative perspective; math was not useful in itself, but was useful only because it told a story. And, to that extent, quantitative analysis owed any success it had to the work of those who were not afraid of telling those stories.

But while both Harrisson and Durant, the two men featured in the pages of *Nature*, sought to bestow upon themselves the laurel wreath of science to justify their methods, thus confirming the notion that "the field of science is a field of struggles," the gendered bias that underpinned such approaches went uncommented on by both.[28] Virginia Woolf was well aware of this problem in *Three Guineas*, claiming that "[s]cience, it would seem, is not sexless; she is a man, a father, and infected."[29] Other women likewise noted the folly of bestowing upon science too firm a claim to authenticity and accuracy. The same year as Mass-Observation published *Britain*, a book trumpeting the need for a revolutionary new science, Naomi Mitchison makes an aside about the subject of statistical analysis in her book *The Moral Basis of Politics* (1938). While tempted to have faith in data and statistics as supposedly unbiased, she stops herself short of such a suggestion: "Socially unbiased mathematics is probably usual, though I should never be surprised to find that there too propaganda has crept in; biased scientific writing and for that matter biased research, is certainly not rare (think of what fun one can have with graphs and charts!)"[30] Borrowing from her friend Gerald Heard, who believed that "ignorance of their own psyche" led scientists to impose false "rationality" on psychological discourse, Mitchison,

---

[26] Nick Hubble notes that "in later life [Charles] Madge acknowledges the importance of Freud's *Psychopathology of Everyday Life* to Mass-Observation." Nick Hubble, *Mass-Observation and Everyday Life* (London: Palgrave, 2006), p. 13.

[27] "Quantitative and Qualitative Method," pp. 517, 514, emphasis added.

[28] Pierre Bourdieu, "The Peculiar History of Scientific Reason," *Sociological Forum* 6, no. 1 (1991), p. 8.

[29] Woolf, *Three Guineas*, p. 139.

[30] Naomi Mitchison, *The Moral Basis of Politics* (London: Constable, 1939), p. 155.

too, finds an inherent bias in the purportedly rationalistic discourse of the sciences.[31] While Durant and Harrisson both feverishly sought the validation the label of "science" proffered in the British Psychological Association debate, plenty of voices—particularly the voices of women—challenged this fetishization of science at its foundations. While science presumes the "objective truth of the product," the product of science, even "the 'purest' science" is born of a "social field like any other, with its distribution of power and its monopolies," a point Pierre Bourdieu is quick to remind us of.[32] And, as women who encountered this discipline recognized, such a social field was highly exclusive, and significantly male-oriented. The conflation between the masculine and the scientific bled into M-O publication practices as well. For one, Celia Fremlin's *War Factory*, published by M-O, was never attributed to her in full, despite the fact that Harrisson asked her to write it, she received only a pittance in payment, and "[Harrisson] never told [publisher] Gollancz who had written it."[33] It is not clear what Harrisson's motivation would have been to deny Fremlin credit for her work, but it is certainly possible that hopes of achieving scientific sanction from traditional academics based on the authority of his sex might have been a factor in his decision.

Despite contemporaneous critiques of the weak underpinnings of science's cultural capital coming from writers like Mitchison and Woolf, the fetish for quantitative analysis was unflappable. On the one side, Durant never relented in advocating Gallup's methods of statistical analysis, reportedly stating that "even one figure arrived at roughly marks an enormous improvement, mathematically an infinite gain."[34] Durant's perspective would eventually win the day in public opinion research. And, in some ways, by the April 1942 meeting of the British Psychological Association, it already had. Despite arguing in 1937 that science suffered "from a bias towards the academic," by 1942 even Mass-Observation had begun to transform under market pressures.[35] Though Harrisson argued that "statistical analysis ran the risk of providing a 'false' picture" of reality, Dorothy Sheridan notes that the collaboration between M-O and the Ministry of

[31] Heard, *The Ascent of Humanity*, p. 29.
[32] Pierre Bourdieu, "The Specificity of the Scientific Field and the Social Conditions of the Progress of Reason," *Social Science Information* 14, no. 6 (1975), p. 19.
[33] Angus Calder interview with Celia Fremlin, 1980, Angus Calder Papers, SxMOA28/7/33, University of Sussex Special Collections.
[34] "Quantitative and Qualitative Method," p. 517.
[35] Harrisson and Madge, *Mass-Observation*, p. 52.

Information would put M-O on track to align itself with the "relentless movement towards large quantitative surveys" in the 1940s and 1950s.[36] Histories of M-O repeatedly note that the Ministry, while hiring M-O to conduct its research, also demanded more palatable and digestible *statistical* data. Harrisson may not have realized it yet, but the sun was setting on M-O's innovative methods of qualitative sociological research.

Scholars have noted that the intersectional approach of M-O leached into literary and aesthetic circles. Obviously, many in literary studies have taken great interest in the convergence of the relationship between M-O's methods and literary movements. Nick Hubble and Thomas Davis have reflected on the relationship between M-O and various aesthetic movements, including experimental documentary and surrealism.[37] M-O's anthropological practices have likewise been tied to a kind of experimental realism in prose form, as argued by James Purdon; still others have discussed Harrisson's history as an anthropologist, or the work of Charles Madge as a poet.[38] But few have addressed the way that M-O was necessarily responding, and reacting, to a cultural environment awash with competing sources of public opinion. Understood in the light of the previous chapters of this book, M-O's history can be understood not only as an innovative form of self-anthropology, which it was, but also as a critical rejoinder to public opinion research to that point. Mass-Observation was not just a mirror against which the British could see themselves; it was also a mirror that reflected early twentieth-century sociology, including its inherent biases.

---

[36] "Quantitative and Qualitative Method," p. 517; Dorothy Sheridan, "Reviewing Mass-Observation: The Archive and its Researchers Thirty Years On," *Forum: Qualitative Social Research* 1, no. 3, 2000.

[37] For more on the intersection between Mass-Observation and literary movements, see Thomas Davis, *The Extinct Scene: Late Modernism and Everyday Life* (Columbia, 2015) and Hubble, *Mass-Observation and Everyday Life*.

[38] James Purdon's "Information Collectives," in *Modernist Informatics: Literature, Information, and the State* (Oxford: Oxford University Press, 2015), addresses the intersection between John Sommerfield's *May Day* and Mass-Observation's methods. More on Tom Harrisson's approach to Mass-Observation can be found in Nick Hubble's *Mass-Observation and Everyday Life*. See also Benjamin Kohlmann, "Social Facts and Poetic Authority: The Political Aesthetic of Mass-Observation," in *Committed Styles: Modernism, Politics, and Left-Wing Literature in the 1930s* (Oxford: Oxford University Press, 2004), Nick Hubble, "The Intermodern Assumption of the Future: William Empson, Charles Madge and Mass-Observation," in *Intermodernism: Literary Culture in Mid-Twentieth-Century Britain*, edited by Kristin Bluemel (Edinburgh: Edinburgh University Press, 2009), pp. 171–88 and James Hinton's chapter on Madge in *The Mass Observers*.

Whose Utopia? Women in 1930s Polling

While public perception relegated women to the periphery of sociological study, politically savvy women were well aware of the exclusionary nature of the field of sociological analysis and keen to find ways to circumvent the traditional institutional apparatuses that overlooked them. The possibility of women breaking into this new field of social analysis attracted writers like Naomi Mitchison, who worked and supported Mass-Observation's efforts in the late 1930s. Mitchison endorsed M-O's efforts to compensate for what she called the "incomplete data" around what people want during wartime; she even encouraged the readers of *The Moral Basis of Politics* to become mass observers themselves.[39] For her, qualitative sociological methods, which included transcribed conversations and local reporting, effectively captured human behavior at its most "irrational"; Mitchison interpreted such unmediated access to political sentiment as key to rooting out fascism.[40] Even before she contributed to M-O, her work alludes to the exclusion of women within fields of hard mathematics and science. Two years before she promoted the work of M-O in *The Moral Basis of Politics*, Mitchison's collection of short stories, *The Delicate Fire* (1933), repeatedly alludes to the inherent social and cultural capital of mathematics and, as biographer Jill Benton argues, it is also "a brave effort to forge a work fully embracing feminine sensibilities."[41] In this early work, Mitchison grapples with the gendered relationship between math and politics. It is only in her later fiction, after she takes up her work with M-O, that Mitchison is able to appropriately diagnose this problem, embracing experiential data as a means of thwarting the exclusionary nature of quantitative social science in the interwar period.

The Delicate Fire, previewing the themes of her 1935 novel *We Have Been Warned*, demonstrated surprising prescience in its diagnosis of the political conflicts which would soon consume Europe and acted, as one early critic wrote, "as a terrible warning to other bourgeois democracies."[42] The stories within *The Delicate Fire* repeatedly address themes of war, authoritarianism, and sexual violence, which she sets within the context of Ancient Greece.

---

[39] Mitchison, *The Moral Basis of Politics*, 320. Also see James Hinton's *The Mass Observers* and "The Mobilisation of Everyday Life," in Nick Hubble's *Mass-Observation in Everyday Life*, pp. 165–200.

[40] Mitchison, *The Moral Basis of Politics*, p. 320.   [41] Benton, *Naomi Mitchison*, p. 90.

[42] Kenneth Wiggins Porter, "Naomi Mitchison: The Development of a Revolutionary Novelist," *Social Science* 14, no. 3 (1939), p. 257.

Most of the allegorical stories in the collection trace the rise and fall of Arkas, a Mantinean who escapes slavery only to become a slave master himself; he behaves cruelly to those who enslaved him and tore him from his family. The series of short stories end with Arkas's slaves, including his sister Kleta, rebelling against the violent slave-turned-slaver, thus restoring a democratic order by the narrative's end. In tracing the transformation of slave to slaveholder, Mitchison narrativizes the banality of evil and warns readers of the creeping nature of social violence. But additionally, and more importantly for my purposes, *The Delicate Fire* sets the stage for her to explore more thoroughly the intersection between politics and statistical science, a theme she takes up again in other works of mid-century fiction.

In the short stories of *The Delicate Fire*, Mitchison links the social and cultural power of mathematics to anti-authoritarianism, but also recognizes that the ability to utilize mathematics as a master-dismantling tool is highly circumscribed by gender. When Aglaos, brother-in-law to Arkas, tells his story of being ripped from his wife Kleta and their newborn child, he imagines a world in which his knowledge of math would raise him above the toil and labor he would face as a slave, wishing he had a "special skill at doctoring or writing quickly in a good hand, or mathematics, or dialectic even."[43] For Aglaos, mastery of such a skill would make him particularly marketable and would substantively change his conditions as a slave. For men, the acquisition of mathematical skills is of immediate practicable use and presents additional opportunities. By opening her series of short stories with a reference to the value of such skills for one male slave, she allows the reader to contrast Aglaos's reflection on mathematics with that of other characters, particularly women.

While Aglaos can imagine his mastery of math saving him from brutal conditions, for women in *The Delicate Fire* the ability to transform knowledge into cultural capital is far more elusive. In another of her linked stories, Mitchison describes the history of brother and sister, Antander and Nikippe, both mathematically minded, tracing their capture and sale as slaves. After her captors sell her, Nikippe desperately tries to avoid being raped by her new male master. Mitchison paints Nikippe as rebellious, independent, strong, and fearless. She takes whippings instead of succumbing to the master's advances, even boldly resisting the slaver's efforts to rape her by

---

[43] Naomi Mitchison, *The Delicate Fire* (Edinburgh: Kennedy & Boyd, [1933] 2012), p. 82.

throwing a rock at a hornet's nest, raising the hornets against her master.[44] But when the slaver threatens to separate her from her brother if she does not relent, Nikippe's confidant Batalé tries to convince her to submit to the sexual aggression she faces. "But you do want to stay with [Antander], don't you?" Batalé asks. When Nikippe assents, Batalé euphemistically requests that she "be a good girl" and that "[t]hings are all right if you don't keep on remembering back so hard."[45] At this point, Nikippe fully accepts the dire fate awaiting her. Faced with the devastating reality of imminent rape, Nikippe turns to math as a method of mental dissociation to manage her internal crisis. She "waited, trying first to think of nothing, and then to think about angles and planes and the startling occurrence of large prime numbers in the orderly world of arithmetic."[46] Nikippe adopts the strategies of dissociation Batalé advises, envisioning the order implied by mathematics and logic as a contrast to the emotional chaos of her victimization. But Nikippe's citation of mathematics differs from Aglaos's; mathematics does not enable her any *actual* escape from rape and torture. Aglaos might leverage his knowledge to secure more amenable conditions under slavery, but Nikippe cannot. For her, mathematics stands as anathema to the complexity of traumatic experience; it flattens and hardens the reality of trauma, allowing her assimilation into the cruelty of patriarchy. Despite her skills, Nikippe's position as a sexual object overdetermines her value within her culture. In showing a comparison between she and her brother, Mitchison obliquely attacks the patriarchal networks of scientific discourse that historically excluded women, a problem she was concretely aware of as a girl growing up in a house of male scientists, precluded from following in their footsteps.[47]

The conspicuous and "orderly world of arithmetic" arises in *The Delicate Fire*'s stories at moments when the crisis of the slave-owning culture

---

[44] This unique method of destabilizing patriarchal authority comes from Mitchison's childhood, where she and other children threw rocks at beehives to distress "distinguished generals and philosophers." Jenni Calder, *The Nine Lives of Naomi Mitchison* (London: Virago, 1997), p. 4.

[45] Mitchison, *The Delicate Fire*, p. 128.   [46] Mitchison, *The Delicate Fire*, p. 128.

[47] Jill Benton's *Naomi Mitchison: A Century of Experiment in Life and Letters* details compelling stories of Mitchison's experiences as a daughter of a scientist and, perhaps, a frustrated scientist herself. She writes: "The young Naomi learnt to be scientifically observant, a skill that has stood her in good stead through a long lifetime of writing. By the age of 11 she was a competent field botanist who wanted to be a scientist when she grew up. This was not to be; she never pursued the education necessary for a career in science, nor was she ever encouraged to do so," Benton, *Naomi Mitchison*, p. 6.

crescendos. Faced with rape, Nikippe fantasizes about the stability mathematics provide, using it as a tool of mental dissociation as she steels herself for her violation. In suggesting the supposedly contradictory relationship between the dissociative impact of mathematics and the experiential richness of social relations, Mitchison alludes to the controversies that hindered social psychology in its earliest stages and would continue to haunt polling methodologies into the interwar period. Social psychologist Hadley Cantril suggested as much when he intoned the problems of applying laboratory conditions of science to "the ordinary affairs of social life."[48] When Cantril wrote this in 1934, he remained unsatisfied that the field had properly synthesized the tools of scientific and mathematical study with the murky, complex world of social relations. Nikippe's mathematical fantasy likewise alludes to the fissure between the worlds of science and society, as she seeks mathematics as a pure escape from the tortures of her sexual violation. For the tortured sister, mathematical purity acts as a means to escape unwieldy social relations, not necessarily master them.

Even in moments where Mitchison suggests scientific and mathematical logic as tools of resistance, men are more apt to access these tools than women. Before a slave rebellion against Arkas, both Aglaos and Kleta suggest that an affinity for mathematics serves as a precondition for revolt against authoritarianism. At this point in the narrative, Akras has taken Nikippe's brother, Antander, as a lover. Meanwhile, the victims of Arkas's cruelty have united against him. Kleta and her husband Aglaos find themselves in compromised positions; they are related to Akras but treated little better than the slaves who conspired to revolt. In the end, both join (and even lead) the ousting of Kleta's brother from power, though they advocate against his slaughter after the uprising succeeds. When the pair are considering likely allies, they think about Antander, wondering if he would side with the slaves or with his admirer Arkas. Aglaos asks Kleta whose side Antander would be on. Kleta states, "He's a mathematician."[49] It goes without saying, then, that the mathematician will join the rebellion against Arkas. She ends up being correct in her assumption that his affinity for math would coincide with a democratic, anti-authoritarian mindset when he joins the insurgency. In the cases of both brother and sister, mathematics acts as both a psychological tool to escape injustice and a possible means to reach a more equitable social structure. Antander's predilection towards mathematical

[48] Cantril, "The Social Psychology of Everyday Life," p. 297.
[49] Mitchison, *The Delicate Fire*, p. 231.

reasoning suggests his psychological resistance to slave-ownership and admiration for a society, as one freed slave states, where one can "do exactly what we like."[50] Alluding to the myriad ways that early 1930s writers compared the new field of political polling to the freedoms and liberties proffered by expanded democratic institutions, Mitchison's short stories in *The Delicate Fire* testify to an increased convergence between a love of liberty and a love of social science, allegorized through the tie between mathematics and slave rebellion. But while mathematics presents a potential means of escaping some of slavery's toil in these short stories, it also assures the continued political disenfranchisement of women within a society prohibiting them from fully weaponizing this form of mathematical democracy. While Mitchison's Greek narratives in *The Delicate Fire* allude to the rise of totalitarianism and fascist thinking in Europe, they also indicate the burgeoning power of sociology as it developed into a kind of science, able to make sense of chaotic social relations and bolster the resistance to socially sanctioned cruelty and violence. But it is only when she involves herself with Mass-Observation that Mitchison conceives of a version of social science capable of the degree of inclusion necessary for women's voices to be heard.

If *The Delicate Fire* suggests the gendered stratification of academic and mathematical discourse, writers who gave life to the quantitatively minded sociological utopias of the 1930s often did so through a highly paternalistic lens without recognizing any inherent bias. The novels of Wells and Stapledon are contingent on the establishment of specialized leaders with technocratic knowledge who kindly guide humanity towards its peaceable future; these guides to the modern paradise, like Dante's Virgil, are exclusively male. H.G. Wells's elevation of the social psychologist Gustave De Windt in *The Shape of Things to Come* (as discussed in Chapter 1) is just one example of this. Wells's novel is furthermore reinforced by a male narrative frame—the diary of Philip Raven—a fictional future historian who relates De Windt's writings to the reader. The framing speaker of Olaf Stapledon's *Star Maker* (discussed in Chapter 3) is also male; despite the fact that the interstellar species he observes are often asexually reproductive, the protagonist opens the novel by describing his marriage and wondering what his role as a part of a heterosexual coupling might say about the experience of love in the wider universe. The masculine framing in these novels reinforces the patriarchal nature of the psychographic revolutions the authors

---

[50] Mitchison, *The Delicate Fire*, p. 268.

dream of. And if these were the futures the authors desired, plenty of people were able to bear witness to their exclusionary nature. Interviewees featured in *Britain* by Mass-Observation cite Wells's utopia as a symptom of cultural elitism, resigning themselves to a technocratic future in which they, as the huddled masses, wielded no real power. As recorded in *Britain*, a shop assistant states, "I saw that film of H.G. Wells'—*Things to Come*. Makes you realize what things are going to be like. *They* know what they're talking about. If you don't know anything about things like that these days you don't get very far, because everything's specialised like."[51] Mass-Observation reports on Wells's *Things to Come* (of which there are several) all carry this tone; the future's scientific advancements are inaccessible to most people; as such, they will only exacerbate, not alleviate, preexisting social inequities. While Wells might have seen scientific achievements, like quantitative sociological study, saving humanity, Mass-Observation was quick to note the exclusionary nature of science in the eye of the public in *Britain*: "There is no indication that any scientist knows (or cares) what the Man in the Street actually thinks about science."[52] In the Wellsian scheme, if statistical analysis of public opinion offers the opportunity to save humanity, the argument follows that the real academic experts in the field, mostly men, will be the ones to lead us into the next stage of human evolution.

As I've suggested, the public perception of Mass-Observation was tainted by the gendered assumptions about academic social psychology. But this gendered bias also replicated itself in the ways that quantitative social analysis was conducted. Within the field of social surveys, particularly those spearheaded by BIPO, the prevalence of gender inequities was striking. For example, whenever BIPO founder Henry Durant mentions his interviewers, he genders them male. Even if one reads this as semantic slippage, Durant makes frequent claims throughout his various articles on polling about the limited use of women as both subjects and interviewers. In his essay on Gallup polling published in *The Journal of The Textile Institute*, he admits to limiting the number of women interviewed "to 30 or 40 per cent, because they are not so easy as men to interview."[53] By cutting down on the women interviewed, the remaining women came to overrepresent the views of women overall. In practice, this would have homogenized the perceived opinions of women in poll results and threatened to delegitimize the value of quantitative polling for capturing the views of women. Durant, furthermore,

---

[51] Mass-Observation, *Britain* (New York: Faber, [1939] 2007), p. 17.
[52] Mass-Observation, *Britain*, p. 14.   [53] Durant, "Gallup Surveys," p. 107.

argued that women, because they shied away from proffering interviews, should be dismissed in favor of their husbands, who might hold more self-assured answers to polling questions. By contrast, M-O made note of the social constraints leading women to avoid expressing opinions on controversial matters but continued, all the same, to record their opinions.[54] Durant's suggestion that women without forcible opinions might damage survey results registers an underlying bias towards those who already see themselves as political and social actors. As Bourdieu notes in his analysis of polling, "the particular propensity of those who were most economically and culturally deprived to abstain from replying to the most properly political questions still had to be related to the tendency to concentrate power in the hands of the leaders."[55] Bourdieu's suggestions about polling bias were realized even in polling's early years; the feedback loop between polling and public engagement meant that the limitation on women interviewees exacerbated any pre-existing alienation from the political process.

Equally distressing findings arise when reviewing Durant's methods of employing interviewers. While some have made the argument that housewives "formed the backbone of Durant's field force," there is plenty of evidence from Durant himself to suggest that this case may be overstated or even inaccurate.[56] When Durant characterized his labor force from the Workers Educational Association (WEA), he described them as an "average minus" group of workers good for the purposes of polling. And while there is evidence that the WEA had become more open to women by the time of the war, women remained underrepresented in WEA's ranks.[57] Whatever role women played in WEA's subcontracting for Durant, his own statements continually excluded women entirely when it came to sensitive polling topics. When discussing surveys about alcohol consumption, Durant expressed concern about the inebriated state of interviewees, noting that the related "danger can be minimized by using *only* male interviewers, since experience has shown to us that men interviewers produce better

---

[54] In *Britain*, Mass-Observation notes that, when asked about whether or not women were in favor of science, "about a third of the women asked, and a sixth of the men, said that they didn't understand about things like that." All the same, M-O did not exclude women for reasons of disinterest and recognizes male disinterest as well. Mass-Observation, *Britain*, p. 15.

[55] Bourdieu, "Opinion Polls: A 'Science' without a Scientist," p. 173.

[56] Roodhouse, "'Fish and Chip' Intelligence," p. 240.

[57] Olaf Stapledon's biographer, in exploring the history of underrepresentation of women as students at the WEA before World War I, notes only 15 percent were women; the student average climbed to nearly 45 percent by the end of the war. Crossley, *Olaf Stapledon*, p. 151.

results in this respect than women interviewers."[58] This tendency to alienate women from roles as interviewers and interviewees, supposedly in order to gather more accurate results, leads to obvious consequences. Having made assumptions about the inevitable social dynamics between men and women, Durant preemptively suggests limiting the role of women in the process of data collection on all sides. These exclusionary practices only reinforce and strengthen the obstacles women faced in their engagement with politics and the public sphere. By suggesting that women might not be suitable for the collection of some data, and by being generally naive as to the need to include women in this process, Durant advocates the underrepresentation of women as both interviewers and interviewees, making the results of his work inevitably biased towards male perspectives. In contrast to Durant's methods, M-O's methods were far more wide-ranging, and tended, as a result, to favor inclusivity. And while Mitchison's *The Delicate Fire* recognizes the reification of gender inequity through statistical analysis, her embrace of qualitative, M-O-oriented, methodologies in her later fiction suggest a necessary corrective to academic sociology's sexist undercurrents.

Naomi Mitchison's *We Have Been Warned*: A Cautionary Psychographic Tale

Despite the active exclusion of women in the burgeoning social sciences, Naomi Mitchison, a student of science within a family of scientists, never stopped imagining the role that scientific discourse might proffer in quelling human suffering. In 1935, Mitchison and Zita Baker traveled across the American south, talking to impoverished sharecroppers. Inspired by this, Mitchison "joined up with Mass-Observation."[59] When Hitler invaded Poland, approximately six years after she published *The Delicate Fire*, Mitchison would pick up the role of burgeoning scientist again by contributing her own observations to the sociological tapestry built by Mass-Observation. It was a far cry from the laboratories her brother and father frequented, but it was, as we have seen regarding gendered division of labor within quantitative social psychology, the most easily available option for her to take in memorializing the home front and capturing public opinion.

---

[58] Henry Durant, "The Gallup Poll and Some of Its Problems," *The Incorporated Statistician* 5, no. 2 (1954), p. 107, emphasis added.
[59] Mitchison, *You May Well Ask*, p. 201.

The highly excerpted diary that followed from her observations, now published as *Among You Taking Notes*, was by no means a mathematical or statistical approach to the war; most of the now published diary is observational, engaging primarily in qualitative analysis of the home front. Women in M-O were not only crucial to the data collection operations, but also to the group's viability.[60] Mitchison describes herself as a patron of Harrisson's, recalling in her memoir that, "I tried to help [young Harrisson], sometimes wondering if it was worthwhile. It was."[61]

By the time Mitchison wrote *We Have Been Warned*, she had garnered a great deal of literary attention. According to Jill Benton, "[a]ny well-read person in Great Britain who grew up during the 1920s and 1930s will have read Naomi Mitchison."[62] As such, the continued emphasis on the value of qualitative social survey methods in her mid-century novel would have caused considerable impact on readers, particularly when compounded by the novel's controversial reception.[63] In the novel, Mitchison rails against the gendered expectation of political silence; as a rare novel in which she concretely and unapologetically presents a political dystopia set in the present day, *We Have Been Warned* (1935) weighs in on the debate about surveillance methodologies. And, ironically, the novel that "ruined Mitchison's literary reputation" may very well provide the most significant literary insight into the way that public opinion data was collected and understood.[64] Despite rejecting the novel for publication, Victor Gollancz called it "the first piece of genuinely social art [...] in our time."[65] Part of this value comes from the novel's interest in theorizing the potential of both qualitative and quantitative public opinion methodologies. If we view this novel in the context of her allusions to the exclusionary power of math in *The Delicate Fire*, *We Have Been Warned* doubles down on the position that qualitative and experiential data enables women to express their opinions freely and grasp the power so long denied them through the fetishization of mathematical and statistical opinion analysis.

Distressingly, *We Have Been Warned* ends with the prediction of a fascist coup in England. The disturbing concluding pages of the novel upends any

---

[60] Nick Hubble also notes the contributions of Mitchison to Mass-Observation as in line with her later utopian fictions. Hubble, *Mass-Observation and Everyday Life*, p. 91.

[61] Mitchison, *You May Well Ask*, p. 201.   [62] Benton, *Naomi Mitchison*, p. 51.

[63] Jill Benton argues that the novel was a "disaster for Naomi," causing a break in her prolific output of novels from 1933 until 1939. Benton, *Naomi Mitchison*, p. 106.

[64] Phyllis Lassner, *British Women Writers of World War II: Battlegrounds of Their Own* (New York: Palgrave, 1998), p. 84.

[65] Mitchison, *You May Well Ask*, pp. 176–7.

rosy vision of Britain as a stalwart anti-fascist stronghold. Rather, Mitchison theorizes a political environment in which all the signs of public opinion are terribly misconstrued; an ethno-nationalist tide arises with little notice by experienced politicians.[66] At the end of a novel whose first act follows the plight of a politician whose wife spends her time trying to better understand his constituency, the novel's conclusion highlights the failure of traditional polling methods to unveil unseemly undercurrents of fascism and British nationalism, making the turn towards fascism at the end both shocking and humbling. And while the novel fictionalizes this tragic misunderstanding of the *vox populi, We Have Been Warned* characterizes a broader skepticism about quantitative polling. For the women in Mitchison's mid-century works, statistical analysis of public opinion not only overlooked the voices of women who were systematically underserved by this method of analysis; quantitative data also flattened the complex, intersectional experiences of women that more qualitative and narrative methods unearthed. In the novel it turns out that only unconventional data, in the form of a ghostly oracle, can accurately warn protagonist Dione Galton of the right-wing radicalism right under her nose. While Dione and her husband Tom knock on doors to gather information from self-censoring constituents, potential voters' true feelings are obscured until a ghost informs Dione that her friends had succumbed to fascistic ideology. For women in a field of public opinion studies increasingly circumscribed by Durant's paternal methods, no such supernatural forces were available; instead, qualitative sociological analysis became a way of un-skewing the polls and discovering the real perspectives behind the flat vision of the public that numbers presented.

Critics often overlook the importance of public opinion assessment in *We Have Been Warned* in favor of its scandalous depictions of sex, abortion, and murder in the second half of the book, as Dione and her husband travel to Russia. But the first half of the work centers on the political career of Tom Galton, who hopes to become the Labour MP for the constituency of Marshbrook Bridge.[67] And while he has four children with his wife Dione,

---

[66] William Davies argues that we might read the "rise of commercial polling in the 1930s" as a means of manufacturing its authority and authenticity. William Davis, "Thoughts on the Sociology of Brexit," in *The Brexit Crisis: A Verso Report*, Kindle Edition (New York: Verso, 2016), loc. 146.

[67] In *You May Well Ask*, Mitchison records her time canvassing for Dick Mitchison in Birmingham, which is the town she fictionalizes as Sallington in *We Have Been Warned*. Mitchison, *You May Well Ask*, p. 186.

as did Mitchison with her husband Dick, he also acts as a symbolic parent of statistics, which he fondly refers to as "a baby science," a term not dissimilar to the many statisticians and social scientists who referred to public opinion polls in the same terms.[68] Along these lines, Mass-Observation even noted that observation was "the beginning of a new epoch of science."[69] Tom is an economics professor, uninspired by his students, and politically motivated by his ideological desire for socialist transformation in the public sphere. But this ideological concern is persistently couched in economical reasoning. During the day he "[tries] to make out what [is] really happening to commodity prices," while at night he delivers emphatic speeches informed by his knowledge of economics.[70] Tom's political ambitions lead his wife Dione to the town of Sallington to canvass for her husband. The drive to master public opinion immediately becomes her master; like a political zombie, Dione walks the streets to canvas for her husband, looks at the fronts of houses, and asks herself "How would they vote?"[71] To help her husband, Dione captures the most flattened piece of information: who constituents will vote for. This aim overlooks the broader mission to understand the constituency and its concerns.

Dione Galton's exhausting political journey is motivated by two sometimes opposing factors: collecting public opinion to help her strategize her husband's campaign and listening to constituents to better understand their concerns. In her enervated state, Dione refers to the polling card as the motivation that helps her overcome physical depletion: "I don't think I ever knew what it was to be tired before. My legs and back and mind are all aching. And yet me, me somewhere in the middle, doesn't mind, doesn't want not to be tired, doesn't, above all, want to stop. I am going to do this little bit of Spark Lane that is on my polling card..."[72] Dione remains subjugated by the call of the polling card, representing the constituents needed to win the election. Not only does the collection of such hard data exhaust her physically, but it also alludes to the sapping of her mental energy, illustrated by the inclusion of extended ellipses. And, of course, even if Dione succeeds it is not *her* political empowerment she works for; it is that of her husband.

---

[68] Like Tom, Dick Mitchison staged a losing bid for a Parliamentary seat in King's Norton where he lost in a "political tide washing parties from the Left, both Labour and Liberal, out of power in favour of the conservative Nationalist party." Benton, *Naomi Mitchison*, p. 80.

[69] Naomi Mitchison, *We Have Been Warned* (Edinburgh: Kennedy & Boyd, [1935] 2012), p. 149; Harrisson and Madge, *Mass-Observation*, p. 11.

[70] Mitchison, *We Have Been Warned*, p. 148.

[71] Mitchison, *We Have Been Warned*, p. 58.   [72] Mitchison, *We Have Been Warned*, p. 63.

Exhausted, Dione listens to the concerns of one potential constituent, but can only stand completely overwhelmed by the statistical impact of her work. In thinking of statistics, she must inevitably fail to absorb anything substantive the constituent is saying: "What am I doing? Must listen. Must think what to say at the cottage meetings to-morrow afternoon, go over the statistics in my head."[73] Working on behalf of her husband, Dione is perpetually engaged in a dialectic between the quantitative and qualitative sides of campaigning, landing—as she indicates—"somewhere in the middle." The narratives she encounters in her daily walks, including the opinions of potential constituents, are juxtaposed with a desire to objectify individuals as data points in the tapestry of a political campaign to survey and control public opinion.

Dione's prevarication between qualitative and quantitative responses to public opinion adroitly characterize the larger tension around polling research in the 1930s and 1940s. Just as only Antander (and not Nikippe) in *The Delicate Fire* can weaponize his mathematical reasoning towards actual revolt, *We Have Been Warned* likewise suggests that the tools available to women and men to resist totalitarianism are markedly different. Mitchison's embrace of the qualitative and subjective methodology of her friend Harrisson in her wartime diary *Among You Taking Notes* emerges in the turn Dione makes from the exhausting and dissatisfying jumble of statistics to more authentic, though circumstantial, methods of inquiry. For Mitchison, the aim of her M-O diary was "to make of it a *picture* of how one family and friends lived during this period of history, what changes they hoped for, and what actually happened."[74] As justification for the dialectic nature of M-O, Harrisson and Madge argue that scientists are "isolated in a vacuum of 'pure' science," and that people see science as "just another of the forces which exploit them and of which they know little or nothing."[75] Mitchison confronted the views of the average man and woman as she tried to help her husband in the election she fictionalized in *We Have Been Warned*. As portrayed in the novel, Dione's interviews with constituents suggest the tension between a perspective of the public fueled by data analytics and one invested in constituents' stories.

While *We Have Been Warned* was published years before the Ministry of Information commissioned Mass-Observation for its Wartime Social Survey,

---

[73] Mitchison, *We Have Been Warned*, p. 67.
[74] Mitchison, *You May Well Ask*, p. 11, emphasis added.
[75] Harrisson and Madge, *Mass-Observation*, p. 10.

it remains striking how Mitchison uses the novel to capture the formal nuance that would characterize the reports M-O produced during the war, and which would feed into the Home Intelligence reports submitted to the Ministry of Information. In an enigmatic series of vignettes early in the novel, Mitchison describes a Labour Party dinner-dance in a way that hierarchizes its priorities in an analogous manner to Mass-Observation's reporting. Time, location, and belief are given—in that order—to report the mood of the room through a variety of individual perspectives. This mirrors the type of information M-O gathered in its myriad reports in both the interwar and wartime periods. An example from the enigmatic passage in the novel provides insight into the visual elements of this type of stream-of-consciousness conceit:

> *Valetta*   TOM GALTON
> They dance this at Labour socials. All over south England and the Midlands.
> Wonder why it is kept on when better ones dropped out. Civil servants
> folk-dance in London and she dons in Oxford. May Day in the High: all
> nonsense. Not even William Morris Behind it.[76]

This snippet typifies a series of formally similar passages, shifting perspective from dance to dance, character to character. Mitchison thus helps us navigate the tenor of the room, through the "time" of the dance (the Valetta), and the "location" of the views (Tom Galton's consciousness). The qualitative structure Mitchison includes for the dances suggests an interest in the discovery of individual experience and its relationship to a collective atmosphere, temporally and historically. The structure of this section is unique and enigmatic in the context of the whole work, but allows Mitchison to suggest the novel's sociological investments, prefiguring the structure of M-O reports not only during the war but also before it. The "National Activities" section of *May the Twelfth*, for example, maintains a similar structure.[77] These reports recorded, in order, the location of the observation, the coded subject number of the observer, as well as the time of the observation. Deeply informed by her own political pursuits and new sociological approaches, Mitchison's aesthetic concerns are thus continuously rooted in the belief that sociological observation can be a tool for understanding public sentiment.

---

[76] Mitchison, *We Have Been Warned*, p. 35.
[77] Mass-Observation, *War Begins at Home*, pp. 167–265.

We Have Been Warned frames qualitative observation as a concern specifically relevant to women. Tom Galton's fetish for the numbers represents the larger connection between politics and mathematics, but his pragmatism is a continual foil to Dione's more eccentric epistemological investments. The novel's first pages feature Dione Galton reading about the urban legend of Jean MacLean, otherwise known as "Green Jean." According to the lore, the Campbell sisters, proclaiming Jean a witch, drive her to her death in a wintry grave. In the novel, Jean's presence is striking; in a novel mainly concerned with political science in the 1930s, repeated reference to Jean awakens an unexpected admiration for the supernatural. Throughout the novel, this ghost provides insights to Dione in the form of visions, many of which are far more accurate than anything she conjured with the help of her statistical analyses. The conflicted relationship between superstition and science thus becomes a central crux of the novel. This topic was also prevalent in Mass-Observation's first publication, where Harrisson and Madge argue that "magical and religions systems" have historically worked to "impede the development of science."[78] Insofar as Dione's visions form a clearer picture of her reality than those gathered by scientifically ascertained knowledges, the emphasis on "magic" over "science" in her fiction marks a slight divergence from the early juxtaposition of M-O's "scientific" methods with superstitious logic. But Harrisson and Madge also note that people turn to magic only when all scientific efforts have failed: "Having taken all the reasonable precautions to ensure success, he goes on to take unreasonable precautions. But when he finds out new scientific precautions which are better than the magical ones, he may be prepared to abandon the latter."[79] To apply this logic to *We Have Been Warned*, Jean's interruptions into the scientific milieu of Dione and Tom suggest an inevitable failure of the trusted scientific methods of analysis to ensure success. Jean comes to represent two positions, both of which challenge the popular quantitative methods of public opinion analysis. On the one hand, Jean represents a magical other, a complete contradiction to any form of scientific reason as determined by the patriarchy. On the other hand, Jean's stories, by revealing the true feelings of those around her, are actually a form of valid qualitative analysis. Perhaps if Dione were not so obsessed with statistics at the expense of truly listening to her family and friends, she might have better identified the fascist undercurrents that Jean eventually describes to Dione. As it

---

[78] Harrisson and Madge, *Mass-Observation*, p. 13.
[79] Harrisson and Madge, *Mass-Observation*, p. 13.

stands, Dione fails to do this, and Jean must become both a symbol of unreason and a voice advocating the validation of qualitative analysis.

Green Jean also represents a two-headed critique of patriarchal politics in the twentieth century. For one, she embodies the position of a woman divorced from any seat of social or political power; the story of Jean is that she was cast out from her community into the snow, having failed to acquiesce to models of femininity expected of her. Jean also exemplifies a strand of anti-rationalism which, throughout the novel, arises to subtly critique the patriarchal fetish for statistics and science. As Dione begins the novel by reading about Green Jean, she constantly envisions men over her shoulder, judging her chimerical thoughts about witchcraft and the ancient past. Her thoughts flow quickly from Jean to her personal life, and even to politics. She imagines having a child after the revolution. But her quixotic daydreaming is abridged by the thought of her practical husband scolding her for her frivolous train of thought: "She mustn't think that either: it was romanticising; it was making personal and little something that was so big and so real that she couldn't think about it properly. What Tom called Realistically. Run away from that, back to Inverary in the seventeenth century."[80] While Dione wants to imagine the utopian vision of revolution, she imagines Tom's rationalistic chastisement of her fantasy. So, Dione runs from the romance of political revolutionary fervor, returning to the story of Jean and the witches, but quickly realizes that this train of thought is no more pragmatic or "realistic" than her last. "[W]hat would father think of me imagining all that, father who was a Fraser and a sceptic and one of the foremost Scottish archaeologists of his day! What would he have thought of Phoebe and me for seeing Green Jean in the nursery corridor? Tom doesn't believe we ever did. But Tom is a lowlander."[81] Even thinking of Green Jean leads her to imagine another shame-inducing rebuke from her father and her husband, both of whom embrace a scientifically inclined patriarchal epistemology antithetical to Dione's more esoteric interest in the story of Green Jean. Dione reports personal experience, only to be rebuked by her practical husband. The novel thus frames the relationship between Dione and Tom as epistemologically oppositional; the types of pragmatic knowledge Tom embraces are at odds with Dione's more mystical beliefs. Such epistemological difference might also mirror the differences between the quantitative approaches of the Gallup polling system, and those of

---

[80] Mitchison, *We Have Been Warned*, pp. 3–4.
[81] Mitchison, *We Have Been Warned*, pp. 4–5.

Mass-Observation in the mid-1930s, which Mitchison contributed to with her own wartime journal. And just as Mass-Observation trusted the input of their observers, Dione trusts the experiences of herself and her sister in opposition to her husband and father, who use science and reason to dismiss the apparition Green Jean.[82] Throughout the novel, Green Jean will suggest this divide; as her predictions become more astute than those of her husband, Jean will validate Dione's untraditional means of interpreting her political environment.

Dione is not the only mid-century character whose unexpected reliance on superstition, witchcraft, or spiritualism turn out to uncover real objective truths. Graham Greene's thrillers *Brighton Rock* and *The Ministry of Fear* allude to occultism as a trope standing in for alternative epistemological frameworks that provide more accurate reflections of reality than reason. *The Ministry of Fear* famously begins when convicted killer Arthur Rowe takes the advice of a female fortune-teller in guessing the weight of a fête-cake and is shortly thereafter framed for another murder in a séance; in *Brighton Rock*, automatic writing is the means by which Ida learns what has happened to the disappeared "Fred" Hale. Allusion to the occult in such novels is prefigured in Mitchison's *We Have Been Warned*, where it stands in for the rise of public opinion polling and the challenge it imposed on women's political power. Unlike the historical trend for séances and the occult, spiritualism in Mitchison's novel is not charlatanism; rather, it leads to more accurate information than more traditional methods proffer. While scientific discourse became increasingly certain about the knowledge it possessed, these other occult voices provided a skeptical check on the omniscience of academic discourse.

Mitchison realized that the scientific objectification of public opinion was neither objective nor apolitical but had the unintended consequence of silencing voices either left out by traditional polling or unwelcome in its discursive parameters. In *We Have Been Warned* the prevalence of anti-realist tropes represents Mitchison's skepticism over so-called objective quantitative analysis. Green Jean's preternatural political prognostications represent a version of reality for which there is no objective or scientific corroboration, but which are all the same proven true. These mystical predictions end up far more accurate than any political surveillance or

---

[82] Phyllis Lassner notes that "female agency is as inseparable from rationality as the latter is from her emotional responses," and that "Dione is still constrained by male-centered interpretations of the law as well as male-dominated lawlessness." Lassner, *British Women Writers*, p. 75.

intelligence gathering. Mitchison's aesthetic interest in prophesy, while potentially undermining the work of M-O, actually aids in its support, as she underscores that the methods of analysis most available to women are often those less valued by the academic scientific community. As I have demonstrated, within the field of public opinion analysis, M-O suffered from the dismissal of many within academic sociology. Women also experienced this level of rejection, and the desire of both Mitchison and M-O to voice opinions of the disenfranchised initially left both to be considered cranks.

Though Green Jean emerges throughout the novel in a variety of contexts, her role in the novel's concluding pages is the most striking. Dione finds herself pregnant, marking a parallel between herself and Green Jean, who bore a baby before her death. In what remained one of the most controversial aspects of the novel, Dione seeks out an abortion, coinciding with the Reichstag fire. All the while, there are hints of local disruption, which the narrative glosses over. Dione's sister, Phoebe, describes someone's political identification as a means of expressing her own: "Dissatisfied Labor. Like a lot of us."[83] Moments like this suggest, but do not diagnose, the larger political unrest of her friends and neighbors. But the terrifying truth about public opinion comes to Dione quickly in the conclusion of the novel. Walking up to a quiet library, Dione sees Green Jean, who states: "I am wanting to help you, Isobel Dione. You have the Campbell Women against you, too [...] You and your coven are in danger."[84] In order to "see" the danger before her, Dione puts her hand on a stone provided by Green Jean. The soothsaying impact of the rock becomes the foundation of the dramatic denouement of the novel.

The pacing of the conclusion is accelerated and unexpected. While much of the novel to this point negotiates romantic entanglements and details the lives of Communist Russians, the final section features a series of dreamlike sequences inspired by Jean's fortune-telling rock. The visions suggest that Dione is endangered by the political outcomes awaiting her at home, each worse than the last. The first is a political victory of the left wherein voters embrace the Labour Party. This vision is akin to what Tom originally wanted before his defeat at Marshbrook: the victory of the centrist left party and an identification, by the constituency, with even some of the more radical aims of the center-left. In this rendition of events, Tom declares,

[83] Mitchison, *We Have Been Warned*, p. 525.
[84] Mitchison, *We Have Been Warned*, p. 529.

"Socialist England...and it's the Labour Movement that's done it," but Jean warns that this outcome represents a deluded optimism: "[T]his might be happening one day," Jean warns, "yet maybe it is not even likely."[85] In the second vision, poison gas portentously launches a counter-revolution, with Russia poised as a haven from political oppression. In this vision, Dione and her husband, having just come from Russia, return there, free from the upcoming political crises in Scotland.

But this is not the worst of the predictions. The final, most ominous, comes as Jean warns: "you will be wiser to take the full warning that's been got ready for you."[86] This future entails personal betrayal and the rise of domestic extremism. In Jean's last prophetic vision, Tom's sister shocks Dione by declaring him a traitor and unveils her previously hidden fascistic beliefs by proposing ethnic cleansing: "We are not like you rebels. We are not concerned with what the foreigner thinks. We are concerned with our English Empire. These executions are necessary. They are a purging. Our country had gone rotten. Now it will be England again."[87] Green Jean's Mosley-esque vision is startling after a novel characterized by optimistic and revolutionary leftism. The novel suggests, by ending with this nationalist version of the future, that the violent right-wing uprising is perhaps a more accurate vision of what is to come than any of the more optimistic versions that preceded it. Still expecting a child, Dione wakes up in a panic from the nightmare of a counter-revolution and her imminent death. The conclusion warns the reader; the alienated leftism of the 1930s may very well be masking a counter-revolutionary oppression. While Tom and Dione were observing their environment using the standard toolkit of political prognostication, they never listened to the stories of their peers, who were increasingly embracing fascist ideology.

A similar concern was shared by Mass-Observation as it squared off against the burgeoning but self-assured field of quantitative social science. Repeatedly, M-O's studies framed themselves in opposition to statistical social analysis. In *May the Twelfth*, the authors indicate that their methods contrast with those of traditional science. Predicting the umbrage of scientists who find the results of the book "premature," the authors write that "Mass-Observation has to attempt more than other sciences...it has to attempt more because more people are involved; because the research is not

---

[85] Mitchison, *We Have Been Warned*, pp. 535, 537.
[86] Mitchison, *We Have Been Warned*, p. 547.
[87] Mitchison, *We Have Been Warned*, p. 550.

being done by one worker, or group of workers, but by a very large number of Observers."[88] Even in the earliest publications, this tension with the body of technocratic scientists reviewing their work is prevalent. This trend continues, and even escalates, in later publications like *Britain* (1939). In response to the results of a national survey from February 1938 about the likelihood of war, editors are quick to note that we cannot take people's responses to a pollster as totally correlative to their actual positions: "Of course this is what people *say* they think. We cannot assume that is what they actually think."[89] Mitchison's Dione Galton, who fails to really understand the beliefs of her local constituency despite her efforts at polling and public opinion assessment, allegorizes the role of Mass-Observation in the interwar period. Only by using unconventional techniques and overhearing the voices of the underrepresented did M-O think it possible to counter the propensity for interviewees to sanitize their worldview. For Dione, it is only by tapping into the spirit world that she can attain a firm grasp on her own social milieu; for M-O, it was the labor of undercover workers like Naomi Mitchison and Celia Fremlin that enabled M-O to speak authentically about the real views of citizens and workers.

Celia Fremlin: Women and Work in Mass-Observation

Green Jean's mystical, clairvoyant approach to public opinion analysis, which recalls so aptly the early spiritualist origins of psychographic discourse, also underscored the value of qualitative analysis and narrativization to polling efforts. But it was not only Mitchison who recognized the way that clairvoyance, sociology, and fiction might work together. Before she was an award-winning writer of thrillers, Mass-Observation worker Celia Fremlin spent the late summer and early autumn of 1940 frequenting psychometrics classes and spiritualist meetings, writing back to Tom Harrisson about her findings. At one point, she even has a medium from the Maryleborne Spiritualist Association access the spirits who wish to contact her. In response to these sessions, Fremlin's skepticism for the spiritualist's methods is palpable, though her notes seem to forecast her future as a novelist, recording that she, too, had "in the past done successful

---

[88]   Mass-Observation, *War Begins at Home*, p. 423.
[89]   Mass-Observation, *Britain*, p. 53, emphasis in original.

character-readings by almost completely fraudulent methods."[90] But the medium in August 1940 sent Fremlin a message from a dead uncle: "Not to take advice which well-meaning people are giving." Fremlin countered that no one, well-meaning or not, was giving her any advice, to which the medium said that "they will do so, and when they do she is to ignore it."[91] While the medium bungled the identification of Fremlin's uncle, he also may have had a point about the well-meaning advice. Sometime in 1941–42 Fremlin would take on a job, after Minister of Labour Ernest Bevin called up M-O to get a "[w]orm's eye view" of war factories staffed by women, which were suffering from "[w]ar fatigue, lack of concentration, and general absence of 'morale.'"[92] Fremlin went undercover for a few months in the Malmesbury Ekco plant, a covert factory specializing in radar, to unearth the problem with morale, producing a book titled *War Factory* (1943), which gave a detailed sociological assessment of her findings.[93] Fremlin claimed that she "felt no discomfort over writing about [the female workers]. They were incognito, could not be identified, and didn't read books anyway."[94] She even described her work with M-O as "terribly exciting and nice."[95] But, getting back to her ghostly uncle's sage advice, Fremlin was never given proper credit for the work she put into producing this critical piece of wartime morale analysis, as I have noted previously in this chapter. Harrisson, in the book's introduction, describes the work being performed by "a highly trained and experienced Cambridge graduate," but Fremlin never received recognition for her work as a professional sociologist.[96]

Soon after writing *War Factory*, Fremlin married, and while her husband "was quite interested in M-O," he "didn't like her going away so much."[97] The same year *War Factory* went to print, Fremlin had a baby; she admitted in a later interview that "[she] would still go out and do interviews, but 'the commitment was gone.'"[98] Aside from some small amount of work during the V-Bomb campaign, Fremlin's wartime work for M-O came to an end.

[90] Celia Fremlin notes on "Psychometry Class," July 31, 1940, Mass-Observation Archive, SxMOA1/2/8/1/B, University of Sussex Special Collections. Reproduced with permission of Curtis Brown Group Ltd, London on behalf of The Trustees of the Mass-Observation Archive, © The Trustees of the Mass-Observation Archive, emphasis in original.
[91] Celia Fremlin notes on "Psychometry Class."
[92] Mass-Observation, *War Factory* (London: Victor Gollancz, 1943), p. 6.
[93] Dorothy Sheridan, "Introduction," in *War Factory* (London: Cresset, 1987).
[94] Angus Calder interview with Celia Fremlin.
[95] Angus Calder interview with Celia Fremlin.
[96] Mass-Observation, *War Factory*, p. 6.   [97] Angus Calder interview with Celia Fremlin.
[98] Angus Calder interview with Celia Fremlin.

But after the war, Fremlin took up novel-writing. As in the fiction of Mitchison, Fremlin's postwar novels repeatedly feature the conflict between the experiential epistemology of women and the intrusions of supposed experts whose failure to hear women's stories leaves them blind to the truths under their noses. As Luke Seaber notes, Fremlin differs from male observers because "what she used in her fiction was not so much material that she had observed [...] as an epistemological stance."[99] This epistemological stance, deeply influenced by the clandestine sociological work of her M-O years, heightened the aesthetic tension in Fremlin's novels between the everyday life experiences of women and the voices of technocratic experts that she sketched in her work for Mass-Observation.

Fremlin's fiction, in highlighting the patronizing, belittling attitudes of patriarchal institutions towards women, also speaks to the utter bungling of the Ministry of Labour's efforts to respond to women's complaints during the war. This fact is testified to in many commissioned studies at the time. In the published version of Home Intelligence's Wartime Social Survey, women are cited as being more "depressed" and "anxious" than their male counterparts about the war effort.[100] Secretary of Home Planning Michael Balfour recalls a radio address by Ernest Bevin, wherein he "call[ed]-up women to industry."[101] What Bevin missed, and that M-O's reports to Home Intelligence suggested, was that there were not enough wartime jobs for women to actually take up, despite the encouragement to do so. Unable to locate the work they were told to seek, part of the anxiety women faced was proportional to the lack of real ability to impact the outcome of the war. A Home Intelligence report from 1940, found that "[a] constant source of dissatisfaction is the failure of professional and middle-class people (especially women) to become fully absorbed in the war effort."[102] Other reports suggested a "[g]rowing feeling that women should be given more work."[103] Bevin's failure to recruit an adequate number of women workers stands in for the immense failures of an institution that overwhelmingly believed in the efficiency of its own bureaucratic efforts at propaganda, despite Tom Harrisson's virulent assertion to Home Intelligence's Mary Adams that the

---

[99] Luke Seaber, *Incognito Social Investigation in British Literature: Certainties in Degradation* (London: Palgrave, 2018), p. 204.
[100] Paul Addison and Jeremy Crang, editors, *Listening to Britain: Home Intelligence Reports on Britain's Finest Hour: May to September 1940* (London: Bodley Head, 2010), p. 19–20.
[101] Addison and Crang, *Listening to Britain*, p. 63.
[102] Addison and Crang, *Listening to Britain*, p. 97.
[103] Addison and Crang, *Listening to Britain*, p. 94.

Ministry of Information "absolutely failed to fulfil its function of collecting information about the effect of the Ministry's influences, instructions, and propaganda."[104] This failure to satisfactorily understand the public led M-O to its job collecting information for Home Intelligence, but also inspired M-O to pursue other efforts to better understand bureaucratic failures of morale during wartime. As Fremlin's *War Factory* would assert, even women who *did* find wartime factory work often found the conditions unsatisfactory. The mobilization of the female workforce, even when successful, did not lead to a corresponding boost in morale. The failure to mobilize women and raise morale, diagnosed by Mass-Observation, was not truly intelligible without the qualitative feedback from the regions that indicated this failure in wartime messaging to women.

In the introductory essay of *War Factory*, Tom Harrisson introduces Fremlin's survey of the experience of women wartime factory workers by having a detailed discussion about methodology. This discussion mirrors, in most respects, the terms of the debate that M-O presented in its early work and that Harrisson himself would later contrast against Henry Durant at the British Psychological Association meeting. Describing the methods, Harrisson argues that "[m]any of the phenomena which face the sociologist *are not* initially amenable to quantitative study until qualitative evaluation has been achieved."[105] He is quick to point out that "[t]here is a strong tendency to regard only the numerical description of humans as scientific." Arguing that most sociologists have been trained in the humanities, trained in "literary, philosophic, historical and other methods," Harrisson argues that the fetish for statistics is a *compensatory* behavior—"a symbol of rectitude."[106] In sum, he claims that "Social Science has been backward," using statistics as a means of providing a false sense of certainty, especially when any person responding to a survey will only reveal what they are comfortable disclosing to a stranger.[107] Harrisson again touts his methods and declares that there is a difference between the statistical social survey and finding out, in reality, what people really do think.

The conclusion of Fremlin's study is a bit dire. "The purpose of this study has been to bring to light something of the human foundations on which any scheme for improving efficiency and increasing output here must be based."[108] She continues to produce a more critical and pessimistic vision of

[104] Tom Harrisson to Mary Adams, October 1939, Mary Adams Papers, SxMOA4/4/6/1, University of Sussex Special Collections.
[105] Mass-Observation, *War Factory*, p. 7, emphasis in original.
[106] Mass-Observation, *War Factory*, p. 7.   [107] Mass-Observation, *War Factory*, p. 7.
[108] Mass-Observation, *War Factory*, p. 113.

the current state of the war factory: "The picture of these foundations is not reassuring. We find as its material, gangs of bewildered and mainly reluctant girls, suddenly cut off from all their former interests and activities; suddenly released from almost all social and material responsibilities which formerly gave their lives order and shape."[109] The expectation for these women was that their work in factories, fulfilling their roles as part of the wartime machinery, would make them feel satisfied and part of the war effort. As Fremlin is quick to say, nothing could have been further from the truth: "Instead of feeling 'in it' (as the newspapers would lead one to suppose working in a war factory makes one feel) they feel out of it, in every way, more than they ever have in their lives. The 'ivory tower' of the intellectuals is not more secure, more insulated from the struggles of real life, than is working twelve hours a day in an unexacting job in a humanely run war factory."[110] Fremlin's argument emphasizes, doubly, the disconnection between the women workers and those managers or elites who consistently declare themselves experts on the experiences of these women. Countering the supposed expertise of journalists, Fremlin rails against press accounts of women war workers, which portrayed them happily and readily diving in to aid in the war effort. She also dismisses the tendency to view lower-class women as more removed from the war effort due to lack of political commitment. By framing these women as similar to the elitist academics in terms of their wartime engagement, Fremlin flattens social hierarchies, declaring that women's experiences cannot be assumed by the elites, but must be gathered through authentic interactions with the workers themselves; this is an argument Fremlin contributed to M-O through her work, having honed her skills on her survey of women in domestic service, *The Seven Chars of Chelsea* (1940).[111]

Fremlin's *The Hours Before Dawn* (1958), among other of her postwar novels, emphasizes this same discrepancy between the supposed experts and the authentic experiences and feelings of women.[112] *The Hours Before Dawn* centers around the wife and mother of three, Louise Henderson, who finds herself in a state of unmitigated exhaustion after the birth of her third

---

[109] Mass-Observation, *War Factory*, p. 113.

[110] Mass-Observation, *War Factory*, p. 113.

[111] *The Seven Chars of Chelsea* was, as Luke Seaber notes, the book that first garnered Harrisson's attention to Fremlin as a sociologist. Seaber, *Incognito Social Investigation*, p. 190.

[112] Many of Fremlin's novels are domestic thrillers centered on the deadening experiences of middle-class housewifery. *The Trouble Makers* (1963) follows the experiences of a woman who stabs her husband out of anger, only to be driven even further mad by the rumor-mongering of fellow housewives. *The Jealous One* (1965) follows a jealous wife, Rosamund, who fears she may have killed a rival for her husband's attentions.

child, Michael, whose night-time cries function as a continual refrain in the novel. His crying keeps Louise from the sleep she so desperately needs. But Louise is not only assailed by her sleeplessness. She is tried from all sides, as her unsympathetic husband harangues her, her nosey neighbors complain about her son's cries, and a mysterious new female tenant behaves in ways that are increasingly suspicious. The mystery of this new tenant, Miss Vera Brandon, introduces the dramatic arc of Fremlin's thriller. Louise first suspects Brandon of espionage after a neighborhood child reports that she has been shuffling through Mr. Henderson's papers on British aircraft design. Later, after Louise discovers her children transcribing notes from Miss Brandon's journal, she begins to suspect Vera of an obsession with her husband, a jealousy further provoked by the tenant's ability to charm her husband with discussions of *Medea*—a haunting reference to the possible murderous repercussions of Louise's jealousy as a wife and exhaustion as a mother.

While Louise's fatigue derives from her experiences as a mother and housewife, the theme of female exhaustion has firm connections to Fremlin's findings in *War Factory*. Fremlin's study emphasizes the twelve-hour days of factory work and the toll these long hours take on women. She notes that the long hours and the subsequent lack of autonomy has a soul-crushing impact on women that disengages them from the social cohesion the war effort means to instill: "From eight in the morning to nine? At night life is taken off one's own hands, completely and absolutely...When a girl gets home at half-past eight or nine at night what awaits her?...Is it surprising that, after a few weeks of this sort of life, a girl should begin to feel isolated from the outside world, and lose her sense of responsibility towards it?"[113] It is not only in Fremlin's summary that we see this sentiment. The workers themselves are quoted at length. One notes the lack of any social contact outside of the workplace: "By the time you've had your supper and had a wash, it's time to go to bed."[114] Beyond the lack of social life, many billeted women found themselves failing to meet the social expectations of their hosts. Like the exhausted Louise, who must constantly juggle the expectations of children, neighbors, and husband, billeted factory workers were constantly in social arrears with hosts due to their overwork. One worker, a twenty-five-year-old woman, makes the point transparent: "I don't know, I get fed up sometimes. Sometimes you come home in the evenings and you

---

[113] Mass-Observation, *War Factory*, p. 47.   [114] Mass-Observation, *War Factory*, p. 52.

don't feel like talking—you know, you're a bit tired. When I'm feeling like that, just come in and sit down sort of thing, they're all whispering to each other, 'Isn't she in a temper?' 'What's the matter with her?' Just because I don't happen to feel like talking to them."[115]

This failure to meet the expectations to embody femininity—to be compliant, kind, genial and welcoming at all times—is a theme that Fremlin returns to in her depiction of Louise, who finds herself repeatedly in circumstances where she frets about the responses of others to her inability to meet expectations. She constantly anticipates her husband's rebukes for her perceived shortcomings; her only shelter from this emotional turmoil is the continued physical turmoil of motherhood:

> Mark was still scowling when Louise rejoined her family, and she could guess at the withering comments hovering on the tip of his tongue. It was something of a relief to know that he would have to postpone them while she fed and changed Michael and put him in his cot; while she dished up supper, while she wrestled with the children's table manners, toothbrushing, and finally got them to bed; while she washed up supper, finished the ironing and ran upstairs to see how it could be that Margery's eiderdown should have slipped off her bed and vanished without a trace in the space of half an hour.[116]

The sentence itself, winding and accretive, exhausts the reader, much as the daily chores exhaust Louise. Fremlin's effort to formally articulate the exhaustion of domestic labour are prefigured by her early critique of women's work in *War Factory*, where this theme of exhaustion arises repeatedly.

The plot of *The Hours Before Dawn* thickens when friends reveal that Miss Brandon had specifically sought out the Henderson's address before she had presented herself as a potential tenant. In the end, Louise discovers the truth behind the mysterious Miss Brandon, about whom she had carried uncanny recollections throughout the novel. After finding and reading Miss Brandon's journal, Louise realizes both she and her husband had indeed seen Miss Brandon before—in the maternity ward during the birth of her child. Miss Brandon was there to have a child too, but the child died shortly after birth. Brandon then fixated on the Henderson's baby, convinced by the appearance of the child that her own baby was still living as

---

[115] Mass-Observation, *War Factory*, p. 102.

[116] Celia Fremlin, *The Hours Before Dawn* (Philadelphia, PA: Lippincott, 1958), p. 20.

Michael Henderson, and that it was Louise's baby who must have died. By presenting Vera's delusions as a plot element, Fremlin presents us with two versions of the female intuitive epistemology to choose from. On the one hand, we are faced with Louise's suspicions, cast as ludicrous by those around her, despite her ability to assess and assert the evidence before her eyes. On the other hand, we have the fully intuitive nature of Brandon's assertion that Louise's child is hers. Both women are operating on an instinctive relationship to the truth value of their beliefs. Fremlin leaves readers with only two valid epistemological frameworks to choose from, neither of which are those of the men who have minimized the concerns and traumas of women; for the readers to fully engage in the drama of the narrative, they, too, must begin to realize the value of such experiential epistemology.

To act on her assumption that baby Michael is hers, Miss Brandon sets up an elaborate scheme to discredit Louise as a mother, taking advantage of circumstances brought on by chronic exhaustion to make her the talk of the neighborhood. Two significant instances in the novel epitomize Louise's public shaming. In the first instance, Louise takes a crying Michael out in a stroller in the middle of the night to avoid further bothering the neighbors or her husband, both of whom have made their frustrations with Michael quite clear. After falling asleep on a park bench next to the stroller, she awakens to a missing stroller and a male police officer, yet another manifestation of male institutional control, questioning Louise's presence. Louise attempts to explain to the officer about her missing baby, only to find that the baby is back at home, crying in his crib. In the second instance, a harried Louise attends to her older children on a fair ride, only to find Michael's stroller missing when she returns. After much searching, the baby is found still at the fair in the missing children's tent. In both instances, it turns out that Miss Brandon moved the baby when Louise was distracted. While Miss Brandon's goal is to gaslight Louise into questioning her own sanity, she also succeeds in making the community suspicious of Louise's hold on reality. Much like in Naomi Mitchison's *We Have Been Warned*, the protagonist is surrounded by voices who discredit her feelings, experiences, and abilities, despite preternatural instincts that reinforce her own suspicions.

The way the self-declared authorities diminish the views of women in *We Have Been Warned* and *The Hours Before Dawn* almost precisely mirrored the experiences of women within wartime administration. The case of Home Intelligence's Mary Adams is a crucial parable of this phenomenon. Adams created the Ministry of Information's Home Intelligence Department after the BBC television branch was shuttered for the war. Her work at Home Intelligence involved the contract with Mass-Observation as well as her own separate survey, the Wartime Social Survey (which employed, at one time, twenty-nine women and only one man, as interviewers).[117] Though Home Intelligence's Wartime Social Survey was more statistically oriented, Adams stood up for M-O's methodologies against the prevailing preference for so-called "hard" data, writing that "quantitative treatment of qualitative material leads to fallacious conclusions because it involves the comparison of [sic] incomparable."[118] But, after hapless male leadership frustrated her, Adams was inevitably precluded from pursuing her vision and pushed out of her position just as M-O was pushed out of their contract with the Ministry of Information; a final letter to Tom Harrisson from the new Home Intelligence director Stephen Taylor demands MoI approval before M-O could share any of their contracted work for the government.[119] Just as Mary Adams, a high-profile female administrator, suffered under administrative obliviousness, so too did the women of a variety of classes who worked in Fremlin's factory.

More specifically, the structure of *War Factory* alludes to this very concern. As the goal of the book was to "improv[e] efficiency and increas[e] output," the book is peppered with administrative responses to the complaints of workers and the findings of Fremlin's investigation. But the author adopts a clever, and creative, method for legitimizing and centralizing the voices of women over those of male bosses. To create textual distance between women and haranguing, male bureaucrats, Fremlin relegates male retorts to footnotes that permeate the text. While the likes of Dione Galton and Louise Henderson may have wished for a reprieve from the attitudes of male technocrats, Fremlin succeeds, in her sociological work, in providing this much-needed relief. She even finds it suitable to provide editorial critique of managerial attitudes towards women. In response to a Works Manager's dismissive attitude towards his workers, Fremlin presents a very strongly worded critique of his leadership. She argues that, despite the "two hundred years of struggle between workers and management," the lack of

---

[117] "Wartime Social Survey," July 30, 1940, The War-time Social Survey Papers, 1940–41, Frederick Brown, SxMOA17/7/11, University of Sussex Special Collections.

[118] "Home Intelligence Notes on Present Condition for the DG," February 7, 1941, Mary Adams Papers, SxMOA4/1/1/1, University of Sussex Special Collections.

[119] Letter from Stephen Taylor to Tom Harrisson, October 2, 1941, Mary Adams Papers, SxMOA4/4/5/2, University of Sussex Special Collections. A letter dating September 1, 1941 informed Harrisson of the end of the contract at the end of September.

this community's awareness of this history "suggest[s] that there is much more scope for *personal* leadership in a factory...than is generally supposed."[120] Speaking as an expert, Fremlin's assault on institutional dismissals of women garners a shocking response from the Works Manager. She relegates his rejoinder to yet another footnote, in which he complains that "subjective thinking is the order of the day," and that a good bedside manner with workers is unlikely to make any significant difference in worker satisfaction. Such "subjective thinking on the part of the management" would be, for the manager, a "cure [...] worse than the evil."[121] This patronizing counterpoint, privileging an impersonal approach to management, captures the methodological conflicts between quantitatively minded managers and those approaching administrative work through a qualitative and humanistic lens. It should be emphasized that the Works Manager's biggest concern is the threat of *subjectivism* that comes to the surface when managers take a personal approach over a more impersonal one.

Fremlin's fiction consistently cites the conflict between self-described field experts and those who suffer under their gazes. When, in the opening paragraphs of *The Hours Before Dawn*, Louise looks around at the other women at the Infant Welfare Clinic, Fremlin draws the reader's attention to the ways that expert discourse corners new mothers and pits them against one another. The perennially exhausted Louise surveys the room and compares herself to other women whose parenting skills exceed her own, including "Mrs What's-her-name in the smart blue suit who's baby did exactly what the books said, for all the world as if he and his mother studied the Behavior Charts and Average Weight Tables together."[122] As Fremlin introduces us to Louise's perspective, we are immediately made aware of the impact her cantankerous child has on her psyche. She begs the nurse for help: "But you see he keeps us awake half the night." Yet the nurse seems to dismiss her concerns, tautologically blaming Louise's worry and exhaustion for her worry and exhaustion: "That's the mistake all you young mothers make. You worry too much. Your worry communicates itself to the baby, and there you are!"[123] Exasperated by Nurse Fordham's reply, Louise leaves the appointment with no foreseeable solution, and only another voice adding to the chorus blaming her for her infant-inspired woes. And others join in to tell Louise how to behave as well. Mrs. Hooper, whose laissez faire

---

[120]   Mass-Observation, *War Factory*, p. 71.   [121]   Mass-Observation, *War Factory*, pp. 71–2.
[122]   Fremlin, *The Hours Before Dawn*, p. 7.   [123]   Fremlin, *The Hours Before Dawn*, p. 9.

approach to parenting involves leaving her child unattended much of the time, takes advantage of Louise's state to berate her for her decisions. When hearing that Louise and her husband are planning to let a room, Mrs. Hooper declares, "'My dear! You're *not* letting that room, are you?' ... 'But how dreadful! I mean, I should have thought you need *more* space now you've got Michael, not less. And then, everyone knows that two women can't share a kitchen...'"[124] Louise must shamefully admit the economic shortfall that has led them to let the room to begin with; it is fair to assume that Hooper designed her lecture solely to extract this embarrassing confession and lower Louise's self-esteem even further.

Fremlin was not only worried about the dismissal of women's concerns as factory workers, but also with the deleterious effects of economic and social displacement; this tension was horribly underrecognized by administrators, who were only interested in the factory itself, and little concerned with women's subjective experience of everyday life after their shifts were over. Fremlin found that women working in the factory were paid quite nicely.[125] But forced to live outside their elements, many of the women were made to be, like Miss Brandon, intruders in the local environment. One of the most major findings in Fremlin's *War Factory* relates to the failure of displaced workers to fully assimilate into the communities where they find themselves. This anxiety cut both ways. Just as the mysterious Miss Brandon's arrival brings with it a series of suspicions that add to Louise's anxiety, billeted war workers produce anxiety in hosts who increasingly criticized their guests. Louise's anxiety over Vera Brandon is a hyperbolic reflection of the kinds of concerns locals had when the workers descended onto their town. As Fremlin records that the "invasion of strangers" was "not only bewildering " but also "annoying, and highly inconvenient,"[126] Fremlin compares the newcomers to a "swarm of locusts" who "eat up the already scarce food supplies" and "cram the local cinema at weekends so that she and her husband can't get near it."[127] Just as Miss Brandon wrought crisis on Louise's home, instilling both jealousy and anxiety, surveys of billeted guests often exposed the tenuous nature of community cohesion; just as locals were annoyed to take in outsiders, those who arrived did not exactly have a friendly demeanor towards their new hosts. Fremlin collects fragments of conversations

---

[124] Fremlin, *The Hours Before Dawn*, p. 12, emphasis in original.
[125] Mass-Observation, *War Factory*, p. 79.
[126] Mass-Observation, *War Factory*, p. 13.
[127] Mass-Observation, *War Factory*, p. 14.

between the women workers complaining about their lodgings, including one who complains, "I expect Mrs. Whats-it here will ration the light to us, or something so we can't read. They're always out to do you down in these places."[128] From the perspective of outsiders, who feel unwelcome and underserved by this new community, what becomes clear is that, in order to make themselves feel at home, billeted guests must necessarily invade the spaces and take the resources of the locals.

The resentment that results from the process of billeting factory workers, particularly women, becomes allegorized in *The Hours Before Dawn* through Vera's mysterious tenancy. The "invasion" of Vera Brandon, the added stress of worrying about the heat of her room or the meals she requires, threatens to break Louise's resolve. Dramatizing the tension between itinerant workers and their hosts, Fremlin uses a postwar setting to reflect on the wartime tensions of the mysterious lodger. In the novel, it turns out that Louise's paranoia and anxieties are well-founded. At the climax of the plot, Miss Brandon finds Louise holding baby Michael in the kitchen, asleep, and then proceeds to turn on the oven in hopes of staging a suicide for the purposes of absconding with the child she believes to be hers. The pilot light catches, and the house erupts in flames. The family barely escape with their lives and, confronted with her failed plot, Vera Brandon throws herself into the fire. The community, retrospectively enlightened by the revelation of Vera's plot, rallies behind Louise, affirming—all too late—her previously rejected beliefs about her suspicious tenant. Not only was her anxiety justified, but she is also acquitted of bad parenting. Michael begins to behave more properly, and the novel closes peaceably enough.

But the emphasis on women's experiences, and the devaluation of that experience at the hands of experts, continues to be a theme that ties Fremlin's work with Mass-Observation to her fiction. Women in Mass-Observation, like Celia Fremlin and Naomi Mitchison, attended to the project as a means of amplifying the voices of those incapable of having their experience validated by the expert and institutional discourses so prevalent to public opinion work in the mid-century. The transition of Mass-Observation from a qualitative arm of analysis to one more bound to the quantitative intentions of bureaucratic institutions and private industry marks the end of a potential alternative path for the methods and practices of polling and public opinion analysis during the war. Ironically, women

---

[128] Mass-Observation, *War Factory*, p. 14.

like Adams, Fremlin, and Mitchison, who wanted to see the fears and anxieties of women highlighted in order to make public institutions more responsive to their concerns, instead were denounced as domestic spies and snoopers. Even in the introduction to *War Factory*, it is clear that Fremlin's anonymity is necessary precisely because of paranoia about domestic espionage. The dissolution of Mass-Observation's original mission was not just a loss for the anthropological experiment that Harrisson, Madge, and Jennings envisioned. It was also a massive loss to those who were systematically underserved by the polling infrastructure that remained.

The quantitative analysis that replaced and supplanted Mass-Observation was insufficient to capture women's experiences. Not only did the lack of narrative and qualitative analysis preclude people sharing the complexity and diversity of their stories, but the Gallup methods that have come to dominate the sphere of public opinion were systematically designed—particularly in the interwar period—to disenfranchise women. If, as the Peace Ballot and the introduction of polling in *News Chronicle* suggested, polling was meant to be a supplement and boon to democratic systems of government, this new practice portended full representation of the people whose opinions it supposedly shared. And yet, as a study of early Gallup methodologies suggest, women were often underserved by this practice, through a lack of male interviewers, a hesitancy to interview women, and a fetishization of the technocratic and male leaders in the polling field. M-O was the one place where women's roles were able to shine, and as the novels of Fremlin and Mitchison demonstrate, the disintegration of M-O's qualitative experiment was a clear detriment to women's morale and valuation during the war.

5

The Morass of Morale

The Ministry of Information in the Works of Cecil Day-Lewis and Elizabeth Bowen

Introduction: Duff Cooper and His Snoopers

On August 4, 1941, the *Daily Mail* reported the shocking mass resignation of twenty-four workers at the Ministry of Information's Home Intelligence Department, provocatively headlined "'Cooper's Snoopers' Have Walked Out."[1] Under the circumstances, one could easily imagine the ebullient faces of the editorial staff as they wrote the headline, touting the quick defeat of a reviled enemy; only one month prior, the *Daily Mail* joined a cohort of newspapers, spearheaded by *The Daily Herald*, in the movement to discredit Home Intelligence, an arm of the Ministry of Information (MoI) designed to research morale during the war.[2] Until the eruption of controversy in the press, Home Intelligence operations consisted primarily in collecting morale reports from a variety of sources, including the BBC, Regional Intelligence Officers, postal censors, and private organizations.[3] Additionally, Home Intelligence conducted its own surveys with the help of professional interviewers, provided via a contract with Mass-Observation (M-O), who worked under the authority of the Ministry of Information. It was this part of Home Intelligence work that would be sensationalized by newspapers when uncovered. M-O interviewers, empowered by the MoI, traversed the country, asking a vast range of questions about topics that impacted the home front. How much milk were people drinking? What was their favorite broadcast this week? If people were told it would help the war effort, would

---

[1] "22 'Coopers Snoopers' have Walked Out," *Daily Mail*, August 4, 1941, The War-time Social Survey Papers, SxMs12/2/2/5, University of Sussex Special Collections.

[2] Ian McLaine's *Ministry of Morale* provides a good account of the Snoopers controversy, which led to a debate in the Commons over the Ministry of Information, The War-time Social Survey, and Mass-Observation. McLaine, *Ministry of Morale*, pp. 84–6.

[3] Papers Describing Structure, Function, and work of War-time Social Survey, August 1940, Mary Adams Papers, SxMOA4/6/1/1, University of Sussex Special Collections.

Public Opinion Polling in Mid-Century British Literature: The Psychographic Turn. Megan Faragher, Oxford University Press. © Megan Faragher 2021. DOI: 10.1093/oso/9780192898975.003.0006

they consider eating brown bread instead of white? The survey experienced, as reported in an internal memo on August 8, 1940, "few difficulties [...] until the publication of the article in the *Daily Herald* of July 25th."[4] But difficulties came in spades after the *Herald* alarmed the public and rallied it against surreptitious investigators working at the behest of the government. Other newspapers, too, castigated the Ministry of Information and Duff Cooper personally for perpetrating an unforgivable invasion of privacy and threatening the freedom of private thought everywhere. The efforts of the press succeeded; the press campaign against Home Intelligence eventually led to a rotating series of new Ministers, the resignation of the Home Intelligence director Mary Adams, and the subsequent mass resignation of Home Intelligence workers in August of the following year. Of course, distrust of polling efforts not only impacted the internal Home Intelligence attempts to assess home front morale; the BBC was also concerned about the Snoopers controversy for its own listener research, citing that the media spectacle "did its best to stir up public antagonism against all form of sample survey," though no interruption in the BBC surveys was cited.[5]

Though the press feigned indignation at the tactics of the government in collecting opinion data, its real motivation was self-serving; up to this point newspapers had been the primary source and outlet for public opinion research. The government had turned itself into a competitor to the newspaper industry in the field of polling—an indignation that could not be suffered. When the Advertising Service Guild (ASG) stepped into the debate about "Cooper's Snoopers," the group was quick to point out that jealousy and competition were two of the primary motivating factors for media uproar. In a pamphlet titled "An Appeal to Reason: Social Surveys Surveyed," the group detailed not only the extant facts about the so-called snoopers, but also dismissed what they saw as a short-sighted press campaign to delegitimize a useful tool for military strategy on the home front.[6] The ASG pamphlet began with a brief example from the papers demonstrating the media's cynical, bad faith efforts to take down a leading competitor. At the beginning of the pamphlet ASG quotes from a truly shoddy "poll" published in the *Sunday Pictorial*, which asked readers a leading question:

---

[4] Papers Describing Structure, Function, and work of War-time Social Survey.
[5] "Listener Research Report," January 18, 1941, BBC Written Archives Collection (WAC), ref 9/1, No. 18.
[6] Advertising Service Guild, "An Appeal to Reason: Social Surveys Surveyed," 1940, The War-time Social Survey Papers, SxMs12/1/5, University of Sussex Special Collections.

"Mr. Duff Cooper is paid £5000 a year by the Government to be Minister of Information. DO YOU CONSIDER THAT HE IS THE RIGHT MAN FOR THE JOB?"[7] The Advertising Service Guild's opening salvo cuts to the quick; it directly highlights the astonishing hypocrisy and immense irony in the *Sunday Pictorial*, which turns to an unprofessional, sensationalist, biased poll in an attempt to discredit Cooper's administration of professional polling. After marking this contrast between the burgeoning professional polling industry and the abuse of the polling form by the papers, the pamphlet ends its introduction by stating, "as professional men we are concerned with the attack which is being made on certain of the activities of the Ministry of Information. In particular we are concerned with the efforts being made in certain newspapers to bring into contempt the science of investigation of public opinion."[8] The Guild pamphlet continues to outline the brief history of public opinion research, begun thirty years prior with "crude" efforts by newspapers to "send out a reporter to interview a dozen or more people about some topic."[9] They go on to chronicle the development of the field, citing first the catastrophic failure of the American *Literary Digest* poll of 1936, then describing the evolution of Gallup's methods, which led to the correct predictions of six by-elections in England.[10] Educating its lay audience as to the benefits of public opinion research, ASG sought to restore polling's damaged reputation.

Of course, just as the press wanted to dismiss governmental polling in part because they preferred to conduct their own sensationalist mock-polls to drum up readership (with the exception of outlets like *News Chronicle*, detailed in Chapter 2), the Advertising Service Guild had its own ulterior motives for defending the MoI.[11] Representing commercial interests and market researchers, the Guild could not very well afford to see the press denigrate polling's status; the success of market research derived from clients paying the ASG to conduct polling on their products; they, too, hired

---

[7] Advertising Service Guild, "An Appeal to Reason: Social Surveys Surveyed."
[8] Advertising Service Guild, "An Appeal to Reason: Social Surveys Surveyed."
[9] Advertising Service Guild, "An Appeal to Reason: Social Surveys Surveyed."
[10] In 1936, the *Literary Digest*, a publication which had been surveying its own readers to engage in political prognostication, failed spectacularly to predict the 1936 election of Roosevelt. As British Institute of Public Opinion's Henry Durant writes, *Literary Digest* could "not get a truly representative cross-section of the population," citing the Gallup method as far more accurate with accurate cross-sections. Durant, "Gallup Surveys," pp. 108–9.
[11] For one, the ASG was given a publicity commission by the Ministry of Information, thus incentivizing their defense of the Ministry of Information. Hinton, *The Mass Observers*, p. 220.

firms like Mass-Observation to conduct research for them.[12] If the *Herald* and its guild succeeded in making polling a disreputable practice, neither brands nor governments would request the service. A ragtag alliance formed among several MPs, Mass-Observation, ASG, and MoI staff, all of whom circled the wagons around polling in response to the newspaper campaign against the "Snoopers." They touted its successes and its ability to aid in coordinating and administering public policy effectively during the war. While these defenders were mildly successful in quelling the revolt against polling, the reactive and conservative approach to Home Intelligence the Ministry adopted after this affair led to the inevitable coup in August 1941.

In part, this upheaval derived from the ever-shifting methodologies preferred by the MoI and, as we have seen thus far, the methodological questions around polling were not lacking in political ramifications. The previous chapter of this book on Mass-Observation (M-O) argued that qualitative data collection, including the recording of overheard conversation and maintenance of personal diaries, enabled women to enter the increasingly professionalized arena of social psychology. Women like Celia Fremlin and Naomi Mitchison used their M-O work to contribute to the war effort as active social scientists, recording their experiences during war and even going undercover to report on civilian morale. While academic studies on public opinion and those in market research required the cultural and educational capital that women often lacked, M-O offered new opportunities for women to contribute to this new field, even if that contribution was tinged by the rogue reputation of Mass-Observation. But while M-O was often considered an outcast from the polling world, its work with the Ministry of Information symbolized the transition of M-O away from its more surrealist, avant-garde roots and towards a more bureaucratic and institutionalized organization.[13] With the help of Home Intelligence director Mary Adams—who became a "key authority" on surveying morale in government circles—M-O received a lucrative contract from the MoI

---

[12] Hinton reports that the ASG began commissioning M-O, paying them a retainer of £30 per week beginning in June 1941, and led to the transition of M-O from a sociological project to a "conventional market research organization" by the 1950s, a point also supported by Dorothy Sheridan. Hinton, *The Mass Observers*, p. 216.

[13] Nick Hubble's *Mass-Observation and Everyday Life* contains an illuminating chapter on the relationship between Mass-Observation and surrealism, looking to Madge and Jennings as defenders of surrealism, and citing the early influence of surrealism on Mass-Observation, including the "centrality of the concept of the coincidence" as a theme that links M-O to the surrealist movement. Similar arguments are put forward in Jeremy MacClancy, "Brief Encounter: The Meeting, in Mass-Observation, of British Surrealism and Popular Anthropology," *The Journal of the Royal Anthropological Institute* 1, no. 3 (September 1995), pp. 495–512.

through some of the war, in exchange for which the group conducted surveys at the behest of the government.[14] Despite a vociferous defense of the Home Intelligence methods and M-O surveys in the House of Commons and in letters to the editor, the press campaign against the MoI indirectly led to the dissolution of the contract between the MoI and M-O. For M-O, the integration of their methods into the institutional apparatus of the MoI led to a shift in their own methodology, a change which followed M-O into the 1940s.[15] For the MoI, the controversy revealed public anxieties about the weaponization of public opinion polling by British governmental institutions, a concern foreshadowing Foucault's critique of polling as part of the *raison d'État*.[16] And while Goebbels used public opinion research to violently repress unsanctioned, anti-government views, those on the British home front feared the national institutionalization of public opinion research would usher in the same censorious results.[17] This chapter examines the struggles of the MoI to incorporate accurate social surveys while also meeting the demand by government agencies for streamlined and simplified data.

This final chapter on the Ministry of Information is a fitting, though tragic, partner to the one prior, as it records the violent backlash against public opinion polling. This backlash is well documented historically, as epitomized by the internal Home Intelligence revolt, but it also emerges in literature, as the coverage of wartime polling led the collection of opinion data to be increasingly viewed as a form of private intrusion. The literary concern with this form of private surveillance emerges particularly in the work of writers whose own war work corresponded with home front morale assessment. As polling disseminated through radio and newspapers, the nature of polling also changed to mirror the sociopolitical dynamism of its mediation. The *Sunday Pictorial* "poll" is a crucial case in point; the newspaper's exploitation of polling's cultural capital is the necessary prerequisite for the use of the Duff Cooper poll as a naked rhetorical device.

---

[14] Angus Calder, *The Myth of the Blitz* (London: Pimlico, 1997), p. 121.

[15] Reference to Mass-Observation's private commissions in the post-war are provided by Dorothy Sheridan in "Reviewing Mass-Observation."

[16] Foucault, *Security, Territory, and Population*, p. 275.

[17] In a 1950 article in *Public Opinion Quarterly*, Doob centralizes the impact of public opinion research for Goebbels' propaganda project, stating that his diaries "maintained that he and his associates could plan and execute propaganda only by constantly referring to existing intelligence." Doob further notes the importance of reports of the *Sicherheits-Dienst* (*SD*) within the secret police. He cites Goebbels' diary, which compares the work of the *SD* to "a statistical investigation...in the manner of the Gallup Institute." See Leonard Doob, "Goebbels' Principles of Propaganda," *The Public Opinion Quarterly* 14, no. 3 (1950), p. 422.

Additionally, the appropriation of polling as a rhetorical tool begins the process of delegitimizing the field's scientific validity in the public eye. Unlike standard scientific polls, the mock poll in the *Pictorial* directly seeks to *form* public opinion, *not reflect* it. The *Pictorial*'s sarcastic poll acknowledges, through negation, the level of respectability polling had achieved in the prior decade. But having established itself as a reputable scientific pursuit, newspaper editors transform polling into a rhetorical device, mirroring the feedback loop between audience and producer likewise experienced in the medium of print journalism and wireless. Floyd Allport provided a diagnosis of this emergent problem when he noted the rise of an "illusion" that what is published as "public opinion" adopts the "character of widespread importance and endorsement" to readers, whether or not the data provided is truly reflective of the sentiments of the nation.[18] In its early days, pollsters wanted to offer a glimpse into the fluctuating life of the chaotic modern mind while also maintaining an anthropological distance from influencing the formation of those opinions. But, in a process that began with the MoI controversy in 1940, the public began to treat polling results as a casted rune, not just demonstrating what people would like to happen, but actively altering public response through the publicity around polling results. The threat to independent private opinion was real, as testified to in Virginia Woolf's *Three Guineas*, where the author frustratedly searches out the conditions under which women could establish their own opinions outside the manipulative influences of capitalism or nationalism; she must eventually settle on a "Society of Outsiders" free from such pressures to provide the possibility for a future free of war.[19] In this moment, the poll transforms from a participatory venue of conversation to an alienating proscription of the future, concretizing the "reification of consciousness" that Theodor Adorno diagnoses in his *Introduction to Sociology* as emerging in the first half of the twentieth century.[20]

While the *Pictorial* poll sought to form of public opinion instead of reflect it, there were other less obvious ways in which wartime polling proactively changed public behavior. The MoI's work in the field of public opinion polling led citizens to adopt different behaviors and attitudes towards such studies during the war. The press sanctified public opinion through allusion to the sanctity of private thought, while the intermingling of

---

[18] Floyd Allport, "Towards a Science of Public Opinion," *Public Opinion Quarterly* 1 (1937), p. 12.
[19] Woolf, *Three Guineas*, p. 50.   [20] Adorno, *Introduction to Sociology*, p. 149.

sociological study and propaganda made the work of interviewers increasingly suspect. The failures of the MoI on both fronts led to increased paranoia and insecurity in citizens who began to mistrust one another and the interviewers who came to their doors. Fiction of the period repeatedly gestures towards this anxiety, particularly as writers in England and Ireland became central to realizing the MoI's vision. For writers familiar with the controversy around the MoI's efforts to assess home front morale, their wartime espionage novels adopted a new tenor. As Elizabeth Bowen gathered information on Irish morale, writing letters to the MoI tracking Irish response to British wartime policy, she also allegorized her tenuous position as a distrusted information worker in her mid-century fiction. In *The Heat of the Day*, the espionage plot surrounding Robert Kelway is frequently superseded by personal rumor and private opinion. While often this has led some to characterize *The Heat of the Day* as a domestic novel shrouded in the veneer of a spy novel, the consideration of Bowen's wartime work reporting to Churchill's administration on civilian morale suggests the inextricability of the private from the political, and her aesthetics reflect the increasing materialization of consciousness realized in her wartime work. Bowen's work in reporting Irish morale was a pseudo-formalized form of wartime labor, and for writers with more formal associations with the MoI, the controversies over public opinion assessment and wartime morale work were even more prevalent. After Cecil Day-Lewis began work in the Publications division of the MoI, his pseudonymous detective fiction concretely reflects the tension between the information-gathering arm of the MoI and the public, who saw the assessment of public opinion as a breach of public trust. Published under the pseudonym Nicholas Blake, Day-Lewis's novels *Malice in Wonderland* and *Minute for Murder* covertly defend the value of Mass Observers and pollsters in their efforts to thwart foreign attack. At the same time, these novels allude to the increasing distrust of the kind of morale reportedly spearheaded by the MoI.

Cecil Day-Lewis's *Malice in Wonderland* and the "Silent Column"

In the midst of the public relations fiasco at the Ministry of Information over their use of Mass Observers, Cecil Day-Lewis published the detective novel *Malice in Wonderland* under his pseudonym Nicholas Blake. That same year, Day-Lewis would take up a role at the Ministry of Information's

Publications Division. But even before Day-Lewis had learned the details of the Ministry's work, *Malice in Wonderland* clearly suggests the important and often controversial role of observers in the interwar period, as he identifies their importance as both social surveyors and agents of the state. In the novel, the detective Nigel Strangeways is accompanied in his duty as detective by another man, Paul Perry, whose role as a Mass Observer has put him in the unique position to amass information used to solve a series of pranks and crimes, eventually leading to the identification of a German espionage plot. Composed in the height of the Phoney War, *Malice in Wonderland* strikes a balance between a story about peacetime leisure and one invested in wartime troubles. The novel takes place in the holiday park "Wonderland," a place of peacetime escapism divorced from the looming prospect of a German conflict. But *Malice* also presents ominous allusions to the war; references to espionage and invasion permeate the text, even as the characters themselves seem to be living in a holiday oasis, isolated from any and all links to political life. It is clear that the convergence of peacetime and wartime tropes in *Malice* is not without purpose; rather, by revealing the plot of an espionage scheme in the world of a holiday camp, Day-Lewis reminds us of the ubiquity of war in the lives of even the most oblivious pleasure-seekers.

The primary, though not only, mystery of *Malice in Wonderland* lies in uncovering the perpetrator of a series of pranks taking place at the expense of Wonderland tourists. The crisis begins when, as the campers go for an ocean swim, several of them are forcibly dragged beneath the water by a mysterious swimmer. These so-called "duckings" are followed by a mysterious note from a villain who calls himself "The Mad Hatter"; it will become clear that many of the pranks and crimes committed by the Hatter are thematically tied to Lewis Carroll's *Alice in Wonderland*. While the Hatter starts his reign of terror by pulling people underwater, he moves on and conducts a series of other pranks. Some of these, like the shooting off of rockets, seem more dangerous, while others, including the covering of tennis balls in treacle, are mere annoyances. All the same, the staff is desperate to save the reputation of Wonderland from the prankster. Luckily, one of the visitors to the camp, the aforementioned Paul Perry, is not just any regular holiday traveler. He is a certified Mass Observer, whose original intention at the camp was to gather as much information as he could about the behaviors of holiday campers for his work.

But Paul's position is wrought with controversy. Before Perry identifies himself as a certified Observer, he is overwhelmed by accusations from other campers, suspicious of his aloofness and surreptitious notetaking. After the campers discover the tennis balls covered in treacle, they immediately begin questioning one another to uncover the culprit. In the subsequent spate of finger-pointing, Sally Thistlethwaite first accuses Paul Perry of espionage: "Oh yes, you did, Paul Pry [...] You go snooping around—yes, I've seen you—putting things down in a little notebook when you think nobody's looking."[21] Sally's accusation, couched in the language of *The Daily Herald* by the citation of his "snooping," leads to increased suspicion of Perry's observations among guests who think he might be responsible for the pranks. Eventually, Perry outs himself to the Wonderland staff as a Mass Observer, being careful to indicate the reason for his secrecy. As accusations fly against Perry, he quickly recognizes the need to justify his behavior by explaining his role as an observer. Aware that "[p]eople are apt to draw in their horns" if they knew they were being observed by a Mass-Observer, Perry quickly outs himself as an Observer, then contemplates shifting roles to, as he puts it, "combine the survey with a bit of detective work."[22] In revealing his observational work, Perry transforms from a mere collector of data to an arbiter of moral culpability; he shifts from being a recorder of reality to the one who judges guilt or innocence. In this transition, *Malice* begins to revive the scientist as a "popular...character in detective fiction," a convergence noted by Mass-Observation in *Britain*.[23] This convergence between social scientist and detective becomes literally true when Perry becomes an assistant to the detective Nigel Strangeways, taking on the case of the Mad Hatter and providing his sociological notes to a state agent for use in detecting a criminal. In part, this transformation of Paul Perry gives credence to the anxieties that clouded the work of Mass-Observation at the height of the war: that innocent people would be judged and disciplined based on their private conversations, and that those judgments would have legal and political consequences.

The methods of Mass-Observation, which emphasized the dynamism between the chaos of social interactions and the proposed orderliness that observational study might impose upon such chaos, addressed more than just sociological problems; they were addressing aesthetic ones as well. As modernist aesthetics had so embraced the specter of impersonality, the combination of the immensely personal nature of observation with the scientific approaches proffered by psychographic methods paralleled aesthetic

---

[21] Nicholas Blake, *Malice in Wonderland* (London: Ipso Books, [1940] 2017), p. 46.
[22] Blake, *Malice in Wonderland*, p. 49.   [23] Mass-Observation, *Britain*, p. 17.

interventions by the 1930s generation of writers. In the Auden and Day-Lewis collaborative preface to *Oxford Poetry 1927*, the pair set forward an aesthetic agenda for the new group, identifying principles that could just as well have been describing Day-Lewis's sociological approach to his detective fiction. Promoting a "new synthesis" between the private and public, which would organize and manage the "chaos of values which is the substance of our environment," the two authors provided a new theory of poetics. Far from the impersonal aesthetics of Pound or Eliot, they wanted to "bring order to self-consciousness," and use poetry to focus on the "psychological conflict [...] between self as subject and self as object."[24] The tacit recognition of this dualism within the psychological landscape—the recognition of the objectification of the self as a psychological phenomenon—could equally apply to methods of aesthetic engagement and those of scientific sociological discourse in the interwar period. As Paul Perry attempts to wrestle the personalities of the holiday-goers with his own role as an object—not a subject—of study, he is duly confronted by his own subjectivity as vacationers attest to his own position as a Wonderland holiday-goer. Paul's wrestling between these two categories throughout the novel recalls the *Oxford Poetry 1927* preface and provides insight into the ramifications of Day-Lewis and Auden's manifesto of psychographic aesthetics.

The seeming bifurcation of Day-Lewis's work starting in the 1930s—the supposed chasm between his deeply private poetry and his pseudonymous, low-brow detective fiction—testifies to the innate conflict between the subjective and objective self. But even in Day-Lewis's poetry we can find tendrils of the psychographic ethos creeping their way into the intimate lines of his verse. Written amidst his work with the MoI, the poems in *Word Over All* (1943) maintain focus on the loss of love and passion amid the tumult of war, as demonstrated in the opening lines of the titular poem "Word Over All":

> Now when drowning imagination clutches
> At old loves driving away,
> Splintered highlights, hope capsized – a wrecked world's
> Flotsam, what can I say
> To cheer the abysmal gulfs, the crests that lift not
> To any land in sight?

[24] Cited in Peter Stanford, *Cecil Day-Lewis: A Life* (London: Continuum, 2007), p. 72.

Despite Day-Lewis's focus on interiority, the "wrecked world's flotsam" is never far from the "drowning imagination."[25] As Day-Lewis recognized in *A Hope for Poetry*, "the specifically modern data of his environment—the political situation, the psychological states, the scientific creations of twentieth-century man—are again and again used to reflect the inner activities of the poet."[26] But Day-Lewis's "Word Over All" asserts that not only can politics reflect the psychological state, but that the psychological state can, itself, be materialized in the political realm. This point is demonstrated later in "Word Over All," when Lewis cites "the politicians weaving / Voluble charms around / This ordeal, conjuring a harvest that shall spring from / Our hearts' all-harrowed ground."[27] While much of his poetry in this time continues to emphasize the inner life of the poet staged against the context of political conflict, moments like this recognize what his pseudonymous fiction declares more overtly: the ways that social analysis has become an institutional tool to weaponize collective psychological interiority.

This tension between subjective and objective social analysis was not just a facet of interwar aesthetics; when *Malice in Wonderland* met its public in 1940, anxieties and fears about observation and observers were at their zenith. While the reception of Mass-Observation as an independent project in autoethnography was not without some critics, as addressed in previous chapters, the venture was originally well-received by segments of the intellectual left. M-O's independence from political institutions meant that the project caused little alarm about security. However, when the MoI began to subcontract M-O to do its work at behest of the government, the tenor of the discussion changed dramatically. While M-O was an independent group, its contractual link to the MoI meant that the recorded work product of observers was going directly to the government. Observers even carried letters from the Ministry, to be used as leverage to encourage participation by interviewees; this was meant to legitimize the M-O workers, but as it did so it also classified them as agents of the state.[28] Subjects of observation were no longer just citizens providing insight into everyday behaviors for a

[25] Cecil Day-Lewis, "Word Over All," *The Complete Poems* (Stanford, CA: Stanford University Press, 1992), p. 325.
[26] Cecil Day-Lewis. *A Hope for Poetry* (Oxford: Basil Blackwell, 1935), p. 37.
[27] Day-Lewis, "Word Over All," p. 326.
[28] An internally produced Home Intelligence department description of The War-time Social Survey describes letters that Mass Observers carried which "they show[ed] only when they encounter[ed] suspicion of their bona fides." "'Wartime Social Survey,' organisation, methods employed," July 7, 1940, The War-time Social Survey Papers, 1940–41, SxMOA17/7/11, University of Sussex Special Collections.

sociological experiment; they were aiding in the government's home front morale initiatives. The shifting role of observers—from freelancers to government contractors—led to an increased level of suspicion and fear during the war, as evinced by the Cooper's Snoopers controversy. Like the tourists at Wonderland, citizens were consumed by "widespread revulsion [...] at the threat to civil liberties posed by the 'police state' methods of observers."[29] These anxieties over domestic espionage on the part of the government were tangible in the media coverage and in public sentiment.[30] The ambivalent response to Perry parallels this shifting attitude precisely. Once Perry becomes an observer-agent empowered to identify the criminal prankster, he is equal parts respected and feared.

In *Malice in Wonderland*, Perry pushes back against great resistance by those who see his work as a form of espionage and even liken him to a kind of spy. Wonderland tourists remain fearful of providing Perry with information, skeptical over the stakes of sharing their observations to a near stranger, knowing it will be fed to the authorities at a moment's notice. In fact, the fear of sharing information suggested in the novel is but an allusion to one facet of the MoI's wartime policy. At the time that the MoI was using Mass Observers like Perry to gather information from everyday citizens about morale and wartime policy, they simultaneously began a public relations campaign that would have devastating effects on their ability to gather such information. In 1940, Duff Cooper's MoI began the infamous "Silent Column" campaign. This campaign was an effort to decrease wartime rumor and make the public conscientious about sharing information with strangers or possible spies, perhaps born of M-O surveys claiming that the country was "awash with alarming rumours about spies, saboteurs, agent provocateurs, and hilltop signallers to enemy planes."[31] But, as one might expect, this also had the unintended effect of producing fear among citizens over their correspondence with Mass Observers. In the end, the Silent Column campaign was derided as inducing needless paranoia and as

---

[29] Calder, *The Myth of the Blitz*, p. 116.

[30] While, despite the Cooper's Snoopers controversy, many respondents were cooperative, some were not. One observer records an interviewee's attitudes as follows: "Hostile and suspicious. Asked what Government department, then asked for authority. Credential letter shown—then said had seen about it in the press—finally asked in, but attitude on defensive all the time and argumentative." "Interviewers' Report on Reception," Papers describing the structure, function and working of The War-time Social Survey, August 10, 1940, Mary Adams Papers, SxMOA4/6/1/1, University of Sussex Special Collections.

[31] Robert Mackay, *Half the Battle: Civilian Morale in Britain during the Second World War* (Manchester: Manchester University Press, 2003), p. 65.

counterproductive to information-gathering efforts, causing a panic about arrest. The tenor of the Silent Column is captured exquisitely by Fougasse's series of "Careless Talk Costs Lives" posters. The posters depict everyday surreptitious listening as the ultimate wartime intelligence risk. The Fougasse posters evince the amorphous nature of espionage anxiety. Listeners might be anywhere. Even the notion of listening in might be alluded to without even a body to listen. Espionage was both embodied or disembodied; it might be conducted by those behind you on the bus, but it might even be the walls themselves that hear your whispered secrets as we see in the poster featuring Hitler's face as a form of sentient wallpaper (see Figures 5.1 and 5.2). Fears of Perry's overhearing in *Malice in Wonderland* thus entered at the precise historical moment when the Fifth Column anxiety was at its apex.

The summer that featured the Battle of Britain and the publication of *Malice in Wonderland* also jump-started this infamous Silent Column campaign. Instigated by Lord Haw-Haw's radio propaganda, including the reading of "spoof instructions" to imaginary Fifth Columnists in England, rumors of traitors spread, with "ample evidence [...] to indicate widespread fears and paranoia" about secret Nazi sympathizers ready to overthrow the country from within.[32] Other than the "Careless Talk" campaign, the Ministry's Silent Column effort included several memorable poster campaigns, including one warning us of Mr. Glumpot, Miss Teapot Whisper, and Miss Leaky Mouth (see Figure 5.3). In mid-1940, Duff Cooper asked BBC listeners to take up their wartime roles as part of what he called the "Silent Column," a group he contrasted to the "Fifth Column" of enemies and spies in their midst.[33] The campaign was rapid and extensive, including over half a million distributed posters, articles in newspapers, special BBC programs on the topic, and security notices during film showings.[34] But it backfired spectacularly, as people became terrified that any idle chatter might be prosecutable under the Civil Defence Act; one woman was even arrested for claiming, *in flagrante*, that Hitler's invasion would be far less intimidating if she could have passionate nights in seedy hotels with her lover.[35] Harold Nicolson lamented that "our anti-rumour campaign has

[32] Calder, *The Myth of the Blitz*, pp. 112, 109.
[33] Jo Fox, "Careless Talk: Tensions within Domestic Propaganda During the Second World War," *Journal of British Studies* 51, no. 4 (2012) p. 944.
[34] Fox, "Careless Talk," p. 938.
[35] Leo McKinstry, *Operation Sea Lion* (London: John Murray, 2014), p. 213.

Figure 5.1   Fougasse (Kenneth Bird), "You Never Know Who's Listening," (1940); © Victoria and Albert Museum, London.

Figure 5.2   Fougasse (Kenneth Bird), "Don't Forget That the Walls Have Ears," (1940); © Victoria and Albert Museum, London.

Do you know one of these?

Mr. Secrecy Hush Hush

He's always got exclusive information — very private, very confidential. He doesn't want to spread it abroad but he doesn't mind whispering it to you — and others he meets. *Tell him to keep it to himself.*

Mr. Knowall

He knows what the Germans are going to do and when they are going to do it. He knows where our ships are. He knows what the Bomber Command is up to. With his large talk he is playing the enemy's game. *Tell him so.*

Miss Leaky Mouth

She simply can't stop talking and since the weather went out as conversation she goes on like a leaky tap about the war. She doesn't know anything, but her chatter can do harm. *Tell her to talk about the neighbours.*

Miss Teacup Whisper

She is a relative of Mr. Secrecy Hush Hush and an equal danger. Everything she knows is so important it must be spoken in whispers all over the town. She's one of Hitler's allies. If she does not know that, *tell her (in a whisper).*

Mr. Pride in Prophecy

Here is the marvellous fellow who knows how it is all going to turn out. Nobody else knows but he does. He's a fool and a public danger. *Give him a look* that tells him what you think of him.

Mr. Glumpot

He is the gloomy brother who is always convinced that everything is going wrong and nothing can go right. He is so worried by the enemy's strength that he never thinks of ours. *Tell him to cheer up and shut up.*

Tell them all to
JOIN BRITAIN'S SILENT COLUMN
the great body of sensible men and women who have pledged themselves not to talk rumour and gossip and to stop others doing it

ISSUED BY THE MINISTRY OF INFORMATION IN THE INTERESTS OF NATIONAL DEFENCE

Figure 5.3 "Join Britain's Silent Column," Ministry of Information (1940).

been a ghastly failure. Altogether the M. of I. is in disgrace again."[36] As a result of discouraging loose lips, not only were people reluctant to speak to Mass Observers, but they expressed fears about government overreach. Mary Adams's Home Intelligence Office warned that concerns were emerging as a result of "prosecutions for defeatist talk and for spreading

---

[36] McLaine, *Ministry of Morale*, p. 83.

rumours."³⁷ The *Manchester Guardian* categorized the Silent Column as "a sort of amateur Gestapo movement in which a few people with nothing better to do would use a lull in the actual operations of war in order to foment baseless suspicions against their neighbors."³⁸ Jo Fox has noted that the Silent Column campaign exposed "shifts and tensions within wartime propaganda," but also indicated how "propaganda campaigns could be undermined from within."³⁹ In a time of war, when mistrust was high, the ability for researchers and interviewers to elicit information from Home Intelligence survey interviewees was severely truncated. The aftermath of this contradictory messaging lasted months. As M-O reported to Home Intelligence in January 1941: "There is not a faintest indication...that any of the anti-rumor campaigns have achieved anything." The M-O, contrarily, noted that the Silent Column campaign "had a considerable temporary effect in frightening people," eliciting "the worst Hitler fantasy for the nervous."⁴⁰

While people feared under-the-table note-takers, like those captured in Fougasse's poster, Mass Observers throughout the country found themselves stymied by an environment of increased fear and paranoia. It is hard to say whether it was this campaign or the Snoopers controversy that finally did Cooper in as a Minister, but surely the combination was too much for one man's reputation at the head of an important wartime Ministry. The Silent Column did not last long, beginning with a public relations contract with ASG in June and ending in July 1940 after it met with massive public outcry.⁴¹ As Ian McLaine reports, the "public resented the well publicised spate of prosecutions for what was regarded as grumbling 'in the British tradition.'"⁴² The press declared, unequivocally, that the public were tired of being told who to talk to or what to talk about. "Savours of the Gestapo," said one Home Intelligence interviewee, "we let people talk in normal times in Hyde park and it does no harm, why cannot they be trusted now?"⁴³ Undoubtedly, the campaign "did more to damage morale than to sustain it."⁴⁴ As much as the campaign failed in its efforts to improve the situation on the home front, it had a little-recognized side effect: it hamstrung the

---

³⁷ McLaine, *Ministry of Morale*, p. 83.   ³⁸ Cited in Fox, "Careless Talk," p. 946.
³⁹ Fox, "Careless Talk," p. 937.
⁴⁰ "Note on Rumour By Mass-Observation," January 7, 1941, Mary Adams Papers, SxMOA4/1/3/1, University of Sussex Special Collections.
⁴¹ Hinton, *The Mass Observers*, p. 221.   ⁴² McLaine, *Ministry of Morale*, p. 83.
⁴³ "The News, Silent Column, the War," August 24, 1940, The War-time Social Survey Papers, 1940–41, SxMs12/5/2/2, University of Sussex Special Collections.
⁴⁴ Mackay, *Half the Battle*, p. 66.

efforts of Home Intelligence to collect the survey data it needed to properly assess morale. As Francis Williams wrote in an editorial for the *Evening Standard*, "people who have been attacking the Wartime Social Survey with one hand, Cooper's Snoopers as they call it, while defending democracy with the other, have got themselves into a hopeless position."[45] Mass-Observation framed the Ministry's famous "Careless Talk Costs Lives" campaign as an abysmal misestimation, arguing that it reinforced "Haw-Haw propaganda" by suggesting that the Germans "know everything, see everything." Thus M-O framed the famous Fougasse project as a real failure, stating that "What is wanted is not a Silent Column to counteract rumor and explain, but a Reassuring Column."[46]

The inherent anxiety over rumor-mongering becomes increasingly centralized as the plot of *Malice in Wonderland* unfolds. In fact, Day-Lewis also seems wary at times about the ability for social surveyors to aid in the public good when they were, in fact, paid by the government. When the pranks begin at Wonderland, Paul Perry offers the Wonderland leadership an opportunity to flesh out the criminal by using a survey, with nine questions related to the preferences of holiday-goers. Most of the questions are seemingly benign ("Do you like your pleasures to be organized for you to the extent they are in Wonderland?"), but others seek to target information about the Mad Hatter: "What is your opinion about the mad hatter? Is he (*a*) a practical joker? (*b*) mad? (*c*) more than one person? (*d*) a stunt on the part of management? (*e*) a person with a grievance against the Wonderland Co.? (*f*) Any other theories."[47] The questionnaire itself is meant to have a calming effect on the visitors, who might be satisfied by the survey's "impersonal" methods.[48] But when discussing the survey, Day-Lewis inserts a crucial passage, seemingly in reference to the kinds of anxieties precipitated by the Fifth Column controversy. As Wonderland management debates the drafted questionnaire, secretary Miss Jones presents the possibility that asking participants whether "they've seen or heard anything suspicious" might be problematic. "[W]ouldn't it be fatal," she asks, "to give them the impression that they're set to spy on one another?"[49] Her boss brushes her off. "Nonsense, Miss Jones," he says. But all the same, Paul becomes "vaguely aware that the semi-official position which his questionnaire had given him in the camp somehow kept him outside their circle. They grinned at him,

---

[45] Francis Williams, "Defend Cooper's Snoopers," *Evening Standard*, August 6, 1940.
[46] "Note on Rumour By Mass-Observation."   [47] Blake, *Malice in Wonderland*, p. 56.
[48] Blake, *Malice in Wonderland*, p. 57.   [49] Blake, *Malice in Wonderland*, p. 58.

friendly enough, but at the same time their attitude was a little self-conscious—as though he were carrying a portable microphone with him and broadcasting their fun as a feature programme to the world."[50]

Like the process of M-O under the MoI, the use of the information gathered by Perry towards the discovery of the prankster leads those who might otherwise be helpful to clam up, silence themselves, and refuse to participate in the very kind of casual conversation which might provide clues as to the Mad Hatter's identity. Furthermore, while the role of scientist first stages Paul as a benevolent outsider to the camp's activity, the public recognition of his exclusion from the camp marks him as something far more threatening once the camp attempts to uncover those who do not belong to the social network of the victimized campers.

Through the novel, Perry is increasingly compromised on two fronts. First, many of the camp-goers, even including Perry himself, slowly become suspicious that he is the prankster. While readers ought to feel secure about the amateur sociologist's innocence, evidence piles up against him. After a series of dead animals are found in campers' beds, the wire used to hang the animals is located under Perry's chalet. At this point even Perry is concerned about his own guilt. He reports to Nigel Strangeways that he "had a nervous breakdown at Cambridge once," and wonders if he hasn't suffered from undiagnosed schizophrenia: "Well, how am I to know if I'm not the split personality? Suppose I've been doing all these vile, stupid things—my other self?"[51] In expressing Perry's fears that his personality has "split"— that he has become both an observer and a participant in the Wonderland plot, Day-Lewis allegorizes the difficult duality of wartime observation. It is also a fictional manifestation of the very same aesthetic concern over the objectification of interiority that Day-Lewis and Auden had theorized in their preface to *Oxford Poetry 1927*, to be mirrored later in Bourdieu's theorization of subjective objectivization.[52] To be sure, Perry *has* divided his allegiances, acting as both a neutral observer and an agent of justice. If we take into account scholarship on the detective genre, which repeatedly reminds us that the detective is little more than the dark double for the

---

[50] Blake, *Malice in Wonderland*, p. 103.   [51] Blake, *Malice in Wonderland*, p. 158.

[52] In theorizing a new praxis of ethnology and sociology that proposes self-reflexivity, Pierre Bourdieu asks, "How can one be both subject and object, the one who acts and the one who, as it were, watches himself acting?" This difficulty, I would say, is at the crux of Perry's crisis. Pierre Bourdieu, "Participant Objectivation," *Journal of the Royal Anthropological Institute: Incorporating "Man"* (2003), p. 281.

criminal, Perry's fears of his unwitting committal of the pranks become fully legible. Likewise, the allusion to the observer as criminal corresponds with the public outcry to the MoI's campaigns, where efforts to better assess morale instead turned normal citizens into fearful ones and observers into aids in the production of a defeatist home front sentiment, thus feeding into narratives promulgated by Nazi propaganda.

Just as Perry is worried that his role as detective has brought him too close to the criminal class of the Mad Hatter, his benevolent domestic espionage becomes embedded in a more serious crime plot centered on international espionage, as the various figures attempting to identify the prankster uncover an even more nefarious scheme directly related to the war. Perry and his love-interest, Sally Thistlethwaite, explore the woods near Wonderland to investigate a curmudgeonly recluse known to have played pranks on Wonderland in the past. When they enter his cabin, they discover aerial photography of the camp and its environs. Later, Sally's father presents his own theory: the recluse, known as Old Ishmael, is a disgruntled citizen turned spy, now purportedly working in cahoots with a local spy to watch naval sites near Wonderland. Sally "vaguely recollected" to her father "that at least one of [the] photographs depicted a dockyard."[53] As "[n]obody's allowed to fly over those docks" and Old Ishmael spends "two days a week in the naval port of Applestock [...] visiting a public house much frequented by naval ratings," Mr. Thistlethwaite, Nigel Strangeways, and Paul Perry all consider that Ishmael has been collecting information on behalf of another spy. Mr. Thistlethwaite argues that one of the "chief tasks of the spy is to collect information [...] Our gallant sailors so rightly nominated 'the Silent Service,' are the last men to accuse of wilful indiscretion. But who could blame them if from time to time they talked a little too freely in the presence of Old Ishmael [...]?"[54] Thus the role of rumor and the Silent Column emerges in *Wonderland* on two fronts. On the one hand, the camp-goers, terrified of being fingered for the pranks by their fellow campers, avoid sharing information, even though such information might lead them to a solution to the mystery. On the other hand, outside of the camp there persists a network of agents whose "careless talk" may very well have contributed to the Wonderland plot. In fact, this ends up being precisely the case. When a shot is fired and hits camper Mr. Arbuthnot, Perry is missing, only to return later with a rifle, but wounded by a gunshot. It turns out that

---

[53] Blake, *Malice in Wonderland*, p. 197.   [54] Blake, *Malice in Wonderland*, p. 197.

Thistlethwaite was correct; someone had been working with foreign intelligence agents to gather sensitive naval information on the ports near Wonderland.

In the end, the purported "crimes"—the series of escalating pranks that include the seaside dunkings, the treacle-laced tennis balls, some slaughtered animals, and a strychnine-poisoned dog—end up being completely unrelated to a real threat to the nation: espionage efforts undertaken at the recluse's camp-adjacent residence. Thistlethwaite's suspicions of the recluse were only partly correct; the man presenting himself as Old Ishmael is, in fact, a spy, who has murdered Ishmael and assumed his identity, procuring aerial photography of the nearby naval base to transmit back to foreign contacts. Posing as the recluse, well-known spy Charles Black gathered information from sailors. Paul Perry realizes this before Strangeways; after leaving the camp, he returns from an encounter with the spy with a bullet-wound to show for his troubles. But Perry shot back, murdering the spy, much to the relief of Strangeways's contacts at Scotland Yard, who have been looking for Black after he successfully evaded surveillance. The violent meeting between Perry and Black thus comes to reinforce the notable duality of Perry's role as observer and spy; when Perry prevails in his spat of spy-on-spy violence with Black, he exonerates himself from suspicion that his form of espionage is malicious while also reprising the notion of the observer as an agent of state espionage.

But while successfully identifying the foreign agent, Perry fails to solve the case of the Mad Hatter. Enamored as he was with Miss Jones, who he credits with "so skillfully bringing the Mad Hatter business into the open, for neutralizing his fantastic activities through the medium of impersonal statistics," he fails to identify Miss Jones as the one responsible for the pranks.[55] Early theories that the pranks are related to company rivals, which turns out to be the truth, are ignored, precisely because Jones dismisses them out of hand. The trust between the observer and the institution, therefore, masks the real culpability of both Jones and the corporate rival. While Perry hopes his methods can chart "new institutions, new modes of behavior [...] shifting, like sandbanks," he ignores (at his peril) the vulnerability of such methods to the dangers of institutional creep, and completely precludes the possibility that such techniques might be used to manipulate public opinion, as Jones does in coordinating the Mad Hatter prank-spree. While

---

[55] Blake, *Malice in Wonderland*, p. 57.

Perry is able to uncover the spy, it is the traditional detective—Strangeways—who ends up being able to unmask Wonderland's institutional figureheads as the actual pranksters.[56] Having identified this threat, Day-Lewis would have first-hand knowledge of this relationship when he took up work with the Ministry of Information during the war.

The Ministry of Morale: Day-Lewis at the Ministry of Information

Before Cecil Day-Lewis took on a position in the Ministry of Information's Publications Division, the Home Intelligence Division hoped he might provide insight into wartime morale amongst young men. The plan for this began a few weeks before Mary Adam's resignation as the founder and director of the Home Intelligence Division, which housed the Cooper's Snoopers. Adams, a former BBC television producer before the fledgling operation was abandoned during the war, corresponded with poet and novelist Stephen Spender to solicit ideas for a new way of assessing home front morale. At the start of March 1941, she wrote to Spender: "You may remember that we spoke about the possibility of getting together a group of young writers to give us their observations and interpretations of morale at home [...] Could you suggest the names of a small group whom we could invite informally?"[57] Adams's solicitation of a writers' focus group was unique and would have provided a new avenue for writers to participate in the war effort. Rather than acting as writers or propagandists in the traditional sense (as with the Wellington House in WWI), the proposed writers were to take on roles philosophically akin to the methods of Mass-Observation, a group Adams enthusiastically supported in her time in Home Intelligence. Ironically, Adams did *not* look to writers for their ability to write, but for their capacity as social observers. In response to her query, Spender wrote back in mid-March with a sense of Adams's vision clearly in mind; he suggested a series of writers "best suited" for the work Adams wanted, though he, too, expressed interest in participating in such a group. His list of potential social observers included Louis MacNeice, Lawrence Little, William Empson ("highbrow + obscure, but also pub crawling + Mass Observant"),

---

[56] Blake, *Malice in Wonderland*, p. 83.
[57] Mary Adams to Stephen Spender, March 6, 1941, Mary Adams Papers, SxMOA4/2/4/1, University of Sussex Special Collections.

Arthur Calder-Marshall, B.L. Coombes, Willy Goldman, John Sommerfield, and Cecil Day-Lewis. The reference to Empson's status as a writer verifiably "Mass Observant" corresponds with others on the list, who were widely known for their aesthetic skills at observation, as noted by several critics.[58] Sadly, Adams never got the chance to gather her focus group of writers in one place. Two days before Spender sent his response, Adams was also writing to Julian Huxley about the possibility of resigning from the Ministry in the wake of the Snoopers controversy. "This wretched place!" Adams exclaimed in her letter to Huxley. She complained about the rapid succession of directors general, stating that Frank Pick's "reign was devastating" and that the new DG Walter Monckton was not much of an improvement. She concludes her letter with a prescient note: "I'll let you know if I resign! I long to get out of this place full of uncongealed misery."[59] Her resignation mere weeks later catalyzed the mass exodus of Home Intelligence staff in August of the same year, when the division was also attempting to navigate the controversy. The resignation, brought about as a result of frustration and increasing denigration of Home Intelligence's work with M-O and a long history of institutional instability, left many possible avenues for institutional research unexplored. Among these was the imagined focus group Adams had wanted to arrange with Spender.

Just as Spender had suggested Cecil Day-Lewis as a possible member of her writers' working group, the latter had already expressed interest in working for the MoI. Despite MI5 notes suggesting the MoI might want to "keep a close watch on him" due to his leftist leanings (MI5 knew he had technically left the Communist party the prior year), he was finally able to secure a wartime position outside the active service.[60] Day-Lewis began working there in March of 1941, following a tug-of-war between the War Office and the MoI.[61] The position was made permanent at the behest of

---

[58] Stephen Spender to Mary Adams, March 17, 1941, Mary Adams Papers, SxMOA4/2/5/2, University of Sussex Special Collections. James Purdon reads Sommerfield's *May Day* as an example of "the collective novel," bringing "together prose-poetic passages with realist narrative" and statistical awareness. Purdon, *Modernist Informatics*, pp. 108, 110. Nick Hubble has done impressive work on John Sommerfield, arguing for his method of documentary-style montage as a critical aesthetic innovation drawn from his work with Mass-Observation. Nick Hubble, *The Proletarian Answer to the Modernist Question* (Edinburgh: Edinburgh University Press, 2017). See also Stuart Laing, "Presenting 'Things as They Are': John Sommerfield's *May Day* and Mass-Observation," in *Class, Culture and Social Change: A New View of the 1940s*, edited by Frank Gloversmith (Brighton: Harvester, 1980), pp. 142–60.

[59] Mary Adams to Julian Huxley, March 15, 1941, Mary Adams Papers, SxMOA4/2/4/1, University of Sussex Special Collections.

[60] Stanford, *Cecil Day-Lewis*, pp. 187, 196.   [61] Stanford, *Cecil Day-Lewis*, p. 187.

his well-connected lover Rosamond Lehmann and the good word of E.M. Forster; Harold Nicolson would also write a letter putting an "end to any suggestion that Day-Lewis should be called up to the front line."[62] The first months of Day-Lewis's tenure at the MoI would have followed upon its most embarrassing era. The Snoopers controversy of mid-1940 had damaged the reputation of the MoI and efforts by the administration under Duff Cooper to manipulate home front morale continued to be misguided, in part because they failed to properly assimilate the research done by Home Intelligence. The press kerfuffle over the Snoopers clouded Day-Lewis's first months at the Publications Division, coming as it did just weeks after Adams's resignation.

The possibility of utilizing writers as ad hoc social surveyors was eviscerated by Adams's resignation, and Day-Lewis entered the Ministry under more traditional auspices, employed as an editor for MoI books, joining writers like Graham Greene, John Betjeman, and V.S. Pritchett, who also worked in the Ministry during the war.[63] As a writer who had long recognized that his poetry contained "a certain amount of (deliberate) doggerel in it, propaganda," and as a poet with the "greatest capacity for producing propaganda" in his generation, it only made sense to put such propaganda talents to use during the war.[64] Rather than engaging in a sociological study of the home front, Day-Lewis had been recruited for the editing and distribution of propaganda. While some of the up-and-coming generation of writers were recruited for print, others were incorporated in the Films Division.[65] The Ministry's Crown Film Unit was intimately linked to the principles of Mass-Observation, with Humphrey Jennings as one of the key directors of many CFU films, integrating the montage techniques inspired by surrealist aesthetics, most famously depicted in *Listen to Britain* (1942).[66] But while much scholarly attention has been given to the Humphrey CFU productions, Day-Lewis, writing under the nom de plume Nicholas Blake, continued to write novels about both M-O and the inner workings of the MoI, which he rechristened the "Ministry of Morale" in his novel *Minute for*

[62] Stanford, *Cecil Day-Lewis*, p. 190.   [63] Stanford, *Cecil Day-Lewis*, p. 190.

[64] Stanford, *Cecil Day-Lewis*, pp. 125, 178.

[65] During his time, Day-Lewis even worked with Basil Wright and Rex Warner on an eventually abandoned film on colliers, the unused dialogue of which eventually found its way into Day-Lewis's writing of a Nigel Strangeways radio play based on his popular detective series. Stanford, *Cecil Day-Lewis*, p. 172.

[66] Notably, when Mass-Observation began to gravitate towards statistical methods of social investigation, Jennings "lost interest" in their work; during his time at the CFU, he was involved in directing seven CFU films (Calder, *The Myth of the Blitz*, p. 236).

Murder (1947). In that novel, Nigel Strangeways takes on a position similar to Day-Lewis, working as an editor for propaganda publications. *Minute for Murder* opens with Strangeways editing a "sheet of draft photo-captions," making the language more direct (altering a writer's use of "pranging" to "attacking," for example). In conversations with colleagues, he is subject to diatribes denouncing "advertising men" and "Public Relations Officers" who "ought to be blotted out," according to the Director's secretary.[67] Not dissimilar to Day-Lewis's own job editing books on esoteric wartime subjects, Strangeways surveys a manuscript "entitled *The War Story of our Four-Legged Friends*, which had been sent to the Minister by an optimistic animal lover."[68] Though the title is facetious, the Ministry's books were often about esoteric and particular aspects of the war effort, including titles like *The Air Battle of Malta*, *The Abyssinian Campaigns*, and *The Mediterranean Fleet*; Day-Lewis himself was responsible for titles like *Bomber Command* and *The Battle of Britain*, making his *Minute for Murder* a charming send-up of the Publications Division.[69]

After the death of the Director's personal secretary by cyanide poisoning, Superintendent Blount is drawn into the plot as Strangeways' aid, which leads to a detailed discussion about the Ministry's methodology in the construction of its propaganda. Strangeways argues that the "first principle of our kind of propaganda is the human touch," but that "to keep pace with the demands, we had to mechanise it—to work out a detailed, inhuman sort of routine for delivering the human touch punctually and in large quantities."[70] This complex blend of rational practicality and falsified humanism—this "mass-emotion factory," as Blount calls it—inevitably leads to institutional dysfunction. Strangeways argues that the insincerity of the material produced in the Propaganda Division encouraged MoI officials to maintain "a certain irresponsibility [...] in their ordinary human relationships."[71] This irresponsibility, Strangeways implies, directly leads to the novel's primary crime; the deceased secretary Nita's barely veiled affair with the Director inspires a bevy of accusations and suspicions, directed at MoI workers. Additionally, Day-Lewis is also quick to point out that these personal peccadilloes diluted the MoI's mission, as the work of the Division becomes "seriously hampered by the police investigation."[72] The in-house poisoning

---

[67] Nicholas Blake, *Minute for Murder* (London: Ipso Books, [1947] 2017), pp. 1, 6.
[68] Blake, *Minute for Murder*, p. 7.   [69] Stanford, *Cecil Day-Lewis*, pp. 19–20.
[70] Blake, *Minute for Murder*, p. 66.   [71] Blake, *Minute for Murder*, p. 66.
[72] Blake, *Minute for Murder*, p. 69.

crime, born of the impersonality and insincerity of propagandistic methods, neuters the institution as it allegorizes the MoI's self-destructive tendencies. Day-Lewis's citation of producing *natural* emotion by *artificial* methods drives straight to the heart of the MoI's public relations crisis, just as it produces the crisis of the novel. Strangeways notes the fact that the artificiality of feelings has led to the dramatic tensions between employees and to the death of Nita. Their inability to properly view reality *as* reality produced a disconnect between the actions of the characters and the emotional effects of their actions.

Polling and the Invasion Panic in *Minute for Murder*

The correlation between interpersonal and institutional dysfunction was relevant to the actual Ministry as well. V.S. Pritchett described the division as "a lunatic asylum, a life of taxis, telephones," with "everyone's office like a street corner."[73] And while Adams complained about the Ministry as a place of "uncongealed misery," hampered by its lack of consistent, coherent leadership, MoI plans to boost home front morale suffered in concrete ways as a result of institutional unrest. *Minute for Murder* is peppered with references on the MoI's efforts to collect public opinion information and use it to inform public information campaigns. At one point, Nigel looks to a poster on the wall illustrating the "public response to the Eat More Potatoes campaign."[74] When Mary Adams was still in control of Home Intelligence, she outlined the goals of the department's public opinion work: to "provide a basis for publicity" facilitated by a "continuous flow of reliable information [...] on what the public is thinking and doing." As Day-Lewis alludes to, the Ministry of Food conducted studies, informed by Home Intelligence work, to better understand consumption; for example, surveys on bread sought to determine if promoting brown bread might yield more consumption. Home Intelligence would manufacture questions, send out questioners throughout the country, collect results, and tabulate them, then send them back to the appropriate ministries alongside a qualitative assessment of the quantitative data. More often than not, in the heyday of Home Intelligence work, these surveys and results were completed in collaboration with Tom Harrisson, who had secured a contract to work with the MoI in April 1940.[75]

---

[73] Cited in Stanford, *Cecil Day-Lewis*, p. 190.   [74] Blake, *Minute for Murder*, p. 162.
[75] Hinton, *The Mass Observers*, p. 128.

This contract, renewed under Mary Adams before her resignation, would last until just after the mass-resignation of the so-called Snoopers, after which point M-O turned to the advertising industry to make ends meet.[76]

Though the MoI eventually thought it could ascertain the kind of information it needed without the use of Adams or Home Intelligence, the department's internal reports had a considerable impact on the home front war effort. Two key examples demonstrate this. The first example was the "Invasion Leaflet." The leaflet informed citizens what to do in the event of German invasion, including to stay put, disbelieve rumors, keep provisions from Germans, and be ready to follow military orders.[77] The Ministry of Home Security and the MoI commissioned Adams to ask people if they had read the leaflet and found the advice salient. So Adams sent a series of interviewers out with a set of questions about the leaflet. Though the data differs by region, in 1940 a little over half (60 percent or so) had read the pamphlet; many of those had never received it at all.[78] Further inquiries by Adams's interviewers revealed that many of these lived in buildings with multiple flats where too few leaflets had been left.[79] Home Intelligence reports estimated that approximately 20 percent of households never even saw the crucial instructions.[80] Moreover, citizens who received the pamphlets had some difficulty with the MoI's instructions. It would be difficult, people argued, to resist giving one's bike to an armed German. Some were unsure how to identify a disguised German officer; still others said they would search out their children in case of emergency, rather than stay put and await governmental instruction.[81] Respondents were also put off by the look of the pamphlet. Observations like these, from Home Intelligence reports, not only helped fix the logistical problems of assessing feedback from

---

[76] Hinton, *The Mass Observers*, p. 215.

[77] The Ministry of Information, "If the Invader Comes," Ministry of Information Propaganda Leaflets, June 1940, The War-time Social Survey Papers, 1940–41, SxMs12/1/4, University of Sussex Special Collections.

[78] 37th Interim Report (N.I.E.S.R), July 1940, The War-time Social Survey Papers, 1940–41, SxMs12/3/1/1, University of Sussex Special Collections.

[79] A sample from one of many reports about the Invasion Leaflet repeats this theme: "Over 60% of the interviewees answered Yes. Of the Noes nearly one half stated that they had not received the leaflet. It is possible that only a single leaflet is placed in a building containing several families and that because of this a complete distribution of separate households is not obtained. If this deficiency cannot be corrected we must reckon that information by leaflet fails to reach about 20% of households." 37th Interim Report (N.I.E.S.R), July 1940, The War-time Social Survey Papers, 1940–41, SxMs12/3/1/1, University of Sussex Special Collections.

[80] 37th Interim Report (N.I.E.S.R), July 1940, The War-time Social Survey Papers, 1940–41, SxMs12/3/1/1, University of Sussex Special Collections.

[81] Angus Calder notes that "more than three to one people were critical of the pamphlet." Calder, *The Myth of the Blitz*, p. 132.

citizens but exposed the over-bureaucratized process of propaganda production to the light of common sense. That people would not agree to be shot over a bicycle stands to reason, though somehow the overambitious Invasion leaflet failed to foresee this variety of reader response. Such efforts by Home Intelligence led to more fine-tuned efforts at propaganda, including far more consideration. As Angus Calder suggests, such reports—which the MoI commissioned from Mass-Observation—might have even strengthened the former's reliance on the latter; the MoI accrued benefit from reports that demonstrated its ability to cull "information about what went on in public opinion 'below the surface.'"[82]

Cecil Day-Lewis would have been well aware of the mishandling of the German invasion threat when he was at the Ministry of Information, and questions of how to manage a German invasion lie at the core of the mystery in *Minute for Murder*. The difficulty in identifying who had poisoned the Director's secretary is exacerbated by the mass panic instigated by invasion fears. At first, Inspector Blount and Nigel Strangeways attempt to locate just one cyanide capsule, kept by Charles Kennington when he escaped from German capture during the war. But the plot becomes more complicated when the detective team learns that Kennington is not the only potential suspect with access to cyanide. As it turns out, cyanide is flowing like so much wine at the Ministry. Blount uncovers that "[a]t least four of the suspects had access to some form of cyanide."[83] While Kennington obtained his during military service, two other potential suspects, Mr. Lake and Mr. Fortescue, received their capsules "when the invasion scare was on."[84] The panic instilled by the Ministry's propaganda campaign leads not only to the crime, but the continued inability to solve the crime on the part of Nigel Strangeways and Inspector Blount. Additionally, the wild goose chase that leads the detectives to hunt down a series of poison capsules masks the true threat of German invasion, as Billson, an employee in the Ministry of Morale, has been blackmailed into giving away photographs with strategic military significance. While Billson's gambling debts make him susceptible to blackmail, his work in photography also gives him access to cyanide. Billson assumed that the requests for information were benign, only suspecting German influence when the blackmailer asked for photographs of "secret apparatus—radar devices on aircrafts, for example."[85] In the end, the

---

[82] Calder, *The Myth of the Blitz*, p. 132.   [83] Blake, *Minute for Murder*, p. 184.
[84] Blake, *Minute for Murder*, p. 185.   [85] Blake, *Minute for Murder*, p. 154.

invasion panic has a real basis, but not in the way the novel depicts from the start—or even in the way that the MoI had depicted it to its citizens. While public relations campaigns created a hysterical image of parachuting Germans, some disguised as nuns, infiltrating the landscape of British sovereignty, both of Day-Lewis's novels revise these narratives. His novels centralize the invasion threat in more personal and even more institutional spaces. Particularly in *Minute for Murder*, the exploitation of Billson's financial condition as a psychological tool for espionage demonstrates that the public relations campaigns are often blind to the very real threats that permeate the institutions so concerned with Nazi espionage.

As in *Malice in Wonderland*, the plot of *Minute for Murder* centers on the failed execution of MoI initiatives. Specifically, the initiatives—whether they were the Silent Column campaign or the Invasion leaflet—had undesirable results because the Ministry failed to consider the importance of public opinion assessment in the course of their work or did so only too late. This stands in direct contradiction to common beliefs about polling technology in the war: that it was effective, innovative, impactful and, perhaps most importantly, prophylactic. While Home Intelligence's work with Mass-Observation and other institutional data-collecting bodies certainly was innovative, and certainly garnered effective data, the overall impact of that data, hampered by the slow machinations of bureaucracy, never reached its fullest potential; it never prevented MoI failures. This is further evinced by the work of Celia Fremlin and her findings about women and work in contrast to the public calls by Balfour to women laborers, who were both desperately needed and wildly under-informed about the mechanisms of war work. In the first decades of the twentieth century, public opinion research had grown leaps and bounds, incorporating a variety of proven methods of assessing morale and gaps in governmental messaging. But data without praxis—perhaps the most apt description of the Ministry's use of its own polling efforts—produced confused and contradictory results, often attested to by the MoI's Home Intelligence branch. The story of Home Intelligence director Mary Adams—her dissatisfaction, disillusion, and ultimate resignation from the Ministry in a fit of disgust—registers both the innate potential of polling technologies in the war and their ultimate failure to reach their highest potential. As continually disastrous as the MoI's incorporation of polling was during the war, the efforts to include polling as a critical war-time strategy led to the continued bolstering of public opinion surveys as a critical part of the government's informational infrastructure.

The Irish "Problem": Morale Assessment in Eire

As blundering as MoI efforts were in England, efforts to assess morale in colonies and former colonies were even further curtailed. In particular, while there was great interest in assessing wartime morale in Ireland, the effort was taken on with great delicacy. In fact, the MoI never had a thorough infrastructure to undergo the challenge of polling Ireland on wartime morale. There were political as well as logistical reasons for this. English reluctance over the use of polling on the island was fueled by "sensitiv[ity] about British attempts to influence Irish public opinion," as any efforts to manipulate public opinion would be seen as an incursion on national psychological sovereignty.[86] But there were also unforeseen reasons why polling the Irish might be more difficult than it would be in England. Mary Adams had first-hand experiences with some of these hurdles, expected and unexpected, in the use of statistical public opinion research abroad. In 1941, Adams received a letter from Felix Hackett, a sociologist at University College Dublin. Not dissimilar to H.G. Wells's confrontation with the Sociological Society reviewed in Chapter 1, Hackett's efforts to introduce quantitative polling in Ireland met with dismay at the meeting of the Statistical and Social Inquiry Society of Ireland. Hackett's presentation appeared as part of the Society's journal.[87] The speech featured a review of the current best practices in polling, a summary of its recent history, and a detailed explanation of Gallup's sampling method. The piece closed with an exploration on topics that any potential Irish Institute of Public Opinion might present in its interviews. The proposed questions were conspicuously benign, particularly under the circumstances of the Emergency; topics included the Irish language, Gaelic sports, and driving tests.[88] But in his letter to Adams, Hackett expressed incredulity that "though called Statistical," the members to whom he presented his research "were disinclined to accept the method of sampling though I have given them a homely example."[89] But the other problem he cited with quantitative polling methods in Ireland presented an almost intractable problem: the Irish language.

---

[86] Clair Wills, *That Neutral Island* (London: Faber, 2007), p. 168.
[87] Felix E. Hackett, "The Sampling Referendum in the Service of Popular Government," *Dublin: Journal of the Statistical and Social Inquiry Society of Ireland* 16, no. 4 (1940/1), pp. 63–90.
[88] Felix E. Hackett to Mary Adams, April 1941, Mary Adams Papers, SxMOA4/2/5/3, University of Sussex Special Collections.
[89] Felix E. Hackett to Mary Adams.

At a time when Ireland was reclaiming its national identity, idiom became a focus of Hackett's concerns: "Another difficulty for members of the audience was the well-known difficulty of getting an Irishman to say 'yes' or 'no.' This is sometimes associated with the fact that no words equivalent to 'yes' or 'no' exist in the Irish language."[90] This was a rather more complex problem to manage. Even within his own exemplar, Hackett included questions like "Would you approve of a decimal coinage for Ireland," the answers for which, "yes" or "no," would necessarily differ were they rephrased in Gaelic. The verbs could certainly be shifted towards affirmation or dismissal ("I approve" or "I do not approve"), but such rephrasing might require new efforts towards the construction of neutral questions. Presenting two polls with divergent phrasing for Irish and English speakers might lead to different results as well. While the MoI had experienced many setbacks in its efforts to institutionalize statistical morale analysis on the home front, this is the first indication of the cultural limitations of this approach in regions outside England.

To supplant the dearth of information about morale reaching London from traditional methods, from 1940 to 1942 Anglo-Irish novelist Elizabeth Bowen began sending a series of letters on Irish morale to the MoI. Her letters proffered the MoI a means to assess how the international situation played out with the circle of Bowen's acquaintances. Like an observer from M-O, Bowen recorded conversations she had overheard in her travels to Ireland and reported back relevant fragments that might alter English policy positions towards Ireland. The tone and content of the letters suggest that Bowen aimed to not only help England understand the Irish position for propaganda purposes, but that understanding the Irish position might ease English hostility against Irish neutrality, arguing that "any hint at a violation of Eire may well be used to implement enemy propaganda and weaken the British case."[91] To some extent, Irish concerns mirrored those in England. Just as Day-Lewis critically reflected on the Silent Column and the invasion panic, Bowen respectively noted both types of anxieties in Ireland, stating that "talk...in this country cuts more ice than anything" and citing equal levels of concern about invasion of Germans *and* the British: "I have

---

[90] Felix E. Hackett to Mary Adams.
[91] Jack Lane and Brendan Clifford, *Elizabeth Bowen: "Notes on Éire": Espionage Reports to Winston Churchill, 1940–2: With a Review of Irish Neutrality in World War 2* (Aubane, Ireland: Aubane Historical Society, 2009), p. 36.

evidence on every side," she writes, "that Eire does intend to fight the British if they land first."[92]

If fears of observation were rife in England, Bowen's participation in this effort to assess Irish morale met (and continues to meet) with vituperative scorn. A book of these letters was published in 1999, and even the name of the collection, "Notes on Éire": Espionage Reports to Winston Churchill, 1940–2 plays up the controversy, with the inclusion of espionage as a key, though controversial, word to characterize her activities. Contrarily, Clair Willis argued that "espionage" was "too strong as well as too narrow a term" for her work in Ireland, which involved "sending secret reports to the [MoI], and meetings at the Dominions and the War Office."[93] Jack Lane, editor of Notes on Éire, states the case against Bowen decisively: "Elizabeth Bowen spied on Ireland for England. That fact, more than any other, shows where her loyalties lay."[94] He writes that, "[l]ike all spies, Bowen basically despised those she spied on, and made that clear towards the end of her life when she told Hubert Butler that she hated Ireland."[95] Turning to a comparison between her letters and fictions, Jack Lane derides her skill as a novelist by claiming that the former "are far more readable than her literary works."[96] Even fifty years after the war ended, this aggressive renunciation of Bowen's war-work proves that, though the common English reader of The Daily Herald might have felt violated by morale questionnaires on occasion, this fear heightened across empire nations, where reporting on morale was linked to continued control of the colonizer. German interventions exacerbated this tension further, as its broadcasts and propaganda emphasized the damage of British imperialism and the possible freedoms that Germany was willing to proffer the Irish in exchange for political allegiance; Lord Haw-Haw's propaganda broadcasts were even broadcast in Irish, as "Irish-speakers were the most nationalist, most anti-British, of de Valera's citizens."[97] While Bowen recorded that pro-German sentiment was minimal, like any good observer she documented sentiments of citizens with multiple perspectives, recalling one person who questioned, "What right have the British to keep denouncing the Nazis? Haven't they been the Nazis to us for centuries, and aren't they trying to be Nazis again now?"[98]

[92] Lane and Clifford, Elizabeth Bowen, p. 13.   [93] Wills, That Neutral Island, p. 117.
[94] Lane and Clifford, Elizabeth Bowen, p. 7.
[95] Lane and Clifford, Elizabeth Bowen, p. 9. Others have noted that there is no sourcing or research on this interaction, so it is hard to calculate the veracity of the statement.
[96] Lane and Clifford, Elizabeth Bowen, p. 7.   [97] Wills, That Neutral Island, p. 193.
[98] Lane and Clifford, Elizabeth Bowen, p. 38.

The styling of Bowen's letters positions her as a keen intermediary between Downing Street and the Dublin streets; this position is well-represented in the female protagonists throughout her fiction.[99] In her work writing letters to the MoI, however, Bowen made a continual point of demonstrating the status of public opinion as *fluid*, capable of being transformed through effective policymaking and better public relations strategies. She reports that, "The stereotyped, or completely conditioned, mind seemed to me rarer in Dublin than in London. (There is also a great deal of bigotry, but this seems to be individual, not mass). Public opinion in Dublin is almost dangerously fluid."[100] Bowen is aware of the tenuous position of Irish support for the English cause, as she demonstrates when she quotes citizens calling the English Nazis or reports that the Irish are willing to defend themselves against English invasion. To facilitate the Irish support of British efforts, she even suggests making commanding policy statements about the Irish position, and asks the MoI to "make an explicit and categoric statement that England has no intention of sending troops to Ireland."[101]

The Heat of the Day and "The Demon Lover": The Materialization of the Mind in Wartime

The novel *The Heat of the Day* allegorizes Bowen's position during the war. As the novel opens, Stella is confronted by the intelligence worker Harrison, who accuses her lover Kelway of being a fascist sympathizer and spy. Working for a vaguely disguised MoI, Stella's relationship with Robert seems stable until Harrison arrives to tell Stella that Robert is collaborating with the Nazis; in a late-night meeting with Stella, Harrison informs her that despite his work at the War Office, Robert was "giving considerably more in another direction," having "traced a leak" back to him through the enemy.[102] But Harrison, too, has a clear ulterior motive: he hopes to woo Stella himself. Stella thus finds herself in a challenging position: she cannot give away her suspicions to Robert, which might lead police to hasten his arrest. She also has to find corroboration of Harrison's claims, completely independent of her romantic investment. Stella is thus caught squarely in

---

[99] Megan Faragher, "The Form of Modernist Propaganda in Elizabeth Bowen's *The Heat of the Day*," *Textual Practice* 27, no. 1 (2013), pp. 49–68.
[100] Lane and Clifford, *Elizabeth Bowen*, p. 14.
[101] Lane and Clifford, *Elizabeth Bowen*, p. 12.
[102] Elizabeth Bowen, *The Heat of the Day* (New York: Anchor Books, [1948] 2002), p. 35.

the middle of a complicated love triangle, compounded by political intrigue, incapable of establishing a moral high ground in any position. As Harrison duly admits, "Trouble is, everyone's so damned cagey."[103]

But further examination of the nature of the cageyness Harrison cites brings us to an unraveling of the most dangerous and precarious ramifications of poll-consciousness. When Harrison confronts Stella with his theory of Robert, Stella wonders why she should not simply inform Robert that he has been found out. Harrison insists that Stella not only keep Robert in the dark, but behave exactly as she would have had she never been tipped off, indicating that if Robert's behavior changed at all, it would be evidence that she had betrayed the state. Put into the position of the surreptitious observer, Stella must simultaneously collect data—listen to Robert and assess his capability for espionage—and remain undetectable. To be perceived in the act of perceiving would, it turns out, alter the subject under observation. To be efficient, Stella's observations must be imperceptible. Thus, Stella slowly transforms from the lover, who assesses the desires of her partner openly and forthrightly, with every expectation that such desires— as data—remain private, to the domestic spy, whose efforts to capture Robert's opinions must be so secret that they make her an agent of the state. Bowen describes Stella's role as that of the spy, "listening for the listener, watching for the watcher."[104] And Stella herself also identifies her role as an unwitting spy when she accuses Harrison of transforming her: "You succeed in making a spy of me."[105]

What is Robert Kelway thinking? Such is the main question of the novel, and the efforts of Stella to answer it fundamentally reveal the conflict between the self as subject and self as object of analysis—the very same concern that Auden and Day-Lewis identified in their psychographic manifesto. After all, if Stella fails in her goal to surreptitiously plumb Kelway's mind, she runs the risk of making Kelway alter his behavior so as to better mask his political position—to make his interiority less legible. To be an observed analyst of the mind is thus to make the mind even more opaque than it was before. Just like Day-Lewis's tourists at Wonderland, who get increasingly cagey when they realize a Mass Observer is in their midst, Stella's observations, to be authentic, must necessarily be undetected. To do otherwise is to risk a transformation of the subject position of the observer, and to realize the perilous fluidity between the positions of the observed and

---

[103] Bowen, *The Heat of the Day*, p. 43.   [104] Bowen, *The Heat of the Day*, p. 140.
[105] Bowen, *The Heat of the Day*, p. 152.

the observer. While Day-Lewis's Paul Perry dramatizes, by suspecting himself of a psychotic break, the way that institutional agents of observations can fall under the power of state apparatuses, Bowen's addition of romantic investment into the dynamic between surveyor and the surveyed heightens the ambiguity between both categories, and suggests the responsibility of institutional agents in the thoughts and behaviors of those they control and observe. Put another way, if Stella fails to properly uphold Kelway's subjective status, not only will the ability to objectively analyze him be at risk, but he, in turn, will transform Stella from subject to object of psychological study, as he play-acts for the analyst and attempts to analyze her responses just as she does his. Of course, Bowen, in her work for the MoI, recognized this all too well. To be recognized as the state-sponsored observer, like Stella, would inevitably taint the results of her surveillance efforts.

Claire Seiler puts the psychographic stakes of *The Heat of the Day* well when she says that "Stella, always of two minds, is a kind of perennially undecided voter."[106] But if we put some pressure on this analogy, we begin to understand its complexity and its stakes. To some extent, Stella is the "voter," trying to decide for herself whether or not Robert is a fascist. But she also acts as an institutional agent of opinion data, the pollster, who collects information about Robert to uncover his hidden political loyalties. Stella, acting as both invested voter and disinvested pollster, maintains an untenable position; this untenability and ambiguity holds itself in play until Robert finally reveals his fascist leanings and mysteriously dies after falling from Stella's roof. Whether you interpret Stella as complicit in Robert's death or not rests almost entirely on whether she was acting in her role as an agent of the institution (the state pollster) or as subject of private affection (the voter). And even at moments when we feel that we can position Stella at one or another side of this divide, Bowen forces us back into the shadows. From the start, Stella is affiliated with a fictionalized MoI. And yet, as Allan Hepburn has noted, when Stella refuses to reveal at the inquest her knowledge that Harrison was a state agent following Kelway, she does little to align herself with the institution she supposedly works for, instead, "inadvertently draw[ing] attention to her possible culpability."[107] Bowen's insistence on the fungibility of the symbolic voter and pollster also has

[106] Claire Seiler, "At Midcentury: Elizabeth Bowen's *The Heat of the Day,*" *Modernism/Modernity* 21, no. 1 (2014), p. 127.
[107] Allan Hepburn, "Trials and Errors: *The Heat of the Day* and Postwar Culpability," in *Intermodernism: Literary Culture in Interwar and Wartime Britain*, edited by Kristin Bluemel (Edinburgh: Edinburgh UP, 2009), p. 133.

impacts on her readers, who, in their efforts to determine Stella's culpability, must inevitably become the very pollster-voter they are dissecting.

The psychographic doubling of roles in *The Heat of the Day* is most clearly dramatized in Kelway's instructions to Stella after he reveals his fascist sympathies: "You'll have to re-read me backwards, figure me out—you will have years to do that in, if you want to."[108] Kelway's phrasing is doing a lot of work here. Kelway first inscribes Stella within the discourse of the institutional analyst. Like the novel's readers, whose reading within the context of the suspenseful narrative is meant to engage in an act of detection and excavation of interiority, staging Stella as the reader marks her as an institutional agent of detection as well. She becomes a human psychograph who can, like the institutional narrator in W.H. Auden's "The Unknown Citizen," look back at the records and ascertain Kelway's authentic interiority as a political subject. And yet there seems more to this quote. "To re-read [...] backwards" is not simply to re-process data in the institutional sense. Rather, it is to process that data from the subject position of the lover in the moment of revelation; that Kelway adds the word "backwards" demands a defamiliarizing type of reading born of familiarity and intimacy, one that blends the institutional with the personal, and cites as a temporal reference point the intimate moment in which he as the lover has revealed himself as the political agent. While to re-read *forwards* is an act of the state institution (to analyze someone's behaviors from birth to death), to re-read *backwards* is to begin from the intimacy of death, and to always be staging the institutional reading with the interpersonal intimacy that will always taint such a reading. It is for this reason, arguably, that he says such a process might take "years" to accomplish.

It is not only in the Kelway plot of *The Heat of the Day* where Bowen uses the intimacy of death as a symbol of the institution's fragility in its assessment of psychological interiority. For Bowen, the war itself facilitates the "exteriorization of an internal conflict" in characters' loyalties as they "at once dread and desire truth in each other."[109] That internal conflict, as demonstrated, is both institutional and psychographic. Just as Bowen's personal connections to her friends in Ireland find themselves tinging her institutional reports to the MoI, the challenge to unbiased institutional

---

[108] Bowen, *The Heat of the Day*, p. 304.
[109] Elizabeth Bowen, "On Writing *The Heat of the Day*," in *The Weight of a World of Feeling: Reviews and Essays by Elizabeth Bowen*, edited by Allan Hepburn (Evanston, IL: Northwestern University Press, 2017), pp. 12, 11.

"reading" comes to play in the Irish subplot of the novel, as Stella's son Roderick inherits an Irish estate called Mount Morris from his deceased cousin Francis. A soldier based in London when not abroad, Roderick allows the estate to fulfill a romantic fantasy of stability for him, establishing what Bowen calls "an historic future."[110] But complicating the Irish part of the narrative, and reinforcing the narrative's ties to Bowen's work with the MoI, Francis represents another Irish citizen "bound by passion and duty" to the property and to Eire, but who considered neutrality "a severe blow."[111] Francis dies in England, having gone there to help the war effort, and passes on his property to his cousin Roderick, who embodies Francis's political aspirations.

But Roderick is already, through the dead, embedded in a psychographic controversy between the intimate and the institutional. In a letter drafted by the lawyers, it indicates that Francis has bequeathed Morris to Roderick "*In the hope that he may care in his own way to carry on the old tradition.*"[112] This phrasing befuddles Roderick, who is not sure whether to place emphasis on "*his own way*" or "*the old tradition.*" It seems impossible to acquiesce to what the institution of the law demands precisely because the will's language requires a level of personal intimacy with the deceased that Roderick lacks. As he wrangles with the language in front of his mother, Stella tries to interrupt to provide Roderick his third way: to sell the property and be freed from any obligations to a person whose intentions he cannot know, thus insisting on a purely institutional, not personal, response to the crisis. Adding to that sentiment, Colonel Pole repeatedly advises against settling at Mount Morris. To Stella he suggests, "I advise you to advise the boy to get rid of it—sell outright, before he ties himself up."[113] The advice against "t[ying] himself up" is tantamount to a rejection of the interpersonal and intimate connection between Roderick and the property—to view property only in its institutional and not its intimate sense. Yet Roderick quickly dismisses the proposal. Stella attempts to outline the impossibility of his position: "They had no idea how it would be for us. If they still had to live, who knows that they might not have disappointed themselves?"[114] Such a passage alludes to the palimpsestic nature of the psychographic impulse. For one, there is the expectation that the dead have for the living and, more

---

[110] Bowen, *The Heat of the Day*, p. 52.   [111] Bowen, *The Heat of the Day*, p. 74.
[112] Bowen, *The Heat of the Day*, p. 95, emphasis in original.
[113] Bowen, *The Heat of the Day*, p. 88.   [114] Bowen, *The Heat of the Day*, p. 96.

importantly, the living's ability to ascertain those very hopes of the dead. The past and present construct a psychological totality, mirroring Bowen's observations in her essay "Ireland Makes Irish" that "a thread of psychological truth knits up Ireland's yesterday with her today."[115] But in this effort to assess the opinions of the deceased, Bowen also touches on polling's early origins in spiritualist psychographic study. The psychographic implications of this passage are doubled, even trebled, when we consider Stella's note that the dead might even disappoint themselves had they lived; the problem is not only that we cannot ascertain the thoughts of the dead, but that even those dead—in troubled times—would fail to fully ascertain their own desires. In Stella's estimation, psychological interiority—including desires, wishes, and expectations—are never stable categories; they are dynamic both interpersonally and diachronically. That one can fail to read the minds of oneself as well as others, across time and space, indicates this inherent impossibility of truly mastering the desires of the other. In other words: no interpersonal polling technology is flawless, either transnationally or transhistorically. Put together, the confused subplot of Roderick's Mount Morris inheritance and Kelway's evocation of "re-reading" allude to more than simply the scarcity of information in a time of war, though they certainly accomplish that. These subplots also invoke psychographics, as both plotlines allude to difficulties in accessing the consciousness of the inaccessible other. Like the early psychograph, supposedly capable of transmitting thoughts accurately through the act of inspired writing, Kelway's "re-reading" simply reminds us of the failures to properly read Kelway the first time. This is even more evident in Roderick's guesswork over Cousin Francis's will, where his efforts to re-read the will repeatedly move beyond the aspects of mere legibility of text, and instead speak to the impossibility of uncovering psychological intent.

For Bowen, the transformation in the aestheticization of psychological interiority directly followed wartime air raids, which reprised the role of psychological interiority as a cultural concern. As the "air whistles and things rock," with objects disintegrating before one's very eyes during bombing campaigns, Bowen marks both psychological and political ramifications of this transformation in her essay "Britain in Autumn." Psychologically, wartime trauma heightened psychographic impulse in fellow citizens:

[115] Elizabeth Bowen, "Ireland Makes Irish," in *People, Places, Things: Essays*, edited by Allan Hepburn (Edinburgh: Edinburgh University Press, 2011), p. 159.

Yes, on the streets we do still look hard at each other, but the look has a different object. You look at eyes. You measure the guts and go. You look for the *someone*—how do *you* feel today? This exchange of searching, speechless, intimate looks between strangers goes on all over the place. But virtually, there are no strangers now. We all touch on the fundamentals we are not speaking about.[116]

This impulse to ascertain feeling from appearance—to manifest interiority materially on the surface of one's face—leads to political ramifications. "[F]or the first time," she writes, "*we are* a democracy."[117] Bolstering the argument of many writers in the mid-century, we see here a connection between the manifestation of collective interiority and democratic praxis. Bowen would later argue that wartime circumstances, including the reprisal of *material* as a core facet of psychological concern, came to indelibly mark literature and culture from the war onwards. In so doing, she puts the emergence of modern psychography in other words, first noting that the more traditionally modernist facets of the interwar novel (which she attributes to Dorothy Richardson and Virginia Woolf) "did not finally diagnose the modern uneasiness" of "dislocation."[118] While such works, as she diagnosed, "stress[ed] the interplay between the consciousness and the exterior world," mid-century novels would turn to the "salutary value of the *exterior*," a reality forced upon them by the prospect of "whole-sale destruction" during the war.[119] As objects, like "streets and houses, tables and chairs" gained "psychological worth," they also transformed the way writers viewed consciousness itself in the postwar. "Up to now, consciousness had been a sheltered product," she writes. "[I]ts interest *as* consciousness diminished now that, at any moment, physical shelter could be gone."[120] Describing consciousness *as* consciousness, Bowen indicates a shift towards psychological materiality not dissimilar in spirit to Day-Lewis and Auden's synthesis of the private and public and suggests a transformation of consciousness away from the private and towards the more public material world of tables and chairs. For Bowen, the mid-century response to the war solidifies what was discovered

---

[116] Elizabeth Bowen, "Britain in Autumn," in *People, Places, Things: Essays*, ed Allan Hepburn (Edinburgh: Edinburgh University Press, 2011), p. 54.

[117] Bowen, "Britain in Autumn," p. 54, emphasis in original.

[118] Elizabeth Bowen, "English Fiction at Mid-Century," in *People, Places, Things: Essays*, edited by Allan Hepburn (Edinburgh: Edinburgh University Press, 2011), p. 323.

[119] Bowen, "English Fiction at Mid-Century," p. 322, emphasis added.

[120] Bowen, "English Fiction at Mid-Century," p. 323, emphasis in original.

in the trauma of the Blitz: that the sanctity of interiority had been replaced by a fledgling effort to make consciousness material, like so many objects that might be destroyed by the bombs. Just as Stella is given a chance to "re-read" Kelway, Bowen "reads" the faces of her fellow Londoners during the war, reviewing her experiences based on a newly found psychographic sensibility.

This unexpected reprisal of Victorian psychographics in *The Heat of the Day*—the thematic emergence of the ghostly, inaccessible interviewee—is similarly mirrored in Bowen's mid-century short stories. "The Demon Lover" stands in as a notable example of the psychographic impulse in Bowen's short fiction, as it dramatizes the conflict between institutional conception of interiority and the inscrutability of the psychological other. The protagonist of the story, Mrs. Kathleen Drover, returns to a bombed-out London to retrieve items from her family's shuttered home. Throughout the story, Bowen suggests Kathleen's inculcation in the psychographic age, repeatedly noting how her self-conception is mediated through an objectification of interiority. As Kathleen is confronted with a mysterious letter from a former lover assumed dead in World War I, she attempts to assuage her horror through the adaptation of a sociological lens—an effort to take up the perspective of the objective observer looking in. Compensating for the fact that there is "no human eye" that sees Kathleen in this isolated, wrecked home, she must look to a mirror to understand herself as a reified, embodied subject: "She felt so much the change in her own face that she went to the mirror, polished a clear patch in it and looked at once urgently and stealthily in. She was confronted by a woman of forty-four, with eyes starting out under a hat-brim that had been rather carelessly pulled down [...] Mrs Drover's most normal expression was one of controlled worry, but of assent."[121] The sensation of her shock upon receiving this dead letter—the feeling of change in her face—is not evidence enough of her interior tumult. Rather, she must see herself as the observer would see her: a woman of a certain middle-age with an expression best described in terms of its normalcy. Like in Mitchison's "The Delicate Fire," where Nikippe turns to the world of mathematics to dissociate herself from the traumatic specter of rape, Kathleen adopts a sociological perspective of the self—an objectivized version of her interiority—to calm her fears. While she desperately wants to flee the house, Bowen again articulates that her social positioning, as seen

---

[121] Elizabeth Bowen, "The Demon Lover," in *The Collected Stories of Elizabeth Bowen* (New York: Random House, 1981), p. 662.

from the sociological observer, influences her decision to stay and complete the task that brought her to the war-ravaged home: "As a woman whose utter dependability was the keystone of her family life she was not willing to return to the country, to her husband, her little boys and her sister, without the objects she had come to fetch."[122] Understanding herself as a representative of a social norm, Kathleen adopts an institutional perspective on the self, articulated through citations of her age, role in the family, "normal" demeanor, and expected behavior.

But while Kathleen attempts to manage her crisis through faith in institutionalized psychographics, memories of the titular demon lover repeatedly "intrude upon" her efforts at self-soothing, and come to represent the innate fragility of these structures of objectivized interiority.[123] Throughout the story, Kathleen struggles to remember the face of her lover. While she can see her own visage in the hastily cleaned mirror and confirm her status as subject assuming the role of self-observer, she can never quite fully observe the remembered other, failing to conjure up the young lover's face after twenty-five years of absence. Recalling the night when they parted for the last time, Bowen describes that "[t]he young girl...had not ever completely seen his face [...] Now and then—for it felt, from not seeing him at this intense moment, as though she had never seen him at all."[124] Though Kathleen is able to decipher herself through the rational discourse of psychographics, the more spectral prehistory of the psychographic impulse surfaces to challenge her security, haunting Kathleen with the prospect of the unknowable other, allowing her only the possibility of "imagining spectral glitters in place of his eyes."[125] Again and again, Kathleen torments herself attempting to summon the face of her lover, who signs his letter with a "K"; her desperation to do so attests to the symbolic value of visualization as a way of mastering the lover's desires, warding them off, and protecting herself from them. But at all such efforts she fails, as "[s]he remembered—but with one white burning blank as where acid has dropped on a photograph: *under no conditions* could she remember his face."[126] Incapable of recalling the lost lover, Kathleen is bound by the inaccessible desires of the dead, which rend her from the collective identity that she had held as protection from the letter's threatening tone. As Bowen describes it, the inability to recall K and therefore anticipate his demands constructs an "unnatural

---

[122]   Bowen, "The Demon Lover," p. 665.   [123]   Bowen, "The Demon Lover," p. 662.
[124]   Bowen, "The Demon Lover," p. 663.   [125]   Bowen, "The Demon Lover," p. 663.
[126]   Bowen, "The Demon Lover," p. 665, emphasis in original.

promise" which "drove down between her and the rest of humanity."[127] It is his unknowable presence that threatens to sever Kathleen from the social normalcy she has managed for herself amidst the war. At the end of the story, Kathleen escapes the house only to find the letter-writer waiting for her as a taxi driver, "[making] off with her into the hinterland of deserted streets."[128]

The setting—the "hinterland of deserted streets" featuring "broken chimneys and parapets"—recalls Bowen's notes in "Britain in Autumn," recognizing the role that the disintegrating physical environment has in the destabilization of psychological legibility.[129] As material objects take on psychological characteristics, psychology itself becomes increasingly important as material. For psychographic enthusiasts like Gerald Heard, emergent studies of haunting in the mid-century were testament to the emergent evolution of collective consciousness.[130] And in the case of both "Britain in Autumn" and "The Demon Lover," the war destabilizes the boundary between materiality and consciousness, as psychology becomes increasingly materialized by the ghostly other, while objects disintegrate into dust. The dead cousin Francis, the demon lover "K" and, to some extent, the inscrutable Robert Kelway, all testify to the fungibility of public opinion revealed in wartime intelligence work. And while the MoI's reliance on public opinion data during World War II concretized the field's institutionalization, it also—as both Bowen and Day-Lewis attest to in their fiction—reveals the fragility of polling as a tool for the production of effective public policy and propaganda strategy. As psychographic study becomes more institutionalized, both the depersonalization of the institutional setting and the destabilizing impact of the war exposes faults, errors, inconsistencies, and aporias that would continue to haunt the psychographic age for decades to follow.

---

[127] Bowen, "The Demon Lover," p. 663.
[128] Bowen, "The Demon Lover," p. 666.
[129] Bowen, "The Demon Lover," p. 661.
[130] Heard, *The Ascent of Humanity*, p. 316.

Afterword

Psychography's Postwar Pivot

In the aftermath of World War II, the assessment of political ideology based on personal taste would find its quantitative match in 1950 with the publication of *The Authoritarian Personality*, a joint effort of Adorno and others at the University of California, Berkeley, forged to better quantify and understand the tendency of authoritarianism in individuals. Graded on the "F-scale"—the "Fascist" scale—questions ascertained the likelihood that any individual could be swayed by the arrival of a totalitarian figurehead like Hitler. The surveys in *The Authoritarian Personality* asked participants to rate statements on a scale of truthfulness; the theory behind this was that, depending on the prompt, individual identification with the truth of certain statements would reveal the likelihood that the respondent harbored fascist tendencies. While some of the prompts highlighted the very obvious racist or anti-Semitic attitudes that might clearly identify a person as fascist or fascist-leaning, other prompts were outwardly unrelated to overtly political content, prompting participants to weigh in about their attitudes to topics that were seemingly apolitical. One prompt, assessing the respondent's ethnocentrism, had volunteers respond to the veracity of statements like: "A child should learn early in life the value of a dollar and the importance of ambition, efficiency, and determination."[1] Another read: "Character, honesty, and ability will tell in the long run; most people get pretty much what they deserve."[2] In a sub-section of the study made to deal with measuring anti-democratic propensities, prompts were even more obtuse. One such prompt asks readers to respond to the statement: "Although many people may scoff, it may yet be shown that astrology can explain a lot of things."[3] According to the study, this question meant to identify an individual's "disposition to think in rigid categories," suggesting that "[t]he belief in

---

[1] Theodor Adorno, *Authoritarian Personality* (American Jewish Committee, 1950), p. 158.
[2] Adorno, *Authoritarian Personality*, p. 158.
[3] Adorno, *Authoritarian Personality*, p. 227.

Public Opinion Polling in Mid-Century British Literature: The Psychographic Turn. Megan Faragher, Oxford University Press. © Megan Faragher 2021. DOI: 10.1093/oso/9780192898975.003.0007

mystical determinant's of an individual's fate" was tied to the tendency to align oneself with political dogma. "[O]pposition to introspection," it was argued, was connected to a weakness of the ego. Therefore, a prompt like "Novels or stories that tell about what people think and feel are more interesting than those which contain mainly action, romance, and adventure" was likely to identify whether or not the respondent was capable of accessing interiority and empathy.[4]

The Authoritarian Personality's innovative work in social psychology, suggesting the connection between seemingly inane opinions and political leanings, symbolized the birth of the next age of social psychology—one which, as of yet, remained unnamed. But by 1975, an old word had surfaced from the depths of late-Victorian spiritualism to identify this latest evolution of psychological science: psychographics. In his essay "Psychographics: A Critical Review," William D. Wells, a commercial advertiser, argued that psychography was a way for marketers to identify what demographics to target for specific advertising campaigns. The fundamental thesis of psychography was that people who share traits beyond mere demographics— lifestyles, attitudes, hobbies, or education—would align in their tastes for consumer products. Just as Adorno moved beyond demography alone, looking to aesthetic preferences and obtuse tastes to ascertain underlying political beliefs, the new psychographics deemed demographics insufficient, arguing for "new, more comprehensive" psychological profiling. William Wells argued that you could successfully ascertain, from asking consumers questions about their "life style[s]" what kinds of activities they were most likely to take up and what kinds of attitudes they held about particular topics, even controversial ones. Wells's psychography was a quintessential example of the radical expansion of market psychology in the postwar period; it was the birth of the *Mad Men*-style marketing campaigns, whose conception sprung from Bernaysian theories of social psychology in the 1920s. But more importantly for my purposes, it represents the inevitable end phase of the psychographic turn which had begun in earnest in the 1930s, and which has become so foundational to our everyday lives nearly a century later.

By taking into account not only demographic data but also "motivation research," postwar researchers made a final reach in their attempts to better understand how consumers make their decisions. William W. Wells uses

---

[4] Adorno, *Authoritarian Personality*, p. 226.

the example of gun ownership to show the difference between demographic and psychographic studies of subjects. While demographic studies might break down gun owners by age, occupation, income, and region, Wells's psychographic analysis goes further. Rather than analyzing propensity for gun ownership by a consumer's positioning in these categories, Wells presents subjects with seemingly unrelated statements to gauge their responses. Responses to statements like "I would like to be a professional football player" and "I like to play poker," he argued, would be just as good at assessing the likelihood of gun ownership as any direct questioning, and would avoid the potential pitfalls of asking politicized questions too directly.[5] Thus, seemingly unrelated personal preferences become shorthand for a series of political, social, and economic realities that capture any particular consumer and place them in multiple possible buckets for the purposes of marketing—not dissimilar to Adorno's surveys in *The Authoritarian Personality*. Though Wells wrote of these innovations in the mid-1970s, it would be this same "new" field of psychographics—a Frankensteinesque reanimation of the detritus of Victorian séance-rooms—that would bear the most poisonous fruit for modern democracies in the subsequent decades.

This book has been framed by the emergence of modern psychographics: the slow transition of psychological interiority from a discourse about opaque individuality to one that embraced the material reality of collective consciousness. By tracing this transition, this book has revised debates on twentieth-century literature that have too long prioritized the sanctity of individual psychology over its commodification in forms of group psychology. As this book has traced the meteoric rise of public opinion studies in the mid-century, we find that discourses on psychology did not just impact works focusing on individual characters, but also transformed the literary field towards a collective aesthetics. This shift in focus to collective over individual psychology unearths writers who have often fallen between the gaps of criticism centered on high modernism. While H.G. Wells has often been seen as either a genre writer or a purveyor of late-Victorian aesthetics, to re-stage his work through the lens of a sociological-awakening is to bring him back to relevance as a key writer of the twentieth century, working within this alternative strand of psychographic aesthetics. Much the same can be said of Olaf Stapledon, Naomi Mitchison, and Celia Fremlin, seldom considered to be critical aesthetic innovators of the period, but each of

---

[5] William D. Wells, "Psychographics: A Critical Review," *Journal of Marketing Research* 7 (May 1975), p. 198.

whom is deeply invested in considering the impact of sociological expansionism on the future of social relations.

For such authors, polling had promise. Statistical analysis of the murky
world of interiority promised stability—even transparency. We see this in
Stapledon's intergalactic telepathic utopias, which outlined the possibility of
liberation from slavery by the statistically minded. The authors examined in
this book, and those who followed in their wake, continually ask: will these
psychographic technologies bring forth a more utopian democracy or a
totalitarian world-state? For the most vociferous proponent of polling in
England, Henry Durant, the answer was simple: the exposure of the public
to private thought could only be a common good. In a very strange anecdote in his book *Behind the Gallup Poll*, Durant recalls a Gallup interviewer
in South London, and a housewife who opened the door, stating, "I'm so
glad you knocked. I was just going to commit suicide."[6] Why include this
anecdote in a supposed detailing of the process behind the Gallup Poll?
Exposing this intimate moment, Durant seems to argue, lets us understand
the immense social benefit of polling for the literal health of the body politic. Such a reading lends new significance to Auden's claim in his dedication
to Stephen Spender in *The Orators*: "private faces in public spaces / Are
wiser and nicer / Than public faces in private spaces."[7] The psychographic
turn had potential to materialize private interiority to the public world.

But while many touted the palliative nature of polling's public face, some
thought that the scientific assessment of interiority threatened to sicken
society, as prefigured in Max Weber's view of science as an "artificial
abstraction...striv[ing] to capture the blood and sap of real life."[8] The eventual embeddedness of powerful institutions with public opinion research,
incipient at its start but (particularly in the British context) accelerated by
the exigencies of war, foretells the narrative of polling that is so familiar to
us now. While the early rhetoric about polling emphasized its potentiality as
a resource to bolster and defend democracy and humanity in dark times,
the final institutional turn of polling's history opened up a new narrative of
its impact on the public sphere. Instead of being seen as an inherent boon to
democratic systems, polling is now part of the political process entirely

---

[6] Henry Durant and W. Gregory, *Behind the Gallup Poll* (London: *The News Chronicle*, 1951), p. 27.

[7] W.H. Auden, 'The Orators,' in *The English Auden*, edited by Edward Mendelson (New York: Random House, 1977), p. 59.

[8] Max Weber, "Science as a Vocation," in *The Vocation Lectures*, translated by Rodney Livingstone (Indianapolis, IN: Hackett Publishing Company, 2004), p. 14.

embedded with the very same institutions that are beleaguered by public mistrust. In his autobiography, Cecil Day-Lewis reflected on the ramification of wartime technologies for the postwar psychology of the citizen in precisely such terms: "Was it desirable that everybody should go everywhere, know everything? Would it only make people more restless and fill them up with a lot of information they did not really understand and could not digest, make them more and more slaves of 'experts,' pundits and commentators who did not understand it either?"[9] If current political discourse can act as our guide, we find in Day-Lewis's question a prescient prognostication of the contemporary dominance of the pundit-class, in which we all play a part as psychographic subjects. Debates about psychographics become even more dominant in the postwar literary canon: Arthur C. Clarke's *Childhood's End* (1953) theorizes the overtaking of humanity by a race of telepathic children; Doris Lessing's *Four-Gated City* (1969), a rejoinder to Clarke, imagines a sub-species of telepathic humans, poisoned by their environments, who can possibly unify in resistance against an increasingly totalitarian government. The debate over psychography's relationship to institutional authority, born of the mid-century, has remained prevalent well after its end.

As society falls to psychographic obsession, polling has come under scrutiny as a way of controlling public opinion, not just reporting upon it. Adorno would argue in *Minima Moralia* that "[i]nstitutions of public opinion accompany what they send forth by a thousand factual proofs and all the plausibility that total power can lay hands on," thus becoming nothing more than a further means of exacting institutional power.[10] As individuals become both subjects and objects of knowledge, this collective auto-reification becomes a force of political influence and persuasion as well. The conclusion of psychography's emergence, epitomized by its institutionalization, foreshadowed the currently troubled position of public opinion in our discourse. The fears of citizens during World War II—that the government would use morale research to censor, discipline, and control citizens—carried through into the late twentieth and even the twenty-first centuries, as citizens continue to both admire and fear the power of research institutions to interpolate, express, and commercialize public will as a resource.

[9] Cecil Day-Lewis, *All My Yesterdays: An Autobiography* (Boston, MA: Element Books, 1993), p. 132.
[10] Theodor Adorno, *Minima Moralia: Reflections on a Damaged Life* (London: Verso, 2010), p. 108.

Even from the late-1930s, scholars identified the harmful ramifications of viewing polling as a form of depersonalized agency, with Floyd Allport writing that too many thought of public opinion as a "super-organic being" or even "some kind of being which dwells in or above the group."[11] And while current discourse about polling and the political milieu suggests that our complicated relationship to public opinion is born of a contemporary moment unique in the way that information technologies have infiltrated our lives and controlled our wills, this book has suggested that our current political moment is prefigured in polling's nascent beginnings. To pay attention to the early years of polling, including its social and cultural impact, is to learn more about our contemporary moment and to understand better how the institutionalization of polling challenged our vision of isolated individuated consciousness. To see ourselves in polling data—represented as just one data point in the sea of other citizens—is to live as the first subjects of polling did: impressed by, inspired by, and fearful of the reconsideration of themselves as psychographic subjects.

Never has the impact of the psychographic turn been as felt as it has in the last decade, a point which—even in this book so centered on the mid-century—I would be remiss to leave undiscussed. Among the perhaps thousands of stories about social media privacy violations for the benefits of marketing and propaganda, the Cambridge Analytica scandal stands alone in validating the pressing fears expressed by mid-century writers about the psychographic turn. When Waugh mused that social psychology "might easily provide a Devil's Handbook for the demagogue," he was only too right.[12] While Facebook's implementation of the "I Voted" status update used peer pressure to help others "carry out their civic duty," it was also an unprecedented "human laboratory," enabling Facebook to harvest information and study the impact of these posts; algorithms create a "feedback loop," where increased reliance on psychographic technologies strengthens their hold on democracy.[13] We recognized this fully when psychographic data harvested from social media by Cambridge Analytica was used to conduct targeted propaganda campaigns, facilitating both the success of Brexit and the election of Donald Trump. As citizens have internalized Waugh's

---

[11] Floyd Allport, "Towards a Science of Public Opinion," *Public Opinion Quarterly* 1 (1937), pp. 7, 8.

[12] Evelyn Waugh, "The Habits of the English," in *The Essays, Articles, and Reviews of Evelyn Waugh*, edited by Gallagher Donat (Harmondsworth: Penguin, 1986), pp. 226–7.

[13] Cathy O'Neill, *Weapons of Math Destruction: How Big Data Increases Inequality and Threatens Democracy* (New York: Broadway Books, 2016), pp. 7 and 180.

skepticism, their cynicism over the polling-industrial complex has led some to avoid participating in polls altogether, only increasing the volatility of polling in the years since 2016. The perilous power of polling was put into sharp relief yet again in 2020; a dearth of institutional trust has led polling to become more unreliable, putting the entire industry under the microscope.

While this book is not about the psychographic work of groups like Cambridge Analytica, I want to suggest that in the age of this new level of consumer data, we are well overdue for an examination of the history of polling and psychography in the twentieth century. Our arrival in this new, risky, data-driven landscape comes as the inevitable result of the transformation of social psychology through the rise of polling in the mid-century. Mapping this cultural history, I hope, also gives us space to imagine the future that might have been, and new ways of understanding the potential of alternative psychographic models. In the early days of polling, the future of the field, and what it would look like, was far from certain. And debates over polling methodology, as fractured a field as it was, seemed to touch on debates happening throughout the world in the mid-century, and which have returned to us now. How do people make their decisions? How do we protect agency and psychological autonomy? What are the risks of new mediatory technologies for group psychology? How do we interrogate group psychology without becoming dogmatic propagandists? Early pollsters quickly realized that the act of acquiring opinion data was, itself, a possible influencer of public opinion. This inevitably produced controversy and debate, both inside the field and outside of it. The public, becoming aware of polling for the first time, expressed a mixture of awe and trepidation at the power of polling. It was both miraculous and highly misunderstood by non-experts. When we read editors from the *News Chronicle* in the 1930s reminding readers that polls are not determinative, but are explanatory, or Theodor Adorno in the postwar period mentioning the correlation between personal questions and political positions, it strikes a note that is eerily resonant in the contemporary moment. I contend that psychography, and its multiple valences over the last century, provide a useful framework from which to show the genealogy of polling culture as it evolved through England and around the world. Where once psychography was a means to assess one kind of inaccessible desire—that of the dead—psychography eventually was meant to represent the study of another somewhat inaccessible desire—that of the masses. And there were many stages in this development along the way, emerging from multiple fronts simultaneously.

But the slow shift towards the psychographic age, the turn that I trace in this book, also awakens more hopeful visions of the field which, for all their utopianism, may do the very work of utopias in, as Jameson puts it "serv[ing] the negative purpose of making us more aware of our mental and ideological imprisonment."[14] We may be far afield from the Stapledonian collective unconscious, which he and Mitchison would dream of in their many luncheons together, having decided that Gerald Heard's séances were a bit hokey.[15] But these ideations of collective community, inspired by theories of telepathy and materialized in early polling practices, led to other kinds of progressive work. Not only did the imaginary opportunities opened up by polling enable political collective action on the left like the Peace Ballot, but they also inspired alternative ways of theorizing collective experience. Already anxious about the power of data-experts over the sanctity of psychological interiority, the emphasis on underserved voices, as evinced by the work of Celia Fremlin and Naomi Mitchison, forwards collective psychological study as a means of demanding political power. And if these psychographic writers were able to imagine, in these nascent technologies, methods by which to manifest political revolutions of peace and democracy, perhaps they can inspire us to reimagine our psychographic age yet again, and push us to reconfigure the psychographic infrastructures of our society towards more egalitarian ends.

---

[14] Fredric Jameson, *Archaeologies of the Future: The Desire Called Utopia and Other Science Fictions* (London: Verso, 2005), p. xiii.
[15] Benton, *Naomi Mitchison*, p. 89.

Archival Materials

Material from the BBC Written Archive Centre is BBC copyright content, used by courtesy of the BBC Broadcasting Corporation. All rights reserved. Passages from Virginia Woolf's Monks House Papers, including fragments from her *Three Guineas* and *Pointz Hall* notebooks, are reproduced courtesy of The Society of Authors as the Literary Representative of the Estate of Virginia Woolf.

Bibliography

Addison, Paul, and Jeremy Crang, editors. *Listening to Britain: Home Intelligence Reports on Britain's Finest Hour: May to September 1940* (London: Bodley Head, 2010).

Adorno, Theodor. *Introduction to Sociology* (Stanford, CA: Stanford University Press, 1999).

Adorno, Theodor. *Minima Moralia: Reflections on a Damaged Life* (London: Verso, 2010).

Adorno, Theodor, Else Frenkel-Brunswik, Daniel J. Levinson, and R. Nevitt Sanford. *The Authoritarian Personality* (American Jewish Committee, 1950).

Afflerbach, Ian. "Surveying Late Modernism: *Partisan Review* and the Cultural Politics of the Questionnaire." *Modernism/Modernity Print Plus* 4, no. 1 (March 2019).

Allport, Floyd. *Social Psychology* (Boston, MA: Houghton Mifflin, 1924).

Allport, Floyd. "Towards a Science of Public Opinion." *Public Opinion Quarterly* 1, no. 1 (1937): 7–23.

Allport, Gordon Willard. *Personality: A Psychological Interpretation* (London: Constable, 1938).

Arnold-Forster, William. "Britain's National Peace Ballot." *World Affairs* 97, no. 4 (December 1934): 226–9.

Ashley, Walter. "The First Million Votes." *Headway: A Monthly Review of the League of Nations* 17, no. 2 (February 1935): 26–7.

Asprem, Egil. "A Nice Arrangement of Heterodoxies: William McDougall and the Professionalization of Psychical Research." *Journal of the History of the Behavioral Sciences* 46, no. 2 (2010): 123–43.

Auden, W.H. "The Unknown Citizen." Copyright 1940 and © renewed 1968 by W.H. Auden; from *Collected Poems* by W.H. Auden, edited by Edward Mendelson, pp. 252–3. Used by permission of Random House, an imprint and division of Penguin Random House LLC. All rights reserved.

Auden, W.H. "The Orators." In *The English Auden: Poems, Essays, and Dramatic Writing: 1927–1939*, edited by Edward Mendelson (New York: Random House, 1977), pp. 61–113.

Avery, Todd. *Radio Modernism* (New York: Routledge, 2006).

Balnaves, Mark and Tom O'Regan. *Rating the Audience: The Business of Media* (London: Bloomsbury, 2012).

Belford, Barbara. *Bram Stoker: A Biography of the Author of Dracula* (New York: Knopf, 1996).

Bell, Duncan. "Pragmatic Utopianism and Race: H.G. Wells as Social Scientist." *Modern Intellectual History* 16, no. 3 (November 2017): 863–95.

Bellamy, William. "The Novels of Wells, Bennett and Galsworthy." In *The Critical Response to H.G. Wells*, edited by William J. Scheick (Westport, CT and London: Greenwood Press, 1995), pp. 71–4.

Benton, Jill. *Naomi Mitchison: A Century of Experiment in Life and Letters* (Kitchener, ON: Pandora Press, 1990).

Berman, Marshall. *All That is Solid Melts Into Air: The Experience of Modernity* (New York: Penguin Books, 1982).

Bernays, Edward. *Propaganda* (New York: IG Publishing, [1928] 2005).

Blake, Nicholas [Cecil Day-Lewis]. *The Beast Must Die* (London: Ipso Books, [1938], 2017).

Blake, Nicholas [Cecil Day-Lewis] [Nicholas Blake]. *The Smiler With the Knife* (New York: Harper & Row, [1939] 1978).

Blake, Nicholas [Cecil Day-Lewis]. *Malice in Wonderland* (London: Ipso Books, [1940] 2017).

Blake, Nicholas, [Cecil Day-Lewis]. *Minute for Murder* (London: Ipso Books, [1947] 2017).

Bouk, Dan. *How Our Days Became Numbered: Risk and the Rise of the Statistical Individual* (Chicago, IL: University of Chicago Press, 2015).

Bourdieu, Pierre. "The Specificity of the Scientific Field and the Social Conditions of the Progress of Reason." *Social Science Information* 14, no. 6 (1975): 19–47.

Bourdieu, Pierre. *Distinction: A Social Critique of the Judgement of Taste*, translated by Richard Nice (Harvard, MA: Harvard University Press, 1984).

Bourdieu, Pierre. "Opinion Polls: A 'Science' Without a Scientist." In *In Other Words: Essays Towards a Reflexive Sociology*, translated by Matthew Anderson (Stanford, CA: Stanford University Press, 1990), pp. 168–77.

Bourdieu, Pierre. "The Peculiar History of Scientific Reason." *Sociological Forum* 6, no. 1 (1991): 3–26.

Bourdieu, Pierre. "Participant Objectivation." *Journal of the Royal Anthropological Institute: Incorporating "Man"* 9, no. 2 (June 2003): 281–94.

Bowen, Elizabeth. "Britain in Autumn." In *People, Places, Things: Essays*, edited by Allan Hepburn (Edinburgh: Edinburgh University Press, 2011), pp. 48–56.

Bowen, Elizabeth. "The Demon Lover." In *The Collected Stories of Elizabeth Bowen* (New York: Random House, 1981), pp. 661–6.

Bowen, Elizabeth. "English Fiction at Mid-Century." In *People, Places, Things: Essays*, edited by Allan Hepburn (Edinburgh: Edinburgh University Press, 2011), pp. 321–4.

Bowen, Elizabeth. *The Heat of the Day* (New York: Anchor Books, [1948] 2002).

Bowen, Elizabeth. "Ireland Makes Irish." In *People, Places, Things: Essays*, edited by Allan Hepburn (Edinburgh: Edinburgh University Press, 2011), pp. 155–61.

Bowen, Elizabeth. "On Writing *The Heat of the Day*." In *The Weight of a World of Feeling: Reviews and Essays by Elizabeth Bowen*, edited by Allan Hepburn (Evanston, IL: Northwestern University Press, 2017), pp. 11–12.

Brabazon, James. *Dorothy L. Sayers* (New York: Scribner's Sons, 1981).

Bradford, Gamaliel. *A Naturalist of Souls* (New York: Dood, Mead, and Company, 1917).

Breton, André. "Surrealism (1924)." In *Modernism: An Anthology of Source Documents*, edited by Vassiliki Kolocotroni, Jane Goldman, and Olga Taxidou (Chicago, IL: University of Chicago Press, 1998), pp. 307–11.

Briggs, Asa. *The History of Broadcasting in the United Kingdom: The Golden Age of Wireless* (Oxford: Oxford University Press, 1995).

British Broadcasting Corporation. *The BBC Year-Book, 1932* (London: The British Broadcasting Corporation, 1932).

British Institute of Public Opinion. "Public Opinion Survey." *Public Opinion Quarterly* 4, no. 1 (1940): 75–82.

Bronson, Leila. *Reading Virginia Woolf's Essays and Journalism: Breaking the Surface of Silence* (Edinburgh: Edinburgh University Press, 1999).

Calder, Angus. *The Myth of the Blitz* (London: Pimlico, 1997).

Calder, Jenni. *The Nine Lives of Naomi Mitchison* (London: Virago, 1997).

Canavan, Gerry. "'A Dread Mystery, Compelling Adoration': Olaf Stapledon, *Star Maker*, and Totality." *Science Fiction Studies* 43 (2014): 310–30.

Cantril, Hadley. "The Social Psychology of Everyday Life." *The Psychological Bulletin* 31, no. 5 (1934): 297–300.

Cantril, Hadley. *The Social Psychology of Everyday Life* (Cambridge, MA: Harvard University Press, 1934).

Cantril, Hadley and Gordon Allport. *The Psychology of Radio* (New York: Harper & Brothers, 1935).

Carney, Michael. *Stoker: The Life of Hilda Matheson, OBE, 1888–1940* (Llangynog: Michael Carney, 1999).

Carr, John Dickson and Val Gielgud. *Inspector Silence Takes the Air*. In *13 to the Gallows*, edited by Tony Medawar (Norfolk, VA: Crippen & Landru, 2008), pp. 17–90.

Carr, John Dickson and Val Gielgud. *Thirteen to the Gallows*. In *13 to the Gallows*, edited by Tony Medawar (Norfolk, VA: Crippen & Landru, 2008), pp. 93–173.

Ceadel, Martin. "The First British Referendum: The Peace Ballot, 1934–5." *The English Historical Review* 95, no. 377 (Oct 1980): 810–39.

Chialant, Maria Teresa. "Dickensian Motifs in Wells's Novels: The Disease Metaphor in *Tono-Bungay*." In *H.G. Wells under Revision: Proceedings of the International*, editors Patrick Parrinder and Christopher Rolfe (London and Toronto: Associated University Press, 1990): 97–109.

Cohen, Debra Rae. "Intermediality and the problem of *The Listener*." *Modernism/Modernity* 19, no. 3 (2012): 569–92.

Cohen, Debra Rae, Michael Coyle, and Jane Lewty. "Introduction: Signing On." In *Broadcasting Modernism* (Gainesville, FL: University Press of Florida, 2013), pp. 1–10.

Cole, Lori. *Surveying the Avant-Garde: Questions on Modernism, Art, and the Americas in Transatlantic Magazines* (Pittsburgh, PA: Pennsylvania University Press, 2018).

Cole, Sarah. *Inventing Tomorrow: H.G. Wells and the Twentieth Century* (New York: Columbia University Press, 2020).

Collier, Patrick. *Modernism on Fleet Street* (Burlington, VT: Ashgate, 2006).

Collyer, Robert. *Psychography, or the Embodiment of Thought* (Philadelphia, PA: Zieber & Co, 1843).

Conley, Katharine. "Surrealism's Ghostly Automatic Body." In *Contemporary French and Francophone Studies* 15, no. 3 (June 2011): 297–304.

Cowling, Maurice. *The Impact of Hitler* (Cambridge: Cambridge University Press, 2009).

Crissell, Andrew. *Understanding Radio* (London: Methuen, 1986).

Crompton, Gerald. " 'Sheer Humbug': The Freedom of the Press and the General Strike." *Twentieth Century British History* 12, no. 1 (2001): 46–68.

Crossley, Robert. *Olaf Stapledon: Speaking for the Future* (Liverpool: Liverpool University Press, 1994).

Cuddy-Keane, Melba. "The Politics of Comic Modes in Virginia Woolf's *Between the Acts*." *PMLA* 105, no. 2 (March 1990): 273–85.

Davis, Thomas. *The Extinct Scene: Late Modernism and Everyday Life* (New York: Columbia University Press, 2015).

Davis, William. "Thoughts on the Sociology of Brexit." *The Brexit Crisis: A Verso Report* (Kindle: Verso, 2016).

Day-Lewis, Cecil. *A Hope for Poetry* (Oxford: Basil Blackwell, 1935).

Day-Lewis, Cecil. "Word Over All." In *The Complete Poems* (Stanford, CA: Stanford University Press, 1992), pp. 325–7.

Day-Lewis, Cecil. *All My Yesterdays: An Autobiography* (Boston, MA: Element Books, 1993).

Deedes, W.F. "The Real Scoop: Who Was Who in Waugh's Cast List and Why." *The Telegraph*, May 28, 2003. https://www.telegraph.co.uk/culture/donotmigrate/3595475/The-real-Scoop-who-was-who-in-Waughs-cast-list-and-why.html.

Deedes, W.F. *At War with Waugh* (London: Pan Books, 2004).

Deleuze, Gilles and Félix Guattari. *A Thousand Plateaus: Capitalism and Schizophrenia*, translated by Brian Massumi (Minneapolis, MN: University of Minnesota Press, 1987).

Doob, Leonard. "Goebbels' Principles of Propaganda." *The Public Opinion Quarterly* 14, no. 3 (1950): 419–22.

Durant, Henry. "Proceedings: Yorkshire Section, Gallup Surveys." *The Journal of the Textile Institute* 32, no. 12 (December 1941): 107–11.

Durant, Henry. "The Cheater Problem." *The Public Opinion Quarterly* 10, no. 2 (1946): 288–91.

Durant, Henry. "The Gallup Poll and Some of Its Problems." *The Incorporated Statistician* 5, no. 2 (1954): 101.

Durant, Henry and W. Gregory. *Behind the Gallup Poll* (London: The News Chronicle, 1951).

Eade, Philip. *Evelyn Waugh: A Life Revisited* (London: Henry Holt and Company, 2017).

Esty, Jed. *A Shrinking Island: Modernism and National Culture in England* (Princeton, NJ: Princeton University Press, 2004), p. 8.

Faragher, Megan. "The Form of Modernist Propaganda in Elizabeth Bowen's *The Heat of the Day*." *Textual Practice* 27, no. 1 (2013): 49–68.

Faragher, Megan. "Big Data and Universal Design in H.G. Wells and *The Home Market*: Are there Market Researchers in Utopia?" In *Humans at Work in the Digital Age*, edited by Andrew Pilsch and Shawna Ross (New York: Routledge, 2019), pp. 55–74.

Foucault, Michel. *"Society Must Be Defended": Lectures at the Collège de France: 1975–1976*, edited by Mauro Bertani and Alessandro Fontana, translated by David Macey (New York: Picador, 1997).

Foucault, Michel. Security, Territory, Population: Lectures at the Collège de France: 1977–1978, edited by Michael Senellart (New York: Palgrave Macmillan, 2007), p. 120.

Foucault, Michel. *Security, Territory, and Population. Lectures at the Collège de France, 1977–1978* (New York: Picador, 2007).

Fox, Jo. "Careless Talk: Tensions within Domestic Propaganda During the Second World War." *Journal of British Studies* 51, no. 4 (2012): 936–66.

Fremlin, Celia. *The Hours Before Dawn* (Philadelphia, PA: Lippincott, 1958).

Freud, Sigmund. "On the Psychical Mechanism of Hysterical Phenomenon." In *Studies on Hysteria*, translated by James Strachey (New York: Basic Books, [1893] 2000).

Freud, Sigmund. *Group Psychology and the Analysis of the Ego*, edited and translated by James Strachey (New York: Norton, 1959).

Gallup, George "Democracy and the Common Man." *Vital Speeches of the Day* 8, iss. 22 (September 1942) pp. 687–8.

Gallup, George. *The Pulse of Democracy* (New York: Simon & Schuster, 1940).

Gielgud, Val. *British Radio Drama, 1922–1956: A Survey* (London: Harrap, 1957).

Habermas, Jürgen. *The Structural Transformation of the Public Sphere: An Inquiry into the Category of a bourgeois Society*, translated by Thomas Burger (Cambridge, MA: MIT Press, 1991).

Hackett, Felix E. "The Sampling Referendum in the Service of Popular Government." *Dublin: Journal of the Statistical and Social Inquiry Society of Ireland* 16, no. 4 (1940): 63–90.

Haraway, Donna. "Situated Knowledges: The Science Question in Feminism and the Privilege of Partial Perspective." *Feminist Studies* 14, no. 3 (1988): 575–99.

Harper, Margaret Mills. *Wisdom of Two: The Spiritual and Literary Collaboration of George and W.B. Yeats* (Oxford: Oxford University Press, 2006).

Harrison, Otis. "Finding the Lush Place: Waugh's Moral Vision in *Scoop*." *Evelyn Waugh Studies* 46, no. 3 (2013): 13–26.

Harrisson, Tom and Charles Madge. *Mass-Observation* (London: Frederick Muller, 1937).

Hasley, A.H. *A History of Sociology in Britain: Science, Literature, and Society* (Oxford: Oxford University Press, 2004).

Hastings, Selina. *Evelyn Waugh: A Biography* (London, Capuchin Classics, 2013).

Haynes. R.D. *H.G. Wells, Discoverer of the Future* (London: Macmillan, 1979).

Heard, Gerald. *The Ascent of Humanity* (New York: Harcourt, Brace and Company, 1929).

Hepburn, Allan. "Trials and Errors: *The Heat of the Day* and Postwar Culpability." In *Intermodernism: Literary Culture in Interwar and Wartime Britain*, edited by Kristin Bluemel (Edinburgh: Edinburgh UP, 2009), pp. 131–49.

Hinton, James. *The Mass Observers: A History, 1937–1949* (Oxford: Oxford University Press, 2013).

Hubble, Nick. "The Mobilisation of Everyday Life." In *Mass-Observation and Everyday Life* (London: Palgrave, 2006), pp. 165–200.

Hubble, Nick. *Mass-Observation and Everyday Life* (London: Palgrave, 2006).

Hubble, Nick. "The Intermodern Assumption of the Future: William Empson, Charles Madge and Mass-Observation." In *Intermodernism: Literary Culture in Mid-Twentieth-Century Britain*, edited by Kristin Bluemel (Edinburgh: Edinburgh UP, 2009), pp. 171–88.

Hubble, Nick. *The Proletarian Answer to the Modernist Question* (Edinburgh: Edinburgh University Press, 2017).

Huxley, Julian. "Preface." In *Mass-Observation* (London: Frederick Muller, 1937).

"If the Invader Comes." The Ministry of Information (June 1940).

Igo, Sarah. *The Averaged American: Surveys, Citizens, and the Making of a Mass Public* (Cambridge, MA: Harvard University Press, 2007).

Jameson, Fredric. "Cognitive Mapping." In *Marxism and the Interpretation of Culture*, edited by Cary Nelson and Lawrence Grossberg (Chicago, IL: University of Illinois Press, 1988), pp. 346–60.

Jameson, Fredric. *Archaeologies of the Future: The Desire Called Utopia and Other Science Fictions* (London: Verso, 2005).

Jameson, Storm. *None Turn Back* (London: Virago, [1936] 1984).

Kerr, Matthew Newsome. *Contagion, Isolation, and Biopolitics in Victorian London* (Cham: Palgrave, 2018).

Kohlmann, Benjamin. *Committed Styles: Modernism, Politics, and Left-Wing Literature in the 1930s* (Oxford: Oxford University Press, 2004).

Kohlmann, Benjamin. "Social Facts and Poetic Authority: The Political Aesthetic of Mass-Observation" In Committed Styles: Modernism, Politics, and Left-Wing Literature in the 1930s (Oxford: Oxford University Press, 2004).

Kulik, Karol. *Alexander Korda: The Man Who Could Work Miracles* (New Rochelle, NY: Arlington House Publishers, 1975).

Kumar, Krishnan. "Wells and 'the So-Called Science of Sociology.'" In *H.G. Wells under Revision: Proceedings of the International*, editors Patrick Parrinder and Christopher Rolfe (London and Toronto: Associated University Press, 1990): 192–217.

Lago, Mary. "E.M. Forster and the BBC." *The Yearbook of English Studies* 20 (1990): 132–51.

Laing, Stuart. "'Presenting 'Things as They Are': John Sommerfield's *May Day* and Mass-Observation." In *Class, Culture and Social Change*, edited by Frank Gloversmith (Sussex: The Harvester Press, 1980), pp. 142–60.

Lane, Jack and Brendan Clifford. *Elizabeth Bowen: "Notes on Éire": Espionage Reports to Winston Churchill, 1940-2 : With a Review of Irish Neutrality in World War 2* (Aubane, Ireland: Aubane Historical Society, 2009).

Lassner, Phyllis. *British Women Writers of World War II: Battlegrounds of Their Own* (New York: Palgrave, 1998).

Lazarsfeld, Paul. "The Use of Detailed Interviews in Market Research." *The Journal of Marketing* 2, no. 1 (1937): 3–8.

Lazarsfeld, Paul and Marjorie Fiske. " 'The 'Panel' as a New Tool for Measuring Opinion." *The Public Opinion Quarterly* 2, no. 4 (1938): 596–612.

Le Bon, Gustave. *The Crowd* (New York: Macmillan, 1897).

Le Fanu, Sarah. *Rose Macaulay: A Biography* (New York: Time Warner Books, 2003).

Lee, Hermione. *Virginia Woolf* (New York: Vintage, 1999).

Lefebvre, Henri. *The Production of Space*, translated by Donald Nicholson-Smith (Malden, MO: Blackwell, 2016).

Levitas, Ruth. "Back to the Future: Wells, Sociology, Utopia and Method." *Sociological Review* 58, no. 4 (2010): 530–47.

Lippmann, Walter. *Public Opinion* (New York: Harcourt, 1922).

Livingstone, Adelaide. *The Peace Ballot: The Official History* (London: Gollancz, 1935).

Lukács, Georg. "Realism in the Balance." In *Aesthetics and Politics* (London, Verso: 1980), pp. 28–60.

Lukowitz, David. "British Pacifists and Appeasement: The Peace Pledge Union." *Journal of Contemporary History* 9, no. 1 (1974): 115–27.

Lurie, Walter. "Statistics and Public Opinion." *The Public Opinion Quarterly* 1, no. 4 (October 1937): 78–83.

MacClancy, Jeremy. "Brief Encounter: The Meeting, in Mass-Observation, of British Surrealism and Popular Anthropology." *The Journal of the Royal Anthropological Institute* 1, no. 3 (September 1995): 495–512.

Mackay, Robert. *Half the Battle: Civilian Morale in Britain during the Second World War* (Manchester: Manchester University Press, 2003).

Maddox, Brenda. *Yeats's Ghosts: The Secret Life of W.B. Yeats* (New York: Harper Collins, 1999).

Mass-Observation. *May the Twelfth*, edited by Humphrey Jennings and Charles Madge (London: Faber and Faber, [1937] 2009), p. iv.

Mass-Observation. *Britain* (New York: Faber, [1939] 2007).

Mass-Observation. *War Begins at Home* (London: Faber & Faber, [1940] 2001).

Mass-Observation. *War Factory* (London: Victor Gollancz, 1943).

Matheson, Hilda. "The Future of BBC Talks." *The Nineteenth Century and After* 111 (1932): 339–51.

Matheson, Hilda. "Listener Research in Broadcasting." *The Sociological Review* 27, no. 4 (1935): 408–22.

McDiarmid, Lucy S. "W.H. Auden's 'In the Year of My Youth...'" *The Review of English Studies* 29, no. 11 (August 1978): 267–312.

McDougall, William. *The Group Mind* (Cambridge: Cambridge University Press, 1927).

McKinstry, Leo. *Operation Sea Lion* (London: John Murray, 2014).

McLaine, Ian. *Ministry of Morale: Home Front Morale and the Ministry of Information in World War II* (London: George Allen & Unwin, 1979).

McLuhan, Marshall. *Understanding Media* (Cambridge, MA: MIT Press, 1994).

Medawar, Tony. "Suspense on Stage." In *13 to the Gallows*, edited by Tony Medawar, (Norfolk, VA: Crippen & Landru, 2008), pp 7–16.

Mendelson, Edward. *Early Auden, Later Auden: A Critical Biography* (Princeton, NJ: Princeton University Press, [1981] 2017).

Miller, Andrew John. "'Our Representative, Our Spokesman': Modernity, Professionalism, and Representation in Virginia Woolf's *Between the Acts*." *Studies in the Novel* 33, no. 1 (2001): 34–50.

Miller, Tyrus. *Late Modernism: Politics, Fiction and the Arts Between the World Wars* (Berkeley, CA: University of California Press, 1999), pp. 18–19.

Milne, A.A. "Peace Ballot." *The Times*, November 16, 1934.

Mitchison, Naomi. *The Delicate Fire* (Edinburgh: Kennedy & Boyd, [1933] 2012).

Mitchison, Naomi. *We Have Been Warned* (Edinburgh: Kennedy & Boyd, [1935] 2012).

Mitchison, Naomi. *The Moral Basis of Politics* (London: Constable, 1939).

Mitchison, Naomi. *You May Well Ask: A Memoir, 1920–1940* (London: Flamingo, 1979).

National Declaration Committee. "Peace or War? A National Declaration on the League of Nations and Armaments." 1934.

News Chronicle. "Britain Thinks," (October 17, 1938), p. 10.

News Chronicle. "A Great New Venture Begins Next Week," (October 15, 1938), p. 1.

News Chronicle. "More Letters to the Editor," (October 5, 1938).

News Chronicle. "Net Sales in 1938," (January 16, 1939), p. 1.

News Chronicle. "Views on Family Needs and Motoring Penalties," (October 28, 1938), p. 1.

News Chronicle. "The Why and the How of 'Britain Thinks,'" (October 28, 1938), p. 12.

News Chronicle. "Widespread Demand for Register in Public Opinion," *News Chronicle* (October 19, 1938), p. 1.

Nicolson, Harold. "British Public Opinion and Foreign Policy." *Public Opinion Quarterly* 1, no. 1 (January 1937): 53–63.

O'Neill, Cathy. *Weapons of Math Destruction: How Big Data Increases Inequality and Threatens Democracy* (New York: Broadway Books, 2016), pp. 180, 9.

Overy, Richard. *The Morbid Age: Britain Between the Wars* (Bristol: Allen Lane, 2009).

Parrinder, Patrick. *Shadows of the Future: H.G. Wells, Science Fiction and Prophesy* (Liverpool: Liverpool University Press, 1995).

Partington, John S. *Building Cosmopolis: The Political Thought of H.G. Wells* (Aldershot: Ashgate, 2003).

Poole, Dewitt Clinton, et al., "Foreword." *Public Opinion Quarterly* 1, no. 1 (January 1937): 3–5.

Porter, Kenneth Wiggins. "Naomi Mitchison: The Development of a Revolutionary Novelist." *Social Science* 14, no. 3 (1939): 252–60.

Pridmore-Brown, Michele. "1939–40: Of Virginia Woolf, Gramophones, and Fascism." *PMLA* 113, no. 3 (1998): 408–21.

Pridmore-Brown, Michele. "Virginia Woolf and the BBC: Public and Private Voices." *Virginia Woolf Miscellany* 56, no. 4 (2000): 3–4.

"Psychography." *The Century Dictionary* (New York: The Century Co, 1889).

"Psychography." *Oxford English Dictionary* (Oxford: Oxford University Press, 2019).

Pugh, Martin. *Hurrah for the Blackshirts! Fascists and Fascism in Britain between the Wars* (London: Pimlico, 2005).

Purdon, James. "Information Collectives." In *Modernist Informatics: Literature, Information, and the State* (Oxford: Oxford University Press, 2016).

Purdon, James. *Modernist Informatics: Literature, Information, and the State* (Oxford: Oxford University Press, 2016).

"Quantitative and Qualitative Method in Sociological Research." *Nature* 149, no. 3784 (1942): 516–18.

Rempel, Richard. "The Dilemmas of British Pacifists During World War II." *The Journal of Modern History* 50, no. 4 (1978): D1213–29.

Robinson, Stanley Kim. "Why isn't Science Fiction Winning any Literary Awards?" *New Scientist* 204, no. 2726 (2009).

Romains, Jules. "Poetry and Unanimous Feelings." translated by Louis Cabri. *The Capilano Review* 3, no. 13 (2011): 46–8.

Roodhouse, Mark. "'Fish and Chip' Intelligence: Henry Durant and the British Institute of Public Opinion 1936–63." *Twentieth Century British History* 24, no. 2 (2012): 224–48.

Salwen, Michael. "Evelyn Waugh's *Scoop*: The Facts Behind the Fiction." *Journalism and Mass Communication Quarterly* 78, no. 1 (2001): 150–71.

Scaggs, John. *Crime Fiction* (London and New York: Routledge, 2005).

Scannell, Paddy and David Cardiff. *A Social History of British Broadcasting: Volume One 1922–1939* (London: Basil Blackwell, 1991).

Schaffer, Talia. "'A Wilde Desire Took Me': The Homoerotic History of *Dracula*." *ELH* 61, no. 2 (1993): 381–425.

Sconce, Jeremy. *Haunted Media: Electronic Presence from Telegraphy to Television* (Durham, NC: Duke University Press, 2000).

Seaber, Luke. *Incognito Social Investigation in British Literature: Certainties in Degradation* (London: Palgrave, 2018).

Seiler, Claire. "At Midcentury: Elizabeth Bowen's *The Heat of the Day*." *Modernism/Modernity* 21, no. 1 (2014): 125–45.

Seldes, George. "Who Fakes Gallup Polls?" *In Fact* 1, no. 12 (October 21, 1940): 1–2.

Sherborne, Michael. *H.G. Wells: Another Kind of Life* (London: Peter Owen, 2012).

Sheridan, Dorothy. "Introduction." In *War Factory* (London: Cresset, 1987).

Sheridan, Dorothy. "Reviewing Mass-Observation: The Archive and its Researchers Thirty Years On." *Forum: Qualitative Social Research* 1, no. 3 (2000). http://www.qualitative-research.net/index.php/fqs/article/viewArticle/1043/2255.

Siepmann, Charles. *Radio in Wartime* (Oxford: Oxford University Press, 1942).

Siepmann, Charles. *Radio's Second Chance* (New York: Little, Brown, 1946).

Silvey, Robert. *Who's Listening? The Story of BBC Audience Research* (London: Allen & Unwin, 1974).

Skal, David. *Something in the Blood* (New York: Liverwright, 2016).

Smith, Constance Babington. *Rose Macaulay* (Stroud: Sutton [1975] 2005).

Stanford, Peter. *Cecil Day-Lewis: A Life* (London: Continuum, 2007).

Stapledon, Olaf. *First and Last Men* (Mineola, NY: Dover, [1930] 2008).

Stapledon, Olaf. *Star Maker* (Middletown, CT: Wesleyan University Press, [1937] 2004).

Stapledon, Olaf. "Sketch-Map of Human Nature." *Philosophy* 17, no. 67 (1942): 210–30.

Stapledon, Olaf. *Far Future Calling: Uncollected Science Fiction and Fantasies of Olaf Stapledon*, edited by Sam Moskowitz and Stephen Fabian (Philadelphia, PA: O. Train, 1979).

Stiles, Ann. "Cerebral Automatism, the Brain, and Soul in Bram Stoker's *Dracula*." *Journal of the History of the Neurosciences* 15, no. 2 (2006): 131–52.

Stoker, Bram. *Dracula*, edited by Nina Auerback and David Skal (New York: Norton, 1997).

Straight, Alyssa. "Giving Birth to a New Nation: Female Mediation and the Spread of Textual Knowledge in *Dracula*." *Victorian Literature and Culture* 45, no. 2 (2017): 381–94.

Tankard, James. "The H.G. Wells Quote on Statistics: A Question of Accuracy." *Historica Mathematica* 6, no. 1 (1979): 30–3.

Taylor, Mark. "Olaf Stapledon and Telepathy in Literature of Cosmic Exploration." *Science Fiction Studies* 47, No. 2 (2020): 175–94.

"Telepathy." *Oxford English Dictionary* (Oxford: Oxford University Press, 2019).

Things to Come, directed by William Cameron Menzies, produced by Alexander Korda, written by H.G. Wells (United Artists, 1936).

Thompson, J.A. "The 'Peace Ballot' and the 'Rainbow' Controversy." *Journal of British Studies* 20, no. 2 (1981): 150–70.

Trotter, Wilfred. *The Instincts of the Herd in Peace and War* (London: Fisher Unwin Ltd, 1916).

Wagar, W. Warren. "Science at the World State: Education as Utopia in the Prophetic Vision of H.G. Wells." In *H.G. Wells under Revision: Proceedings of the International*, editors Patrick Parrinder and Christopher Rolfe (London and Toronto: Associated University Press, 1990), pp. 40–53.

Wagner, Adolphus Theodore. "Apparatus for Indicating a Person's Thoughts by the Agency of Nervous Electricity." In: Provisional Specification, Office of the Commissioners of Patents, no. 173 (London: Eyre and Spottiswood, January 23, 1854).

Waugh, Evelyn. *Waugh in Abyssinia* (London: Methuen, [1936] 1984).

Waugh, Evelyn. "Strange Rites of the Islanders." *Night and Day*, October 14, 1937, pp. 28–30.

Waugh, Evelyn. *Scoop* (New York: Little, Brown, [1937] 2012).

Waugh, Evelyn. "The Habits of the English." *The Essays, Articles, and Reviews of Evelyn Waugh*, edited by Donat Gallagher (London: Methuen, 1984), pp. 226–8.

Waugh, Evelyn. *The Letters of Evelyn Waugh*, edited by Mark Amory (London: Phoenix, 2009).

Waugh, Evelyn. "An Englishman's Home." In *The Complete Stories* (New York: Little, Brown and Co., 2012), pp. 217–37.

Weber, Matthew. "Those Dots: Suspension and Interruption in Virginia Woolf's *Three Guineas* and *Between the Acts*." *Journal of Modern Literature* 40, no. 3 (2017): 18.

Weber, Max. "Science as a Vocation." In *The Vocation Lectures*, translated by Rodney Livingstone (Indianapolis, IN: Hackett Publishing Company, 2004), pp. 1–31.

Weiss, Allen. *Phantasmic Radio* (Durham, NC: Duke University Press, 1995).

Wells, H.G. *Anticipations of the Mechanical and Scientific Progress upon Human Life and Thought* (London: Chapman & Hall, 1902).

Wells, H.G. *Mankind in the Making* (London: Chapman & Hall, 1904).

Wells, H.G. *The New Machiavelli* (London: Everyman, [1911] 1994).

Wells, H.G. *An Englishman Looks at the World* (London: Cassell and Company, 1914).

Wells, H.G. *The Shape of Things to Come* (New York: Penguin, [1933] 2005).

Wells, H.G. *An Experiment in Autobiography* (London: Victor Gollancz, 1934).

Wells, H.G. *World Brain* (New York: Doubleday, 1938).

Wells, H.G. *The Correspondence of H.G. Wells: Volume 2*, edited by David C. Smith (London: Pickering and Chatto, 1998).

Wells, H.G. *In the Days of the Comet* (Lincoln, NE: University of Nebraska Press, [1906] 2001).

Wells, H.G. *Things to Come: A Critical Text of the 1935 London first edition, with an introduction and appendices*, edited by Leon Stover (Jefferson, NC: McFarland, 2012).

Wells, William D. "Psychographics: A Critical Review." *Journal of Marketing Research* 12, no. 2 (May 1975): 196.

Whittington, Ian. *Writing the Radio War: Literature, Politics, and the BBC, 1939–1945* (Edinburgh: Edinburgh University Press, 2018).

Wilks, Samuel. "Undergraduate Statistical Education." *Journal of the American Statistical Association* 46 no. 253 (March 1951): 1–18.

Williams, Francis. "Defend Cooper's Snoopers." *Evening Standard*, August 6, 1940.

Williams, Keith. *H.G. Wells, Modernity and the Movies* (Liverpool: Liverpool University Press, 2007).

Williams, Raymond. *The Politics of Modernism* (New York: Verso, [1989] 2007).

Wills, Clair. *That Neutral Island* (London: Faber, 2007).

Winter, Alison. *Mesmerized: Powers of Mind in Victorian Britain* (Chicago, IL: University of Chicago Press, 2000).

Woolf, Virginia. *Three Guineas* (New York: Harcourt, [1939] 2006).

Woolf, Virginia. *Between the Acts* (New York: Harcourt, [1941] 2008).

Woolf, Virginia. *The Diary of Virginia Woolf: Volume Five, 1936–1941*, edited by Anne Olivier Bell (New York: Harcourt, 1943), p. 231.

Woolf, Virginia. "Character in Fiction." In *The Essays of Virginia Woolf: Volume 3*, edited by Andrew McNeille (London: Hogarth Press, 1966), pp. 420–38.

Woolf, Virginia. *The Letters of Virginia Woolf, Volume 6: 1936–1941*, edited by Nigel Nicolson and Joanne Trautmann (London: Harcourt, 1980).

Woolf, Virginia. "Modern Fiction." *The Essays of Virginia Woolf. Volume 4: 1925 to 1928*, edited by Andrew McNeille (London: The Hogarth Press, 1984), pp. 157–65.

Woolf, Virginia. "The New Biography." In *The Essays of Virginia Woolf. Volume 4: 1925 to 1928*, edited by Andrew McNeille (London: The Hogarth Press, 1984), pp. 473–80.

Index

For the benefit of digital users, indexed terms that span two pages (e.g., 52–53) may, on occasion, appear on only one of those pages.